Critical Events in
Teaching and Learning

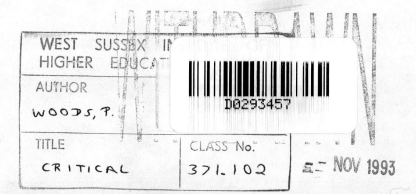

To my sister, Betty

Critical Events in Teaching and Learning

Peter Woods

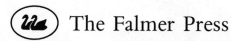 The Falmer Press

(A member of the Taylor & Francis Group)
London • Washington, D.C.

UK   The Falmer Press, 4 John Street, London WC1N 2ET

USA   The Falmer Press, Taylor & Francis Inc., 1900 Frost Road, Suite 101, Bristol, PA 19007

© Peter Woods 1993

First published 1993

A catalogue record for this book is available from the British Library

Library of Congress Cataloging-in-Publication Data are available on request

ISBN 0 75070 232 x cased
ISBN 0 75070 233 8 paper

Jacket design by Caroline Archer

Typeset in 9.5/11 pt Bembo
by Graphicraft Typesetters Ltd., Hong Kong.

Printed in Great Britain by Burgess Science Press, Basingstoke on paper which has a specified pH value on final paper manufacture of not less than 7.5 and is therefore 'acid free'.

Contents

Acknowledgments		vi
Preface		vii
Chapter 1	The Nature and Significance of Critical Educational Events	1
Chapter 2	An Educational Bluebird: the Making of *Rushavenn Time*	14
Chapter 3	Filming a Village Life: Community Education in Action	44
Chapter 4	The Chippindale Venture: Real Learning in the Making	72
Chapter 5	The Magic of Godspell: the Educational Significance of a Dramatic Event	104
Chapter 6	Conclusion: Outcomes and Prospects	141
Appendix	Researching Critical Events	157
References		166
Name Index		177
Subject Index		180

Acknowledgments

The book would not have been possible without the input of 'critical agents' and 'critical others'. Among these, I am especially grateful to Peter J. Woods, Theresa Whistler, Stephen King, Dawne Fleet, Sarah Goodwin, Melanie Pike, Doug Gosling, Charles Freeman, pupils of Laxfield Primary School, villagers of Laxfield, Dot Browning, Debbie Kerr, Pam Turner, Joy Williams, Philip Turner, Nigel Green, architects from Plincke, Leaman and Browning of Winchester, the pupils of Western Primary School and of All Saints Community Primary School, Winchester, Sally Mackey, Lesley Fielding, Ian Willison, and the cast of the Roade School production of 'Godspell'. I thank them for their time, freely given, for their enthusiasm, successfully conveyed, for their revealing insights into teaching and learning, and, not least, for their generous hospitality. I hope this book does justice to their work.

I am grateful to Donald Mackinnon and Barbara Mayor for their comments on drafts of parts of the text. I have received valuable secretarial assistance from Jan Giddings and Lynn Kent. A special thanks to Sheila Gilks who has typed the whole script through several drafts; and to Kath for her support and encouragement.

Preface

This book goes back to my initiation into teaching over thirty years ago. I taught for a term in a primary school as an untrained graduate, taking the place of a full-time teacher who was on maternity leave. I was not there long enough either to become part of the school culture as an insider, or to understand it more analytically as an observer. I stumbled through the term in a haze of bewilderment. For this, I was paid more than the rest of the staff, who were trained and who did know what they were doing, but were non-graduates. Not only did they know what they were doing, but they seemed to me to do it extraordinarily well. What was the secret? How did the school, with over 500 pupils and complicated and myriad activities going on simultaneously, work? What held the school together as a social unit? How did the teachers achieve such remarkable results, far beyond my own capabilities? What special knowledge, skills and experience did these teachers possess, and how was it acquired? How was the sense of excitement, activity and immediacy generated and maintained? It was all very mysterious.

These questions remained unanswered, but I was sufficiently captivated by the society of an educational unit to undertake training. I went in for secondary teaching as I thought that more suited to my longer-term interests at the time, and there I remained for the next twenty years, teaching during the first half of that period and researching during the other. The great problem in secondary schools was the recalcitrant clientele in the older forms, and that was my first research interest. Inevitably, the research revealed that earlier experiences had been influential, so, in due course, I studied the earlier years of secondary school. That led, in turn, to studying the transition between primary and secondary schools. It was then but a small step back into the full mysteries of primary school. Hence, there is both a logic to the current study in terms of my research career, and a motivation deriving from the kind of fascination lying dormant since my initiation into the profession.

To this personal inspiration was added other factors which seemed to me to make the subject of study a pressing current issue. One of these was the comparative lack of qualitative research in primary schools, especially detailed delineation and evaluation of teaching and learning activities. Yet primary school teaching has been a matter of great debate for some time. Traditional or progressive? Child-centred or knowledge-centred? Instructional or constructivist? Whole-class teaching or group and individual work? The debate, always apparently in polarized terms, which surfaces and induces a major moral panic every few years, features more politics and ideology than evidence and reasoned argument. As Alexander (1992) argues, therefore, there is a clear need for the application of 'conceptual and empirical tests' (p. 194).

There was also a political motive in the research. Teachers have been coming under increasing pressure in recent years. There is talk of intensification of their work, of deskilling, and of demoralization. There are said to be crises of confidence in professional knowledge and in the teacher role. Some fear the loss of work that is most meaningful to them, having to work to others' instrumental agendas, being hidebound by tests and record-keeping. If, therefore, we can document and evaluate some of their exceptional work, it might sharpen general views of its efficacy, demonstrate the nature and degree of teacher skills and help justify particular conceptions of the teacher role which allows scope for these particular endeavours.

The methodology also involves a particular conception of the teacher role. The teachers involved in these events have been collaboratively involved in the research. The stories told here are a combination of their lived experiences and my conceptual and organizational overview. The synthesis should meet the test of recapturing the facts, feelings, mood and magic, as the participants experienced and perceived them, that is, of telling the story 'as it was'; and also meet other measures of validity as far as they are applicable. This seems a sound basis for combining theory and practice, which, in turn, makes for strength in the formulation of policy. This, then, was the background to the research.

Once back into primary schools, I found them as perplexing and exciting as ever. Now, however, I had the advantage of a number of years of teaching and researching, yet of still being the 'stranger' (Schutz, 1964) in these particular schools, able to study them at arm's length as it were, and to seek answers to those earlier questions that so intrigued me. One thing that caught my attention was the inventiveness and creativity of primary teachers, and my first attempt to understand this is recorded in Woods (1990a). This book is the second product of that research. I noticed that, occasionally, some very exciting things happened in primary schools. They were ambitious, complicated projects, with high risk factors. Yet on the whole they worked, and some worked uncommonly well. Certain events were particularly productive. They were radical, cathartic, inducing profound change in pupils and teachers alike. For many, they represented a turning-point in development, some pupils showing hidden, unsuspected talents or abilities; and some teachers professing they would 'never be the same again'. I term them 'critical events' — critical in the sense of crucial, key, and momentous, rather than being problematic. Some have suggested 'exceptional events', to avoid any possible confusion over 'critical'. This would certainly describe them as they are out of the ordinary, but not all extraordinary events are critical in their consequences.

I expand on these issues in Chapter 1, and in particular examine the concept of critical events in greater length. Chapters 2–5 contain detailed analyses of the four events selected for study and seek to assess their criticality in terms of educational outcomes. One of these is from the secondary sphere. This is to show that critical events are not limited to primary schools though those are the main focus here. It also has some interesting properties of its own, thus enabling extension of the concept. Chapter 6 summarizes the outcomes in general, and considers the viability of this kind of teaching and learning in the National Curriculum. A discussion of the research methods used in the study is included as an appendix. Readers particularly interested in methodology might prefer to read this section with Chapter 1.

The Nature and Significance of Critical Educational Events

During recent work on creative teaching in primary schools, my attention was drawn to certain outstanding events. They had won wide acclaim from teachers, other professionals, pupils, parents, academics, advisers, and other members of the public. Some of them had won an award. Initially I was interested in them as individual, exciting educational events. Eventually, however, it became clear that they had common properties, and that they were all examples of the same kind of activity. I term this activity 'critical event'. In the rest of this chapter, I outline a model of how such events are constructed, how they work, and the conditions attending them, The model was derived from the study of the events examined in Chapters 2–5. It is grounded in the empirical data there presented (Glaser and Strauss, 1967). The coding procedures were similar to those recommended by Strauss and Corbin (1990), involving the derivation of a core category (critical event), and its specification in terms of the conditions which give rise to it, the context in which it is embedded, the strategies by which it is handled, and the consequences of those strategies. As far as the sequence of the research went, therefore, it came last. However, it seems necessary to present it first as the central integrating feature of the book. It helps, I hope, to illuminate what follows, and to highlight the features which the events have in common. I concentrate, therefore, on the main pattern of events here. Its substantiation and further particular details will follow with the examples.

The Significance of Critical Events

The significance of critical *incidents* in people's lives has been noted (Strauss, 1959; Becker, 1966; Walker, 1976; Measor, 1985; Sparkes, 1988). We have observed critical incidents and periods in teacher careers (Sikes, Measor and Woods, 1985). These are 'highly charged moments and episodes that have enormous consequences for personal change and development' (p. 230). They are unplanned, unanticipated and uncontrolled. They are flash-points that illuminate in an electrifying instant some key problematic aspect or aspects of the teacher's role, and which contain, in the same instant, the solution. There might be a higher proportion of such incidents during critical periods, such as one's initiation into teaching. They are key factors in the socialization of teachers and in 'the process of establishment'

(Ball, 1980) in the classroom. Critical events are a related phenomenon. They lie between the flash-point incidents and the career-phase periods. They are integrated and focused programmes of educational activities which may last from a number of weeks to over a year. Some might be known internally as themes, projects or topics, though by no means all of these are critical in their effects (Avann, 1982; Tann, 1988; DES, 1989; Gammage, 1990; Alexander, 1992). They cover a multitude of different kinds of activity (Stewart, 1986, p. 122). There are both positive and negative events. The latter are the equivalent of the 'counter incidents' described in Sikes, Measor and Woods (1985), and lead to personal or educationally retrogressive consequences. I have described some of these in Woods (1990a). Here I concentrate on positive events that all involved regard as critical in the manner defined. What, then, makes them critical?

First, they promote children's education and development in uncommonly accelerated ways. They are times of outstanding advance, in a number of ways — attitudes towards learning, understanding of the self, relationships with others, acquisition of knowledge, development of skills. McLaren (1986, p. 236) talks of 'the great moment of teachability'. Some children make great leaps forward, discover new things about the self, are changed radically. As Pring (1985, p. 130) remarks, education is about 'the development of persons'. We can train them in certain skills without affecting them as persons. 'In educating people, we have in mind a transformation of how they see and understand the world and themselves within that world' (ibid.). It is this kind of holistic change in a comparatively giant leap that is involved here. Such events, then, help pupils (and teachers) become persons, aiding conceptual and moral development, promoting both self-determined action and relations with others, enabling them to 'transcend their own self-interest' and acquire 'a sense of justice that enables young persons to look critically at conventional morality and to establish a set of more universal principles which they are able to make their own' (Pring, 1987, p. 16; see also Carr, 1989).

Secondly, these events can be critical for *teacher* change. As Eisner (1979, p. 166) points out, teachers also have needs that must be met through teaching, ranging from pride in their craftsmanship and in securing results, to realization of the self. Others have argued that the role of teacher necessarily implies the role of learner (Schaefer, 1967; Schön, 1987; Nias, Southworth and Campbell, 1992). Unlike critical incidents, critical events are in large measure intended, planned and controlled. But the plans contain within them seeds for growth and scope for opportunities. There are elements, therefore, that are largely unforeseen, and unpredictable new pastures that all, teachers and pupils alike, are venturing into, with what consequences no one exactly knows. As G.H. Mead says, 'The possibilities in our nature . . . are possibilities of the self that lie beyond our own immediate presentation. We do not know just what they are. They are in a certain sense the most fascinating contents that we can contemplate, so far as we can get hold of them' (1934, p. 204). Nias (1989) quotes from Connell (1985, p. 127) on the metaphors reached for to describe the heights of the feeling of teaching well — 'chemical reactions, currents, setting alight, taking fire'. She mentioned William James' moments when he feels 'most deeply and intensely active and alive [when] there is a voice inside which speaks and says, "This is the real me." Nias (p. 200) goes on, 'Perhaps it is in the precious moments when primary teachers become creative artists that they transcend the contradictions of the job and achieve the "peak experience" of which Maslow (1973, p. 177) writes and in which they, like

James, become aware of their full identity.' So the teacher also learns and develops in fulfilling ways, either as pedagogue in understanding of children's learning and refinement of teaching methods and techniques; or as self, in relation to one's own knowledge, powers, aptitudes and abilities.

Thirdly, critical events can also have an important preservation and confirmatory function for teachers. They maintain a particular definition of reality and identity against the pressure of contrary forces (Berger and Kellner, 1964). Consider, for example, a teacher with high ideals working in a severely constrained situation — a not untypical scenario. Common strategies in such a situation are to adjust one's ideals, transpose them to some other form of activity outside teaching, or renounce them altogether (Woods, 1990a). Critical events permit teachers to retain their ideals in spite of the assaults that might more customarily be made on them. Just as they are peaks that launch new fields of learning for teachers and pupils, so they are peaks that sustain the teachers' vision, restore their faith, confirm their own personal practical philosophy (Connelly and Clandinin, 1985), show them that, when the conjuncture of circumstances is right, their principles work. Like oases in the desert, these experiences can sustain them through less productive periods, and keep the prospect of the highest standards, as they define them, within view. After a period of doubt, they can be signally restorative. They allow them to 'strategically comply' while holding in mind the real prospect of 'strategic redefinition' (Lacey, 1977). In this sense they act as a coping strategy (A. Hargreaves, 1978; Pollard, 1982; Woods, 1979), where coping is to do with 'personal dignity, integrity, values and aims. Thus coping is linked to preserving and developing the attributes which individuals identify as being part of themselves' (Pollard, 1990a, p. 75). Critical events have this rather paradoxical feature, therefore, that though peripheral in the sense that they may occur but rarely, they are absolutely central in terms of the teacher's sense of self and professionalism, as indeed they are to pupil learning.

Fourthly, these events can be critical for the profession as a whole. Currently, teachers appear to be at a crucial juncture. Since the failed 'Teacher Action' of the 1980s and the gamut of reforms imposed by the Government during the 1980s, teachers have lost status and a large measure of control. There is fear of 'intensification' (Larson, 1980; Apple, 1986; A. Hargreaves, 1991a) and deskilling; of being reduced to technicians whose task is simply to deliver the National Curriculum. Teachers in primary schools have recently been under attack for alleged blind adherence to outmoded 'dogmas' (Alexander, Rose, and Woodhead, 1992) and 'sacred cows and shibboleths', among which 'thematic work, topics, enquiry methods, and group work' figure prominently (Alexander, 1992, p. 194). If critical events can still be shown to be possible, even perhaps, when all has settled down, to have even better chances, it would be a considerable morale-booster for teachers in general. Even if not the instigator of such events, therefore, one can derive succour and inspiration from them.

Features of Critical Events

The events studied are informed by a particular learning theory, and generate a distinctive form of relationships.

Real Learning

The learning that takes place is real learning, which builds on pupils' own needs and relevancies, and their existing cognitive and affective structures. There is a strong emphasis on reality, on a real problem or issue of importance or value, on constructing situations that are the same as those they purport to represent, on using real professionals, on collecting first-hand evidence and materials, on doing things oneself, on having as realistic aim. As in research, this heightens the validity of the output. Learning is integrated in the self, which helps further to ensure coherence within, and across, subject areas (D. Hargreaves, 1991). An expression of this in primary schools is described by Best (1991) as 'Personal Enquiry':

> It is primarily concerned to develop qualities such as curiosity, original-
> ity, initiative, cooperation, perseverance, open-mindedness, self-criticism,
> responsibility, self-confidence and independence. This is achieved by the
> child's involvement, in a personally meaningful way, in an enquiry, or
> more aptly a congeries of related enquiries, which grow out of an issue
> which attracts his (*sic*) interest. There is both co-operative and individual
> work, and success is assessed in terms of the development of individual
> potential. The overriding aim is to help and encourage children to learn
> how to learn; to develop their own ability to think; to develop a lively,
> enquiring attitude. (Best, 1991, p. 275)

As Best points out, this is not to be equated with some versions of the 'discovery' method with flexibility amounting to laxity, but involves 'carefully and ingeniously structured work, and the development of *self*-discipline'. Its main strength is that it not only leads to an acquisition of knowledge, but also, and more importantly, develops 'a grasp or understanding of that which gives sense to knowledge' (ibid., p. 261). This understanding includes 'developing a feel, a sensitivity, a grasp, and a love for a subject, entering creatively into the *spirit* of an area of enquiry' (p. 269). It is less important, Best feels, that we should aim to teach students *about* a subject, than that we should encourage them to *be* creative writers, scientists, historians etc. The former will follow from the latter, with sounder conceptual grasp.

This is in line with reformulated notions of 'progressivism'. As summarized by Galton (1989, pp. 140–42), 'choice is no longer about *what* task to do but more importantly about *how* to do it:' The pupil needs to feel a 'degree of control' over the process. The teacher will 'build upon the child's partial understandings so that the pupil can reconstruct their knowledge and ideas in ways that make them more generally applicable'. There may be some instruction, but usually in relation to 'lower-order cognitive tasks', and blended skilfully and seamlessly into children's own activities. The outcomes are assessed by 'critical dialogue, in which the teacher's and other pupils' views are offered as part of an ongoing debate about the quality of the final product'. This kind of supportive, constructive criticism calls for great skill on the part of the teacher, and presupposes a 'negotiated' teacher–pupil relationship to reflect what Galton calls 'the negotiated learning model' (see also Armstrong, 1980, 1981; Rowland, 1984, 1987; Nias, 1988). This contrasts with a traditional mode of control which confused attempts to implement the progressive ideology associated with the Plowden Report (1967).

The philosophy, with the emphasis on experience and discovery, is that of Dewey (1934), the learning theory constructivist (Vygotsky, 1962; Donaldson, 1978; Bruner, 1986; Bruner and Haste, 1987; Edwards and Mercer, 1987; Wood, 1988; Pollard, 1990b). While there might be talk of child-centredness, it denotes a pedagogy largely validated in action and containing a number of fitness-for-purpose techniques, rather than simply being the language of ideology (Alexander, 1984). It is not a free-floating child-centredness, but one that involves negotiation with the teachers over aims and activities (Pollard, 1991b). Nor does it eschew learning through instruction. Vygotsky (1978) sees the teacher as being more active, as being a kind of mediator. He points to the importance to learning of cooperation with teachers and other pupils.

> Learning awakens a variety of developmental processes that are able to operate only when the child is interacting with people in his environment and in co-operation with peers. Once these processes are internalised they become part of the child's development achievement. (Vygotsky, 1978, p. 90)

Edwards and Mercer (1987), similarly, point to the cultural and communicative aspects of context. Teachers develop 'a framework for shared understanding with children based on joint knowledge and action which provided its own rationale for present activity and a strong foundation for future developments. This contextual edifice is the "scaffolding" for children's mental explorations, a cognitive climbing-frame' (p. 167; see also Wood, Bruner and Ross, 1976; Bruner, 1983; and Wood, 1986). Joint, negotiative discussion helps build this construction. Authoritarian teaching can leave pupils 'scaffolded' and 'unable to function independently' (ibid. See also Bruner, 1983). The method is to develop a support structure for children's own learning based on their own needs, interests and relevancies; not, therefore, to 'direct' but to 'lead by following' (Wood, 1986, p. 202), and to aim for children's learning to stand on its own when the structure is removed. A key process, therefore, becomes 'handover' of control of learning from teacher to pupil. If it works, therefore, it follows that the children have a large amount of control over their own learning, and they own the products of it. They are not learning, therefore, for the teacher or for any other external source, but for themselves. Moreover, the learning and development that occurs is not peripheral and cosmetic, but central and radical. It counts for something; it changes and empowers the person. Not surprisingly, therefore, there is strong commitment and motivation to securing the aims of the enterprise. The teaching and learning reflects the holistic nature of the teacher's view of the child (Pollard, 1990b). It covers not only rationalist, algorithmic modes of thinking which are so dominant in the official curriculum at present but also aesthetic experience (D. Hargreaves, 1982; 1983) and 'poetic' thinking. Bonnett (1991) argues that the latter

> . . . seeks harmony rather than power, receptiveness rather than imposition, is affected rather than effective, is openly curious and wondering rather than goal-orientated, accepts mystery as against seeking transparency, intuits the wholeness of things as against analysing them into specific problems to be solved, and stays with things in their inherent

strangeness rather than turn them into defined objects — manageable and familiar. In essence, poetic thinking attempts to re-establish a direct living in, and with, things which is largely destroyed by the distanced analytic approach of rational-calculative thought. (Bonnet, 1991, pp. 282–3)

While this might seem the preferred mode of thinking for artistic pursuits, Bonnett suggests that 'it may represent the only truly respectful way of relating to people and things around us' (ibid.). It can also be applied with profit to other areas of the curriculum: science, mathematics, technology, for example. In this respect, science and art can both enrich each other (Waller, 1934; Nisbet, 1962).

This teaching philosophy applies equally to the teachers' learning. These changes would not occur if teachers did not feel that they 'owned' the conception and management of curriculum and pedagogy. Bertrand Russell (1950) remarked that

The teacher, like the artist, the philosopher and the man of letters, can only perform his work adequately if he feels himself to be an individual directed by an inner creative impulse, not dominated and fettered by an outside authority. (Russell, 1950, p. 159)

Thus the needs of the teachers in the schools of Nias, Southworth and Campbell (1992, p. 45) were met since they felt that they 'owned' the curriculum, in the sense of 1) controlling those aspects for which they were responsible; and 2) of having internalized it. The curriculum 'came from within them or was part of them'. Fullan (1982) points out that teachers need room to experiment, modify, select and absorb proposed changes that are being instituted from without. The same applies to changes from within (see also Nias, 1989) Teachers also sometimes learn constructively alongside the children (ibid.).

'Communitas'

Aiding the escalation is the fact that it is invariably a group effort. The teachers involved are of common accord. They have similar values, aims, aspirations, and they are deeply held. Nias' (1989) teachers stressed the importance of this if they were to 'pull together' (p. 160). 'They could cooperate with people whom they did not perceive as part of their own self-confirming reference group, but they could not collaborate with them, either in the formation of common curricular or disciplinary policies or in translating these into action' (ibid.). Elsewhere, Nias, Southworth and Yeomans (1989) have illustrated the nature of 'collaborative cultures' in some primary schools, showing how they valued individuals as well as groups, pervaded the whole of school activity, were based in the bedrock of mutual support and esteem, and promoted both teacher and pupil development. Nias, Southworth and Campbell (1992, p. 135) describe how 'a sense of unity' developed during the production of a school concert: 'The whole staff and sub-groups worked together, people learnt more about one another's strengths and talents, everyone was valued for his/her particular contribution . . . [and] their sense of collective purpose was strengthened . . .' (see also Hartley, 1985; Little, 1990; Biott and Nias, 1992; Fullan and Hargreaves, 1992). Collaborative teaching or 'TTT' (teachers teaching together) if well-conceived, has been commended for its potential by Alexander (1992). Similarly, it has been argued that collaborative work among pupils has many benefits, though managerially it might be difficult to bring off at times. Summarizing the work on this, Galton and Williamson (1992, p. 16) state that it is claimed that pupils learn from each other, work at their own pace, lose the fear and stigma of failure, improve their self-image, learn respect from others, gain confidence. In critical events, these two groups — of teachers and pupils — working at their best come together to form a highly productive, integrated group of teachers and learners where the roles are less clearly demarcated and all are involved in the pursuit of learning and all are contributing according to their means. Close collaboration was a prominent feature of the events that I researched such that these requirements were writ large. It was not simply a matter of like-mindedness, however. The teachers and other adults involved complemented each other on the skills, experiences and knowledge they brought to the enterprise. Individually, they would be considered by many to be excellent teachers. Collectively, they were formidable units.

The creative energy produced by these relationships then embraced the pupils, who, once aroused, contributed their own enthusiasm to constitute a most productive group. The group grows together, develops a group identity and culture. Children prime each other's enthusiasm, complement each other's knowledge and expertise, develop new ways of working together. They gain new understandings of others, and from others they develop new conceptions of their own selves. Though the learning experiences might be reckoned in individual terms, the major accomplishment is a collective one. This includes the teachers and any others that have been involved. All have reached heights of uncommon excellence that appear, in large part, to have superseded standard discriminators such as age, gender and social class. Pollard (1985), and Nias (1988, 1989), among others, have also pointed to the educational merits of collaborative cultures among not only teachers, but between teachers and pupils. Anning (1991, p. 63) feels that 'we need studies of classrooms where this kind of working consensus between the teacher and the children has been achieved — where children are producing high standards of work and where teachers are functioning effectively'. Bruner (1986, p. 127) observes that 'most learning in most settings is a communal activity, a sharing of the culture'. The efficacy of this is well illustrated in critical events. They have something of the spirit of what Turner (1974) calls 'communitas'. The essential characteristic of this according to Musgrove (1977, p. 155) is 'a relationship between concrete, idiosyncratic individuals stripped of both status and role'. It contrasts with social structure, and therefore is sometimes called social anti-structure, which McLaren (1986, p. 259) states is 'composed of human bonds that exist outside the structure of roles, statuses and positions within the society. The antistructure is a state of undifferentiated, homogeneous human kindness'. 'Communitas' has something magical about it. Outside, above and beyond structure, it has a quality that is both intensely real and intensely unreal. Latent or suppressed feelings, abilities, thoughts, aspirations are suddenly set free. New persons are born, and, almost in celebration, a new collective spirit. Uncommon excitement and expectations are generated. All know that this is something special, though exactly why is difficult to explain. Something is always lost in the attempt. After all, the more successful the magic, the more impenetrable the solution.

I should make clear that these are features of the critical events that I have observed. I cannot claim that they are essential features of all such events. We know that teachers differ in their teaching and learning philosophies; that they are divided, for example, on the extent that children should own their own knowledge (King, 1978; Pollard, 1985; Hartley, 1985; A. Hargreaves, 1986). It may be that other teaching approaches also have such events of their own, or their proponents might argue that they have little distinctive merit within the general efficacy of the approach.

The Structure of Critical Events

These events go through fairly well-defined stages:

1 Conceptualization. The process is set in motion by an initial spark, or moment of conception: the creative moment that comes from inspired thought. It might be a single person's idea or dream, or the product of discussion among several. Whichever the case, there is a gestation period as the possibilities in the idea are considered.

2 Preparation and Planning. This stage involves briefing, resourcing and enskilling. Aims and objectives are clarified, plans made, routes through the event plotted. People who might contribute are contacted, roles are assigned and materials are assembled. If necessary, basic knowledge and skills are imparted to the children to equip them to be constructively creative.

3 Divergence. This is an 'explosion' stage when the children are encouraged to be innovative and creative, explore opportunities, stretch their abilities, experiment with different media and forms of expression to find the optimum ways of working, test and develop their relationships with others. Tight planning within this phase would be counter-productive. There is a strong element of serendipity. Unforecastable things happen. New, and completely unforeseen, teaching and learning opportunities arise.

4 Convergence. This is an integrating stage, where the products of the previous stage are examined to find those that best serve the aims of the enterprise. Many good ideas in themselves may be discarded if they are deemed to be a less appropriate fit within the collective scheme. But this will not happen until all attempts have been made to integrate them, perhaps by blending them with others.

5 Consolidation. The work is refined in the writing-up, editing, picture-mounting, performance or whatever medium or means of expression is being used. The artistic beauty of the composition, with all parts having their own unique properties but all enhanced by the harmony with each other, becomes clear.

   The distribution of time and energies among these phases depends on the constraints on the group involved and the resources available. In some instances, groups may be 'given their heads' in an extended divergent phase. Elsewhere, with large number of pupils, perhaps, and complicated tasks, convergence may receive more emphasis.

6 Celebration. This marks the end of the event. It may be an exhibition, a performance of a play, a showing of a film, the launch of a book, a

concert, and so on. The celebration has an air of excitement and something special about it. Within the structure of the event it serves two functions. The first is its clear signalling of the end of the event throughout its course. Critical events by their nature involve, at times, apparently chaotic activity which presents considerable problems of co-ordination. The celebration, though far distant, helps to structure this activity. It is something to look forward to, a goal, taking place at a prescribed time. One can count back from there in structuring the other phases. They become geared to the final product. It gives a sense of 'working towards' and thus helps also to sustain motivation. The second function is that is serves as a rite of passage out of the critical event and back into normality. This might otherwise be difficult to do. The problem of 're-entry' especially from a temporary higher to a more permanent lower status is a common one in all walks of social life. The passage is eased by appropriate rites.

Seen in this way, critical events have a neat and logical kind of symmetry, a distinctive underlying pattern, though on the surface this might not be too apparent. On occasions there might be a multiple event, which builds upon each successive event (see Chapter 5), though these will need some special device to counter the re-entry syndrome precipitated by the previous celebration, and to re-ignite the spark to set the new series in motion.

How does learning proceed through these stages? Prawat (1992, p. 357) writes 'There is a rhythm and flow to learning; periods of equilibrium precede sudden disequilibrium. Students need to mull things over in their minds — to try alternatives, to disagree, and to reflect. This promotes change'. Learning in critical events has a 'rhythm and flow' typically following a 'layering' process. Education does not take place all at one level, but spirals and accumulates and becomes more complex as the event unfolds. Whitehead (in Gershman, 1988) argued that students learn in a rhythm of three stages: through 'Romance', a stage of free adventure, experiment and discovery; through 'Precision', wherein the teachers equip students with detailed knowledge of the subject and train them in skills — there is inevitably a large element of instruction here — finally to the 'Freedom' stage, wherein the new knowledge is actively applied. The student's mind 'responds to the richness of illustration and general truth of the Precision stage; and in response to a 'natural' progression, it seeks fruition of the effort in the Freedom stage. The teacher has begun by 'evoking initiative and ends by encouraging it'. (Gershman, 1988, p. 258) Whitehead's three essential stages can be seen in those depicted above, though not necessarily in that order. Typically, in critical events student learning proceeds along these lines (with 'Romance' and Precision' interchangeable) through all the broad stages above, with more 'Romance' in the early stages and more 'Precision' in the later. A critical event proceeds like a qualitative research study, where initial conceptions prompt data collection which is then analysed, which then, in turn, prompts more data collection, which fills out and refines ideas, and so on. The creativity is thus founded on an increasingly solid basis, which in turn promotes creativity of a higher order.

Each stage thus builds on the preceding one in increasing involvement and intensity, with new depths of knowledge and higher levels of skill, some of them, perhaps, unforeseen. This contrasts with the widespread view among some teachers that 'children's capacity to learn is relatively fixed and broadly estimable'

(King, 1989, p. 15). It is not just a matter of cognition. It involves the whole person of both pupil and teacher. Both sets of interests are being served and there is mutual respect. Both feel strong motivation, identification and emotional involvement. A great deal of excitement and enthusiasm is generated. As John Holt has remarked, 'True education does not quiet things down, it stirs them up. It awakens consciousness. It destroys myth. It empowers people' (quoted in Meighan, 1991, p. 18). This kind of spirit makes light of the hard work involved, and creates time and space for doing things where none otherwise would seem to exist. Typically, no distinction is drawn between school and non-school areas, work and time. The world, city, or village is the school. There is a recognition of the power of learning out of school, and that 'classrooms are far from ideal learning environments' as currently constituted, and that opening them up to the outside provides a broader vision (Desforges, 1990). Critical events are part of the mainstream of life.

The process is not dissimilar to the 'positive cycle of teaching and learning' identified by Pollard (1985, p. 239). Here, teacher and child strategies mesh together. Through teacher initiatives, children enjoy a sense of their own dignity and value. They are stimulated and challenged by the activities provided, their interests are served, and the procedures are judged as fair, in allowing them a say and degree of negotiability. This produces children's enjoyment, which promotes 'real' learning. This in turn, meets teachers' interests, fuels their sense of achievement, which serves as a basis for new inspiration to ignite a new spark and set the process in motion again. 'A cyclical process of reinforcement is created which can then spiral upwards into a higher and higher quality of learning experiences' (ibid.). 'Sometimes', Pollard says, 'Teaching in primary schools goes just like this'.

Conditions for Critical Events

Clearly these events cannot occur very often. Nor is it necessarily educationally desirable that they should. The process of layering takes place outside, as well as inside, the event, so that it has to be contextualized within the pupil's whole scheme of learning. In other words, a period of consolidation typically follows the end of the event. Also, high levels of intensity are achieved, and it is dubious whether these could be sustained more continuously. As it is, the constraints that teachers have to operate under in the state system almost guarantees that such events will be rare occurrences (A. Hargreaves, 1988). At certain times, and in certain schools perhaps, they will be almost impossible. So what do they need?

First, they require legitimation within the curriculum structure. In the days when teachers had more influence over curriculum content and objectives, they had more latitude. With the National Curriculum, the compartmentalization into subjects, specification of attainment targets, and national assessment, there is, at least for the moment, less scope for experimentation. Current political trends against 'progressive' and 'child-centred' education, group work as compared to whole-class instruction, and against topic work, are creating an unfavourable climate. The educational arguments in the debate clearly allow room for such activity (see Chapter 6), but the point becomes occluded in the political rhetoric (Alexander, 1992; Alexander, Rose and Woodhead, 1992). The events are too costly in terms of time, energies and resources to be totally extra-curricular.

If there were general scope for such activity, teachers would need the support of their schools, and particularly the headteachers. Critical events are usually supported by whole-school policy informed by compatible learning theories. It would be difficult for teachers to engage in such practices where that was not the case. They need moral and material support. Some of this is gained, too, from school culture and ethos (Nias, *et al.*, 1989). The experience and support of colleagues is a valued resource. Their activities help produce a climate congenial to the practice. That context is important for pupils is well known (see, for example, Donaldson, 1978). Different rules of conduct and interpretation that can apply among different situations can transform basically similar tasks and activities (Wood, 1986). This had led some to argue that true education does not occur in school, as it is too hidebound by structures, control, constraint, selection procedures and bureaucracy, a popular theme among the de-schoolers. Reimer (1971), for example, was of the opinion that, 'Some true educational experiences are bound to occur in schools. They occur, however, despite and not because of, school'. The best of many people's genius is devoted to hobbies and spare time interests which owe nothing to formal education or to one's work. This is not to say, however, that schools cannot, at times, touch on and nurture this genius. School can be a considerable resource. The question is how we can make best use of it. Critical events help do that, for they place school within the broader and more educative context of pupil learning and development and prioritize that against the other major function of schools, which is to select and control.

Resources are needed — time, energy, money, materials, equipment — often in excess of normal requirements. Inspiration and enthusiasm provides some of these, but there are still basic costs that have to be met if the event is to meet its targets. There is no special fund for such claims, which have to compete with other worthy causes. Entrepreneurial activity often comes to the rescue.

Above all, these events require a 'critical agent', such as a teacher, or teachers, with the vision, commitment, faith, skills and relationships to conceptualize and plan the project, orchestrate it, promote it and bring it to fruition, often in the face of considerable difficulties. They have strong commitment, like Nias' (1989) teachers feeling that teaching is central to their lives, that their identities are enhanced by their work, that it makes them feel 'whole' and 'themselves'. Far from being technicians and deliverers of curriculum, they are reflective practitioners (Schön, 1983; Pollard, 1988), extended professionals (Hoyle, 1980), teacher-researchers (Stenhouse, 1975), continually seeking to improve their work in the best interests of the children they teach. Typically, the teachers concerned with the events which feature in this book, were not seeking plaudits but were self-critical in their appraisal, trying to identify ways in which things could be improved in the future.

They hold a particular conception of teaching, designed to promote 'real learning'. While theoretically-minded, their theory is absorbed and translated into their practical activity, which is a matter continuously of seeking better ways of educational values and bringing them to fruition in classroom practice (Schwab, 1969). They are teacher-artists working to a process rather than objectives model of curriculum development (Stenhouse, 1975; Schön, 1983; Jackson, 1977; Eisner, 1985; Rudduck 1985). Critical teachers are person-centred, as opposed to knowledge-centred. They are concerned with the development of the child's own scheme of relevancies.

They consider context extremely important, being mindful of the social construction of identity, and the impact of situation on motivation, perspectives and view of self. This is not 'dogmatic' child-centredness but one that is based in one's own personal practical knowledge which is supported by tried and tested experience, and is theoretically sound in its own terms. The person-centredness is a structured one, in the sense that it recognizes that all children may not be in an equal position with regard to the teaching aims, and this applies to values, as well as knowledge and skills. There is quite a significant element, therefore, of planning, programming and instruction. Indeed, the art of these teachers lies, to a large extent, in their almost instinctive skill in holding the balance between structure and openness, between instruction and discovery, between direction and freedom.

The management style in keeping with person-centredness is one of 'democratic participation' (Carrington and Short, 1989). This has been found generally effective also in relation to curriculum change by comparison with top-down models (Fullan, 1982). There is an emphasis on cooperation rather than competition, collaboration rather than discrete individualism. Children may work in pairs, small teams or large groups, all contributing in various ways and at various levels to the collective endeavour. The adults concerned — teachers, other professionals, parents, advisers and so on — contribute a range of complementary skills and knowledge, that are blended together by consultation and debate. Critical teachers typically have high-order personal-management skills, which again, strike a note of delicate balance between providing direction and guidance and maximizing personal inputs from others; between securing the best for the children, and promoting the personal development of all. In theory, there should be no distinction between these latter, but, in practice, their relatedness is not always fully evident (for further elaboration of this model of teaching, see Grugeon and Woods, 1990, pp. 211–28).

There are also 'critical others': people who might not be the driving forces, but nonetheless play a significant role in the exercise. They are frequently from outside the school. They might provide specialist skills not otherwise available to the teachers; aid the transition between stages; help with key resource; give general coordination assistance. They contribute to the sense of holism, bringing the outside, real work into the school, incorporating the school into the real world. They provide a new kind of role-model for students, extending their horizons, and making bridges between professional and person. They are part of a team which is enhanced by their presence, and which becomes stronger than the sum of its parts. They act both as validator and motive-spring (Perinbanayagam, 1975), playing their part in the joint construction of meaning.

The particular conjuncture of circumstances and factors is in itself critical for the success of the project. The more these conditions are met, the more the educational outputs stand to be maximized. The more they are circumscribed, the stronger the possibility that any higher aims will be compromised. The project then either takes on a technical-rationalist (Schön, 1983) character, bounded by teacher-imposed rules and guided by strong teacher direction; or falls into a looser and more ill-defined activity which is fun to do in parts but has unclear educational benefits.

I have elsewhere (Woods, 1990a) suggested a model of teaching on an opportunities–constraints dimension. At the hypothetical pure end where opportunities are legion, teachers are free to put their ideas into practice without restraint. At the other, totally constrained, end, teachers do as directed, or suffer unbearable stress or burn-out. In between — the circumstances of by far the greater majority — are a mixture of opportunities and constraints with teachers seeking to maximize their interests through a range of strategies (Woods, 1979; A. Hargreaves, 1978; Pollard, 1982). It will be seen that critical events belong at the opportunities end of the dimension. There might be a moment in a teacher's career when the extreme positive end is reached and golden opportunities are presented — the chance of a lifetime. If seized, the results can be spectacular. They can put down a marker for future aspirations, and through fluctuations of fortune that might equally, on occasions, veer towards the opposite pole, present an experience of possibility and hope to keep in store for better times.

In the following four chapters, I present examples of critical events. The events chosen for study either came to my attention through the media or my existing relationships with schools; or were brought to my notice by colleagues in other institutions. Of those investigated, I select four here for detailed examination, the selection being governed by two criteria. Firstly they are the ones that illustrate most completely and vividly the nature and significance of critical events. Secondly, these four represent major media of expression: book (Chapter 1), film (Chapter 2), planning and design (Chapter 3), and drama, dance and music (Chapter 4). Eisner (1985, p. 211) argues that teachers should seek to 'provide the conditions that enable students to secure deep and diverse forms of meaning in their lives,' and in order to do this, we 'must develop multiple forms of literacy'. These four events provide a range of such 'forms of literacy', and offer opportunities to substantiate some of those 'deep and diverse forms of literacy'. The emphasis here on the creative arts does not mean that critical events are a preserve of that part of the curriculum. As it is, however, the subject matter of the events provides another point of integration in the book. I shall examine each event in the same way. First, I shall introduce the event with some brief details about its composition, reception and evaluation (for more general and detailed consideration of research methodology, see the Appendix). I shall then explore the nature of its criticality: what students, teachers and others gained from it, the radical changes, the cathartic boost to development. Finally, I shall consider the conditions promoting this exceptional boost to learning and development, including teaching methods, organization of the event, critical agents and others, and any further resources.

Chapter 2

An Educational Bluebird:
the Making of *Rushavenn Time*

Rushavenn Time

Rushavenn Time is a book written by Theresa Whistler with the assistance of fifteen children from Brixworth Primary School in Northamptonshire. The children were all volunteers, and not chosen for any academic considerations. The only qualification was a desire to take part, deriving from their own inclinations and an earlier acquaintance with Theresa's *The River Boy*. There were seven girls and eight boys, aged between 8 and 12. Their parents were mainly professional people. They met for ten Saturdays over the period of a year, discussing the book's features, contents and characters, creating events, interaction and dialogue, writing, acting, drafting and re-drafting, with Theresa coordinating the activity, providing the initial inspiration and direction and writing the chapters. The project was the brainchild of the headteacher of the school, Peter J. Woods[1], and was the culmination of a series of events designed and organized by him to maximize children's creative potential. Peter is a firm believer in children having a special quality of insight and perception that all too frequently is dulled by our schooling process. He wanted to set up something that would take that quality to the limit, that would open up new horizons for the 'vision of childhood'. It would, in effect, be a celebration of childhood. It would be fun, but it would also be hard work, and require great dedication and commitment from all concerned. In the process, much else stood to be learned, for example, knowledge of self and others, relating and working together, particular skills of oral and written expression. A number of practising writers had been to work in the school already with great success. Theresa, however, had been a favourite of Peter's since his reading of *The River Boy* in 1956 and he had a more ambitious project in mind. A letter to her publishers eventually found her, and after correspondence and a meeting, the 'Rushavenn project' was born. The aim was to produce a full-length children's story, encouraging and giving free rein to their creative abilities. Thus, while the process was important, there would be a very real, significant outcome which would stand for all time as a testimony to the skill and ingenuity of which children are capable. Clearly the task required the services of a real author — and one who had good understanding of children. Peter provided teaching and administrative support. Jonothan Neelands, a drama expert, completed the team.

The work took place in 1982. Publication had not been an initial aim, but it became more of a reality as time went on. With sponsorship, support and persistence, the book was finally published in 1988 when it won a prestigious, national award. One of the judges described it as 'one of the most outstanding publishing achievements of its kind in recent times'. The story is of two cousins, Sam and Rebecca, who go to stay with their uncles in the West Country. Together they play in the ruined remains of a house ('Rushavenn') which had belonged to a family who were all killed in a bombing raid in London during the blitz. As they play, they meet the family and the house as they were, recreating a rich sequence of encounters and making friends with some of the children. Place and Time are crucial features of the book. There are special properties attaching to Rushavenn, and the persistence and accessibility of the past is demonstrated in the children's play and imagination.

Speaking at the launch of the book, Professor Robert Gibson, a specialist in children's literature, compared the book with classics of the genre, and he 'honestly believed it could hold up its head in their company'. It was 'marvellously well-written'. He insisted that it was not fantasy, but very much 'rooted in the real world, the world you can see, hear, smell and touch'. The characters, both in present and past were 'entirely credible, beautifully observed and rounded out with all sorts of deft touches', with the children 'particularly lively and normal'. Speaking to the children present, he said that if they owned a copy of the book, they would find it 'a magic talisman of great power', that would 'enrich their lives for always, just as the lives of Sam and Rebecca will be enriched for always because of what they saw and felt at Rushavenn'. Clearly this is a special and unique piece of work.

I contacted Peter in December 1988. From that time until the present we have had a number of discussions both at the school and at our homes about the making of the book, his educational philosophy, and about his life and career. Most of these discussions were taped and transcribed. I also had one two-hour discussion with Theresa Whistler, and talks ranging from three-quarters of an hour to two hours at the school with each of three of the children involved, now teenagers and studying for their A levels, reflecting back on their experiences (Stephen, Dawn, and Sarah). In addition, I had the benefit of a certain amount of documentary evidence (including the book itself, but also other work done by the children at the time), and a number of tapes recorded at the time (including a discussion with the children reflecting on the project, a recording of one of the sessions, and interviews with other authors who had been working at the school in other activities).

Radical Change and Development

Critical progress was made by students in two broad areas, to do with knowledge of the self, and skills associated with the art of learning.

Knowledge of the Self

Two sides of this are: the internal construction of self (personal development), and the self in relation to others (social development).

Personal Development

All claimed a great increase in confidence, a willingness to talk and to risk expression of ideas; heightened motivation; a growth in sense of self-worth and self-esteem; a feeling of control of the learning process; a sense of achievement, thrill and pride in a job well done, a record of which had been preserved for posterity.

Theresa told me about Stephen, who had written an extended sunset description in the book. When he started 'he didn't think he could write, he'd brought a sheet of drawings. A group of younger boys who obviously looked up to him echoed it too — "Stephen has very good ideas but he draws them, he doesn't write them." ' After a while, however, 'Stephen produced a story about a magic paintbox or pencil, and it was full of inventiveness and imagination. His parents wrote us a delightful letter afterwards saying they'd never seen him so enthusiastic about a thing like this — he used to write a great deal at home and he never missed a single session'.

Looking back on the project nine years later, Stephen drew attention to the significant factors bringing about this change: meaningfulness and relevance. He said it gave him

> confidence to write, whereas before writing was like maths, was number crunching. You had to be given a task and you had to do it, and the teacher would look at the spelling, that sort of thing. That's what I thought up to that point what writing was about, just to say what you had to say and then hand it in. It taught me that's not what writing is about at all. There's no point in writing something down if you're not going to mean what you say . . . you've got to feel inside that you're telling the truth.

Children's abilities were not foreclosed upon, but recognized and encouraged. Peter remarked 'That rigid distinction between more and less able was doing an injustice to them, because the better we got to know the children the more and more they demonstrated to us that they all had individual abilities of one kind or another and it was not until we really began to identify and recognize their particular abilities that they really began to make a contribution to the sessions'. It is not just a question of ability, therefore. It is so much a matter of attitudes and feelings, confidence, recognition by others. Theresa also mentioned how some had discovered new chances in the project. There was 'one little boy who never missed a single session and was most attentive and when he contributed in talk it was always very much to the point, but I don't think he ever wrote at all; and there was one boy who I found afterwards was dyslexic, and it had meant a lot to him to be with a group doing this because it gave him confidence. And so their contributions were whatever they felt like . . .' On the day of the prize-giving 'the parents of the dyslexic one came up to me and thanked us for the amount we had done for John's confidence; it was lovely to know'. Sarah had told her of the excitement of finding 'that they could contribute what grown-ups were interested in, that their own thoughts and feelings about things that probably they hadn't much put into words, — memories and things that meant something to them — that these were of real value'.

Sarah told me that she and some others had been rather shy to begin with. She overcame it because Peter and Theresa made us feel that everybody was worthwhile. If we had a suggestion to make it was listened to. That played a major part in making everybody feel that it was worth their being there and that you weren't just somebody there to make up the numbers. You were an important part of the group and once you had that security then it was easier to work with people. I'm sure there must have been times when teachers would say, 'Right, we're going to do this, that and the other' and you'd think, 'Oh no! cringe, cringe, hide behind your hands in the corner', but I don't remember that at all from the project.

Asked if she discovered anything about herself, Sarah said:

I think it gave me a lot of confidence, speaking in a group and telling people my ideas and it gave me probably confidence with the work I was doing. It made me feel that my pieces of paper weren't inferior to anybody else's. It made me feel it was worthwhile trying to do my best and it certainly made me take an interest in other books . . .

She remembers the total participation, and that if somebody was 'normally really quiet . . . nobody was like that, even if they were like that in the classroom, nobody ever sat in a corner and didn't say anything'. She herself recalls being 'really reluctant to share ideas in the same way we'd done with Theresa'. She had been 'using her ideas more' as a result, giving an example in art work: 'I'm the world's worst drawer, but if I have an idea I can put it down, I can talk it through.'

Stephen commented that the idea of the book was not to make a group of twenty small authors. It was more subtle than that:

I think it was to expand you as a person, as an individual, not just in areas of writing and illustrations and that sort of thing. If that's what it set out to do, then it's achieved its goal, because that set me off realising that there was more to life than just a teacher imparting knowledge upon you in terms of education.

Peter pointed out that the span of the project from inception and preparation, through execution to, eventually, publication, had given the students new perspective:

That gave them an insight into the protracted nature of an artist's work, and it probably contributed to their growing awareness that education is a lifelong experience; that it touches all parts of your chronology and is not just something which is linked to what happens at school.

As if to bear this out, the students, and especially Stephen, situated Rushavenn within their whole lives and educational careers. Stephen depicted the event as an apogee, a high point in his career. The first year in secondary school was particularly traumatic, as he had to adjust to what he called 'number crunching'. The more successful his primary school in 'creative encouragement', the more the blow at secondary.

I'd say my transformation from primary to secondary was horrific, devastating. My first year at secondary school — I hated it . . . You then have to lose it all, and then have to start all over again in the new atmosphere where things that I'd enjoyed weren't encouraged any more, and were quite positively ignored. That was fairly painful.

The transition from primary to secondary school is a difficult one for many pupils (Measor and Woods, 1984). Projects like Rushavenn can compound the problem. Critics might argue that they are divorced from the real world (an argument used by both sides!), and that primary schools inadequately prepare their pupils for the secondary stage of learning. Stephen has no doubt where the problem lies:

If I'm going to lay the fault on somebody, it's because the secondary school is geared to passing a thousand pupils a year through the education system and get as good a quality result at the end of that as they could. Whereas at primary school there's no 11+, there's no exam to pass or fail, there's no leaving test or anything and there's no pressure on the staff to have to convey the type of quality and volume of knowledge that you have to at secondary school.[2] I wasn't even aware of a curriculum at primary school. I don't know if there is now or if it's just a broad group of headings or what happens . . . But my education was far broader than that at primary school. Putting an exam at the end of the primary school would stop the horrible gap between primary and secondary but it would destroy primary education in the way that it should be . . . School is your life until a certain age and therefore it's responsible not just for reaching this ceiling of education, but for you in society as well. It's got a responsibility to you as a person to educate you more than just the number-crunching exam way. I think most teachers shirk that responsibility at secondary school and I don't think they're too interested in it . . . I think this sort of project, whether it's going to be extracurricular by the teachers and the pupils, or actually worked into a curriculum, is very important. I'm not just talking about a book project, but anything. If you can work that in to the education of a young person it would be invaluable.

Social Development
As Stephen remarked, the group had to work as a group not as a collection of individuals. New skills, knowledge and attitudes had to be developed for this to happen. At the start there were differences of power and authority, age, sex, aptitude and ability, and some individuals had phobias deriving from earlier more formal education. But, in time, some distinctive features of 'communitas' began to appear. For example, there was an equalizing of the sexes in the sense that members of the group rose above the pressures of gender cultures and roles to a new realization of their potential. Peter said that the girls were more willing to express their ideas and emotions in the early stages, and seemed more advanced than the boys. But as time went on the boys grew more confident, realized no-one would laugh at them and that people were 'really interested in their ideas and their feelings'. By the end of the project Peter felt there was no difference in this respect between boys and girls, but he did notice that it was difficult for the boys

to carry these gains over into the normal school context, where they became subject to different peer pressure.

The students confirmed these observations. Sarah said that some of the boys were 'really outgoing, and this might have had a bearing on some who would have felt embarrassed about that sort of thing.' As for herself, 'at that age there's almost a barrier between the two sexes. I wouldn't go anywhere near a boy at that age . . . (but) we all worked together. I mean I don't remember standing back and saying, gracious me, look I'm sitting at a table talking about things with boys'.

Stephen said the boys in the group all surprised each other with what they could do. They would probably be ridiculed, if, in the classroom where everybody's talking about getting out at break time and playing football, you suddenly mentioned 'this wonderful poem I've written'.

I suppose it's embarrassment within the classroom — to write a great descriptive piece about a flower blowing in the wind or something. As a young person whose only aim in life is to score a hat-trick or run faster than the next person, to have this as well was very interesting.

Theresa also noticed none of 'that boy and girl thing' in the group. She recalled that at the very first session when they were asked which characters they would like to develop, the eldest boy picked on the 16-year-old girl Carlie, which she thought surprising. She 'felt he had a slight romantic feeling about her — it brought out that side in him anyway'. Theresa also recalls that age was no barrier. She recalls 'the youngest boy speaking up to the oldest with his own ideas. He didn't feel that because this boy was four years older than him he'd better keep quiet. He would send him off on an errand like an older boy would to get something for him, but they had a lovely respect for each other . . . stratification by age didn't seem to be applying at all.' Stephen recalled that it had a humanizing effect in that you 'got behind the scenes in the school' and you related to the adults as people, not as in their formal roles. Above all it was a 'very social thing. The thing that kept me coming every week was the social atmosphere of it. It was fabulous!'

There were gains here for individuals, but at heart it was a collective accomplishment. Dawn remarked that 'we all got on really well'. Sarah felt that 'the satisfaction was that we were working together really. Looking back that was where it had really shown up, when we were working together.' Theresa spoke of a 'unity of purpose'.

The children would go away and discuss among themselves, sometimes worked on their own . . . but when writing poetry, it was much more like the kind of undefined but strong thing that makes one try to write a poem which you can't put into words until the words are there, and the children seemed to pick that up and be completely in tune with it. I have never collaborated with anybody over writing and I was surprised. I don't think I could do it except with children in this kind of way. It was as if we were seeing the same thing and after the same thing.

The children developed enormous respect for each other and for their teachers. Stephen remarked that there were people in the group who I not only grew to like as friends, but admire as individuals, as writers. Somebody who was better at something than me and I actually looked up to. Andrew was one of them. He's a really interesting person — somebody who I quite admire as a human being. I didn't know the man before we started. The same with Peter. He is somebody I admire greatly now . . . If you go away on a field trip with a teacher, your whole perception of them changes. The relationship becomes educational, it improves incredibly, because the person is no longer this dictator . . . Complete change, black and white almost . . . Usually you don't expect to see the Headmaster teaching even. You just expect to see him strolling around being officious . . . But at the weekends to see him come in jeans and be human was great.

Sara remembered that:

it was so different to anything that we'd done before and it was sort of teacher on our level — there were no barriers anywhere. The only barrier was that we were all shy of each other to start off with. Theresa was a grown-up but we didn't ever feel intimidated by her, and I would always be quite prepared to go and talk to her about things, and tell her my secrets. The same with Mr Woods. It wasn't, 'I'm going to sit here and tell you what to do and you're going to benefit children and come and do it.' I think it was important for them, too, to work *with* us rather than *at* us.

This feeling of 'communitas', doing things together, working for each other without inhibition or the restraints of hierarchy or external culture was one of the prominent features for those taking part. Moreover it was a long-term effect. Peter said 'The special bond between all members of the group still prevails today. This is equally true of my (and Theresa's) relationship with the individual members of the group and the interrelationships within that group'.

The Art of Learning

Learning is not just a matter of absorption, but is an interactional process with strong cultural influences. In order to learn, the child must understand messages, perceive them as relevant and be open to their initial reception. They must also be able to evaluate their learning. At times it seems easy to learn, at others, most difficult. The combination of factors has to be right. So often in the normal school system one or more factors is not right. The objective may not be clear, its purpose to one's own aspirations obscure. The routine nature of much teaching and learning invites a routinized response which may well become established as the norm, learning senses and receptivity becoming dulled. But when something excites, all the faculties come into play, sensitivities are sharpened, insights generated, opportunities created in the recognition. This is essentially an artistic accomplishment. The project refined their learning skills in several ways.

I draw first from a tape of a discussion held by Peter with the group shortly after the completion of the project at the time. They were considering what they had got out of the project. Julia said that it had helped her with the use of words. It gave her ideas as to what words to use to express feelings of people, and it had helped her to make her descriptions more vivid. She had entered for a short-story competition which she would never have done before. Jennifer had never thought of the characters in books she read being real. 'But those in *Rushavenn* were real flesh and blood. You got to know them better, really created people out of words and you gave them life. Also, having a book read to you, it tells you how to imagine it. Since I've had *Rushavenn* read to me, when I'm reading *River Boy* I imagine it all. I can just see River Boy . . .'

Stephen said his writing used to be 'like a child's', now it sounds and feels more creative. Dawn, Jennifer and Julie were all getting better marks for English. Several remarked that they had found new gratification. Andrew, for example, 'used to dread writing, but I quite enjoy writing now'. He had explored a range of books, and had developed an interest in the authors as well as their texts. Some of the boys remarked that it gave them something productive to do on Saturdays, as opposed to lying in bed, or washing-up. Graham found the project exciting, though he had expected it to be boring. It gave him practice at getting up in the morning, and he used this as an example of the life of an author. He could now read longer texts, more quickly.

Several of the girls listed the books they ware reading — an impressive number and range. Julia used to have trouble reading a text, retaining understanding and deciphering a text, but these things began to come together after several sessions of *Rushavenn*. She 'now knew what she was looking for'. Sarah also found that 'the story stays with her better.' Lorraine, too, could 'understand these books more easily than I could before'.

These comments suggest considerable gains in literary appreciation, in the skills of reading and writing, and in the general disposition toward pursuits of this nature. The project gave them a glimpse of the artist at work and of the artist's mind. Seeing things from the inside, as it were, offered a new perspective and opened their eyes to new vistas. Simultaneously, it unlocked the doors to their own childhood vision, which they were given an opportunity to express in both a free and a disciplined way — free in the sense that all were encouraged to contribute what they could and how they would do so; and disciplined by the democratic appreciation of the collective group and its general aims.

Nine years on, Peter said that one of the most important things that he felt the children got out of the experience was the ability to listen, especially 'to listen to other children's perceptions of a particular text or a particular situation, and through listening to other viewpoints to give depth to their own feelings and their own interpretations. They developed the ability to consider objectively the alternative viewpoints and to modify their own, and hence to broaden their experience'. Most did not have this ability to being with. Dawn, looking back, agreed. It had made her

> able to discuss things in front of people, and people you don't really know. That played an important role, especially when we were doing O levels. Also being able to listen to everybody else and what they had to say, and giving constructive criticism.

They learned also to formulate and express ideas, ideas 'which may have been sublimated for years and years because of inappropriate context and environments they had been subjected to' (Peter). Sarah spoke of the special quality of these ideas. She was doing work experience in the school, and

> I never cease to be amazed by the many different ideas that children have. If you give them one idea in a class of twenty, you have twenty different ideas. I think that's incredible, and there must be a lot of people who don't realise how many ideas children have. When you're young, the ideas you have are totally different from the ideas you're going to have when you're older, and there are lots of things that you don't know and lots of things that you forget when you grow older, and it's lovely that they have been got down in a book.

Sarah is talking of a special quality of childhood that was brought out by the project and preserved in the book. When she came to read the book, she read it through about three times, and this brought back to her all the ideas she had had.

> I read something and I remember the day that they had that, and there it is in my little diary, this is what we did. I can remember that happening, and what I was thinking, and places when my ideas have been mentioned. I'd completely forgotten that I ever thought those things and it was incredible, because I don't think I could ever think them up again now.

Theresa also noticed this special quality of childhood. She thought 'you should let children go over the top.' She quoted a poem of Sarah's which she felt 'had grown for her out of the feeling of the child who was always wanting to come back to this house. It fitted perfectly because it had grown out of the same thing that was the whole germ of the story'. Theresa felt that many children have 'a strong, Wordsworthian sort of feeling — instinctive and not necessarily conscious — about childhood, and that they know this is something they are leaving behind. It has a kind of poignancy for them, and the form of the story allowed a play to that.' They were thus 'valuing their own childhood' at a time when they were on the verge of leaving it for adolescence.

Theresa recalled a comment from a neighbour of hers about his 12-year-old son:

> 'He's in the absolute prime of his childhood, the sort of old age of his childhood.' That's just what they have at that age, I think — just before puberty when it's stirring. That gives them a new emotional perspective but they haven't yet got to cope with all the business of adolescence.

Much was made of this point at the launch of *Rushavenn Time*. Peter spoke of the need not only to recognize the existence of the childhood vision, but also to create an environment in which it could find expression, in which 'children could find their own voices instead of imitating ours.' Despite all the debate about child-centredness, little had been done to acknowledge or recognize the vision of childhood, which has 'not yet been clouded by the mists of adulthood'. They do 'not only do things differently, but they do them better, because they are seeing with greater clarity'. Edward Storey, the resident author for the county, spoke of the development of the child's imagination, and quoted from the poet John Clare, whose 'childhood cast a spell over my imagination for the rest of my life' and who thought that childhood was a 'magic world'.

There is a danger here, perhaps, that one might become carried away with romanticizing childhood. That would be an adult indulgence in conceptualizing the principles behind the project. Whatever romanticism was involved — and the nature of the project made it a desirable element — was firmly controlled. As Stephen remarked:

> This was a real, proper book . . . written for children. It isn't a book designed to show how cute 10-year-olds can be when they write poems about butterflies. It's a book that shows that children of 9, 10, 11-years-old really do have something to offer in a poetic and literary way.

Peter recalled how the children gradually came to realize that integrity in writing was important. Then

> you had other children in the group interrupting and saying 'Well, we can't say that because it isn't consistent'. At first this sort of comment was based on consistency of context or what had been said previously about a character, but as time went on their observations became more subtle and sophisticated. They began asking their partners, 'Do you really feel that they would have said that or done that?' Occasionally they might have a slight suspicion that their partner wasn't being totally honest about their feelings for the character . . . They had become so closely knit as a group that they were becoming more familiar with each other's feelings . . .

So not only were they owning and controlling their own knowledge-production, but its quality in certain key respects was subject to the scrutiny of their peers. Peter felt this sharpened their critical powers to evaluate any book.

They learned a great deal about the generation, process, structure and mechanics of writing. Stephen used to have 'quite a problem with spelling and punctuation' but the contact with Theresa worked wonders:

> To write something and then to have somebody who I knew as an author and knew what she was talking about, to say 'Ah, I like that, that's quite interesting, well done, if you could just change it'. She'd then give a bit of active criticism towards it and say if you did this, that and the other then I think you could probably come up with something quite good there . . . So from that, from the encouragement there, I went on to write a lot more within lessons. Whereas before, essays would be 'Get it done!', they became interesting because of Theresa's influence as a teacher . . .

Quality also improved as he

> was able to write more creatively and honestly . . . It was the actual teaching that went on in the groups that equipped me with new tools to

then take out and use in the classroom . . . The actual mechanics of writing were taught within the groups . . . It's like painting. If you go to an art class they'll teach you that you do a different brush stroke for a flower than you would for a house or a solid structure. And then within that you're advised to develop your own start towards a faster brush stroke, if you want to do that, or your own mix of colours, and that's the personal thing. But before you can put in that personal touch, there's the basics that you need to learn. That's what it equipped me with.

At the other extreme, knowledge was gained about the power and structure of writing, and the grand design of producing a work of art. Books are the materials of the school's trade, but pupils and teachers generally have little chance of being actively involved in their production, of experiencing the writer's drive and inspiration, seeing the author's vision, rehearsing the myriad possibilities in one's own mind and in discussion with others, doing the hard work of drafting and re-drafting, taking responsibility for a part, and seeing how the whole of it is coordinated.

Dawn commented that the exercise had given her an enjoyment of English as a subject (if she wasn't doing Music, she would have quite liked to do English):

By having to sit down and write the basis of the book, it gave you an opportunity to not take books for granted anymore. You could see what went into it and enjoyed it more by understanding more. By doing the project it taught you more than you could ever be told in the classroom.

Theresa observed that

children who have made a book have experience of managing to complete a story. It gives them a different attitude towards reading, because they see how people did it. They talked about this a bit themselves, and I remember Sarah and Dawn, they saw more in other books because now they began to see how you do it, why you made the choices, why certain things happen in the structure of a book, or the way it produces its effect, without their having to do it through laid-down rules of criticism. You see, it's so much more instinctive, and I think really much more enriching an experience to do it through trying to make the thing yourself.

They came, too, to more of an appreciation of the artist's mind almost in the act of creation and what actually drives it. They had gained insights into the working of Theresa's mind. Through her, too, they had gained an appreciation of other adults' perspectives and intergenerational links. Peter thought that

this enabled them to be much more at home with the older, more adult characters in the book when they came to create and develop them . . . I'm sure that when those children go on to do their A level work they will be much more able to identify the areas of common ground between one age and another, one person and another . . . and be much more efficient at applying knowledge to other apparently often unrelated situations, which is so important at A level standards.

Above all, perhaps, was the motivation and inspiration unleashed by the project which acted as a catalyst for much of the accomplishment. There was a great deal of excitement felt by all in doing the project. It was conducted at a high level of awareness, with acute sensitivities and deep personal involvement and commitment. This brought out hidden depths and abilities in people, and created time in the sense that much high quality use was made of it. Dawn '. . . enjoyed it. Instead of going out into town, or whatever you used to do on Saturdays, it gave you something to look forward to.' The book gave her pleasure and pride '. . . and other people reading it. It feels nice knowing that you've achieved something that very few people have the opportunity of actually doing'. Yes, her parents had read the book '. . . and her grandparents, aunts and uncles . . .' Rating it among her achievements at school, she said, 'It's got to be very near the top of everything I've done. It's the only thing I can remember from primary school, and from first and second year of secondary school, so it was a fairly important activity'. The only things it compared with were big musical events in her life, like her 'first appearance at the Derngate, or at the Albert Hall with the County Youth Orchestra'.

Stephen, looking back, said:

I'm still proud of it. . . . I've seen copies (of the book) at libraries. I go in and underline my name, . . . I remember when Theresa used to read a piece out to us. One time she read about when the house was in ruins (this is something I did with two others) and a flock of birds flew over the house. We drew a simile between that and the original planes that might have destroyed it, and the atmosphere, and that was almost in there word for word. The excitement of knowing that was going to be published was pretty good. I liked that. I was very proud at the time and I still am now nine years later. My current friends can't understand why I should be proud of something that's so . . . but I remember it as it was. It was wonderful, it was great. It was sad when it finished really; It was one of those events where you probably didn't want to go but once you got there you could stay until the sun went down. The worst thing was when it finished . . . It was just so fresh and interesting, and actually talking to people like Theresa and other authors/visitors who came in who we hadn't met before or were just interesting characters.

Teacher Development

To Peter, *Rushavenn* represents his most gratifying achievement as a teacher. There are ultimates here, things often aimed for, but rarely achieved. For a moment in time, and in his career, the opportunity came for him to turn theory into practice, dream into reality. This then unlocked further possibilities.

Peter mentioned 'going right back to childhood', and in the desire to explain the thinking and *life* behind *Rushavenn* that is exactly what he did. *Rushavenn* is an important part of his life and has to be seen in that context. He remembers his own schooldays of almost entirely formal, and, to him, meaningless, schooling, and the true education he received from his visits to favourite parts of the local countryside from labourers and wardens — the 'critical agents' of his youth.

There is a note of confinement about his youth, behind walls, within schools, within certain school subjects and modes of working; punctuated with the occasional blissful escape. No wonder he is keen on 'opening doors' for the children in his charge.

As an introspective and reserved child, he felt much inner conflict about the duality of his life. Marginality became enshrined in his self and continued with him into later life, for in some teaching posts he had little scope to put his ideas into action. But the marginal person can have uncommon insight. Berger (1971) comments that to move into the margins may be to experience ecstasy. Turner (1974) argues that 'threshold experiences liberate us and renew our humanity' (see also Musgrove, 1976). Aoki (1983, p. 325) commenting on his probing for the essence of what it means to be human, remarks that 'this kind of opportunity for probing does not come easily to a person flowing within the mainstream. It comes more readily to one who lives at the margin.' *Rushavenn*, therefore, had it origins deep within Peter's own past and within his self. His success can be measured by the comparison between himself at school age and Stephen. The project, and Stephen's primary education in general had helped to fashion a perspective which gave him a head start over Peter when at the same stage. Peter had been alienated, confused and reserved when a pupil at school. Stephen, and the others involved in *Rushavenn*, had vision, confidence and the power of expression. Consequently they had the ability to evaluate their schooling for what it was. They could articulate their views, and had the courage to state them. It is not unreasonable to conclude that *Rushavenn*, and the educational ethos that surrounded it, had been a major instrument in fashioning this perspective.

Why had it not occurred before? Peter said:

> I don't think I really understood in my own mind or could put some kind of configuration to all of those various experiences which I picked up along the way — going right back to childhood. What happened really was that up to the time of Rushavenn, there had been a number of incidents which set up warning signals or queries in my mind which made me want to question some basic concepts about education and strategies used in teaching. In the early stages certainly I did not have wide enough experience of teaching and education in general to actually formalise all of those things and it really wasn't until we embarked upon *Rushavenn* that many of those things began to fall into place and I could see a way in which the whole situation in the classroom could, to a certain extent, be changed and improved to the advantage of everyone. Certainly I would regard the Rushavenn project as providing the key to a whole range of earlier experiences. . . . The more I think about the project and those incidents prior to it, the more I feel that had it not been for the almost accidental idea of looking at the situation where a practising writer and a group of children worked together, many of those initial experiences would still be perhaps dangling in mid-air. So I would regard *Rushavenn* as very important in my own educational development.

He conveys through imagery its special significance to him. He told me about a trip he had made to the Craters of the Moon in Idaho, USA.

This volcanic plain struck me as being analogous to large parts of the traditional British educational system: the overpowering aridity — sterility — of the landscape. Barely anything could be seen living or growing. The sudden appearance of a mountain bluebird, however, demonstrated that there was life amongst all this desolation. It merely had to be sought out and pursued. It was Idaho's national emblem — the bluebird — that particularly interested me and this small, but colourful bird was to achieve a particular symbolism for me in that barren landscape. The Rushavenn Project was, in effect, an attempt to chart the flight of one such educational bluebird.

As the project developed and his relationship with the children changed, so he began to introduce Rushavenn techniques more into his everyday teaching. He had done this to a certain extent before, but was now 'able to approach this kind of teaching with increased confidence', and was able 'to pass on some of the benefits of Rushavenn to those children who had not participated'. He arranged classrooms more informally; developed the use of role-play; arranged for more discussion about literary texts. The Rushavenn group 'became catalysts for all manner of developments in our day-to-day life in the school . . . Their active involvement and enthusiasm for such developments, helped to enrich our curriculum'.

What happened with Rushavenn has remained thoroughly enshrined in the philosophy of Brixworth School in that we have always been more interested since that time in a child-centred approach . . . It is in our documentation, our guidelines for new staff. It is not simply restricted to the language side of things; it invests our approach to the whole curriculum, from Science to Mathematics and Religious Education.

He constantly sought opportunities to

quietly introduce some of the Rushavenn thinking into staff-meetings and in-service training sessions, to the lasting benefit of all concerned. Notwithstanding educational revolutions, in whatever form they take, the achievements of the past cannot be denied if they are truly worthwhile.

The Critical Conditions

How was the Rushavenn Project accomplished? I identified prominent features to do with context; the use of multi-methods; roles and relationships; critical agents; content and 'drawing out'.

Context

Peter puts great emphasis on the situation and ambience where teaching and learning take place. It is well-known that children can assume different identities in different circumstances, and that some are not at all favourable to their educational development (Brice-Heath, 1982; Turner, 1983). Peter recognized the restrictions of the ordinary classroom with its arrangements of chairs and desks, its style of furniture, its central point the teacher's desk and the teacher's possessions, 'regular patterns which bring a regular pattern of response from the children'. This may be necessary at times, but at others it inhibited an 'honest and in-depth response'. It was significant, therefore, that the event took place on Saturdays, outside normal school hours, and that the main room used was the staffroom. There . . . each of us were part of a circle, so that no-one in that circle occupied a position which was more important than anyone else.' When he first took over as headteacher, he did not think about such a grandiose project. His time was largely taken up with administration, but there were a number of sessions during the week when he had some spare time. He would split one of the larger classes and take half in rota to the Rural School's Project building, beside Brixworth's famous Saxon church. There they would look at books like *Joby* and *Beowolf*. The proximity of the church was particularly meaningful with the latter text. It was rather like 'being present at a production of Prometheus in the open-air theatre at Delphi with birds of prey circling above'. It was here that he began to evolve the idea of changing the typical school environment. Authors came to discuss their work, often staying on in the evening, when parents joined them. The level of the children's communicative competence, I was told, surprised both authors and parents. Theresa picks up these points and relates them to the ethos of the school. Brixworth may have had its bureaucratic constraints from Peter's point of view, but Theresa thought it quite distinctive. From early on she found the children 'enormously responsive', and saw this as

> very much a feature of that school, that they'll come out to meet your ideas and answer. There was never that sort of dumb silence — the semi-circle of shut faces — never once, and that was there right from the beginning. I'm sure that's from the general atmosphere in the school and the way they're taught.

She also referred to the fact that

> they do so much creative work, these children; so much of their ordinary lessons is grouped round projects. They produce the most wonderfully imaginatively decorated school books and things of all kinds. They've been used to it individually. You'd have a great deal more loosening up to alter the set attitudes of children who have been taught on the basis of teacher doing all the input and the child writing it down or memorising it. I can't believe it would work in any school.

How did the project appear to the children and how did it compare with 'normal' school? Stephen recalls his impressions of the environment:

> It was a strange atmosphere really . . . It definitely was an educational experience but it was as far away from the classroom as you could get. In a classroom the teacher has to teach one idea to 30 pupils and he can only teach it in one way. He can't say 'you five at the back, you can write

a poem because I know you enjoy poetry and you at the front can put some illustrations in because I know you enjoy illustrating.' Whereas in the group sessions we had what was needed to actually get the idea in as many different forms as possible and in the best way possible. So it was a far better learning experience because of the one-to-one bouncing of ideas and encouraging something that you felt quite confident with.

On the actual situation, he said:

It was never Theresa and Peter at the desk and the children sitting in front of the desk. I think that was the idea of going in the staff room because it's quite a big space, comfortable chairs and we all just sat where you wanted. I still remember it as being quite a grown-up activity, the whole thing about it; if you fancied getting up and getting a drink of water or coffee you didn't have to put your hand up . . .

Multi-Methods

Peter emphasized the importance of instilling confidence into all members of the group. Some, he felt, were being held back because of apprehension about their abilities deriving from their experience of traditional schooling. Some were more confident expressing their ideas in an oral form, some using their hands.

So at an early stage we introduced a range of media: pencils, paints, colouring pencils and so on. . . . We also urged as great a variety of response as possible through the poetic, narrative and cartoon forms. One member of the group was particularly good at drawing cartoons and so that was a way in for that particular child. Others, and we hadn't investigated this to any extent within the school at that time, responded to role play and through drama. During some of the mime sessions, when the children were encouraged to create photographic frames, sort of *tableaux vivants*, of the next stage of the story's development, those who couldn't get their ideas down on paper and didn't have the confidence to respond orally, often came up with some absolutely wonderful ideas. The resultant expressions of appreciation of the contribution by the other members of the group increasingly gave these children the confidence to expound their ideas orally. The developing oral confidence of such children was one of the venture's most notable achievements.

At the end of the year, therefore, there was much less distinction between oral and writing ability among members of the group than there had been at the beginning. In Peter's opinion, this was less a matter of transfer of skills than one of new-found confidence in expressing one's nascent abilities. By providing a range of methods, maximum opportunity had been given for each member to excel. The appreciation of that by the group then encouraged them in other fields.

Peter talked of some children facing brick walls in their normal schooling, and the project 'opening up doors' for them by providing alternative methods. Two of the favourite children's books were *The Secret Garden* and *Tom's Midnight*

Garden in both of which children achieve heightened awareness of the totality of their lives when they discover the door in an intimidating high wall and gain access into the 'secret garden' beyond. As a teacher, he is constantly trying to find the right 'door' for each child. It took some time to identify the appropriate ones for individual children. Peter gave the example of one girl (Dawn) who wanted to express certain ideas. She tried writing it down in prose, but being a perfection-ist wasn't satisfied with that so then tried a poetic form, then drama, then drawing and painting. One day she revealed that she enjoyed playing the flute (it was her most treasured possession). Theresa suggested introducing a musical element into the story, and Dawn writing a piece of music for that. She did, and

> achieved the level of response with the words which she wrote and the music to accompany it in a way she hadn't been able to do in any other area, and from that point on she was a different girl. She had found the medium that was appropriate to her, but having achieved that success with the flute become more confident and achieved similar successes in the written word, especially in poetry, as the poetic element came closer to music . . .

Other ways in which the changes were wrung were in the groups within which they worked and the materials they used. After the general discussion in the staffroom, they would break up into groups and go off to various classrooms to pursue ideas on particular items further. Peter went round, because 'it fascinated him how it worked':

> There were some children who were much more confident working in a group of two or three. Others were far happier working on their own. Others preferred to work with a blank piece of paper in front of them to start with, some preferred the blackboard so that they could use the board-rubber to erase their work and try a different phrase, a different word . . . And then I had some very interesting sessions with the children where, having let them work individually or in pairs or in slightly larger groups, we all came together as a group and I went to the blackboard and said, 'Now, let's have a wide range of responses, ideas from you about the next passage or chapter.' I collected the ideas from them, jotted them down on the blackboard and then we used this summary as a basis for further work and discussion.

Comparing their usual schoolwork, Sarah said:

> I think the one difference was that we had so much freedom within the project . . . We used to do these Social and Environmental Studies, and everything we did in one half-term would be based round that. But the stuff we did with Theresa, it could have been on anything and that was a big difference.

Stimulation might come from some surprising quarters. For some ideas to take root and blossom, many had to be sown and cultivated. Theresa mentioned a boy whose father was an architect, and who produced a drawing of a house out of which came the incident of Sam drawing his idea for the rebuilt house. Things often work like that, you see. I get an idea from something at a tangent from what we were doing . . .

It is consequently difficult to analyse the process and to be precise. Theresa said that 'In a way I can't tell you how we did it. It went well, so it grew . . . I didn't write the story of how it would be beyond the session we were at. I had no idea how it would work'.

This kind of 'structured openness' seemed to be particularly productive, as did the combination of the children's ideas and Theresa's skill, insight and experience in pulling them together:

I remember this happening in family paper games. On occasions people, almost telepathically, suddenly get going. It was rather more like, I suppose, children who are writing and producing a play or an opera or something of that kind. It had that element of excitement in it. I wanted, if possible, to set free everything that they could do and not give them the burden of sustaining a long written piece which is too much at that age.

Peter described it as

a bit like an amoeba in that you would push out in one direction and if we found we met an obstruction and something didn't work we would withdraw and try something else. This might entail branching out in an entirely different direction altogether. Sometimes we would find that part of the shape was able to continue, but other parts met an obstruction. Thus, amoeba-like we would continue pushing forward in that direction until we felt that we were in danger of becoming too isolated, too far removed from the central structure . . . We wanted to test the ultimate extent of it, but we had to bear in mind that we were involved in writing a story and that there had to be an overall structure, a framework in which we could continue operating. This was particularly important with group authorship.

At times, they allowed things to develop outside the framework because they felt it was contributing to the development of the children concerned, and to their own knowledge of children and their potential. Peter gave the example of 'photographic frames', an idea Jonothan introduced:

Here, a moment in the story was crystallized by children taking up certain postures, the idea being that they would then act out the next sequence in the story. They would divide up into individual groups of four or five, pool their ideas and work out a sequence of events which they would enact. They would then decide on a representative moment of time in that particular sequence and they would assume miming postures, just as though a shutter had come down in a camera and had fixed them there and then. The other groups would try to interpret their postures.

31

The members of the miming group then gave their explanation. By this time they had become so involved in the story itself that the characters had almost become real people to them and they recounted not only what they were doing, but how they were feeling, and the kind of smells which were in the room at the time. For example, we had some wonderful descriptions of what autumnal apples are like, and apples which have been wrapped up and put in the attic. Often their descriptions of things like that and of the emotions which they evoked, were so mature that we just let them go on and on talking about them. . . . Sometimes they became so involved with a character they were almost speaking with that person's voice and there were points when it was a rather eerie experience . . . There were times at the end of those sessions when we had to take time out to de-role, both the children and ourselves.

This was revealing for the teachers as well as for the pupils:

It seemed to underline the fact that we were beginning to feel, more and more, that we just didn't know the children that we had been teaching, or that we'd been seeing them in such a shallow way and had been greatly underestimating their capabilities. It was as if, at that moment of time, we had been given an insight into their true potential which, because of a combination of circumstances, we had very briefly released . . . Our experience has led us to believe that the more you investigate the potential of children the more limitless it seems to be.

Role-play is, in fact, a powerful educational tool. Moreno (1972), for example, sees the possibility for using this powerful response to produce personal development, seeing the function of role adoption as 'to enter the unconscious from the social world, and bring shape and order into it'. Heathcote (1972) discusses the importance of 'living through' the experience of others not otherwise available to them. It is the process that is important, not the product, requiring 'the provision of situations which challenge the energies, the intelligence and the efforts of the child in his class'.

Roles and Relationships

The book was the result of teamwork. Relationships among and between the teachers and children were vital. The basis of the teacher–pupil relationship was democratic, and based on mutual trust and regard. It was this, together with some special qualities of the participants, that generated the 'communitas'. They inspired each other, 'sparked each other off', probed, complemented, extended, evaluated, applauded. Individuals, already lifted by initial recognition, were further lifted by their involvement in the activities of the group.

Amongst this group, the teachers were guides, facilitators and human beings. So often in schools teachers are not regarded as human beings or 'proper persons' (Blackie, 1980). The role has dehumanized them in the eyes of pupils. This divide was crossed, and in some respects a close, family feeling was developed. Theresa, of course, was not a teacher in the formal sense. But she was an adult, which could have brought its own barriers, and she could have adopted 'teacherly' tactics. Instead, she adopted the children:

> I felt about them that they were children of my own. I got immensely fond of them and found them all without exception delightful to be with . . . It was lovely sitting there like a fisherman, because you put your rod out and wait and quite often they would supply special ideas in a break. I would sit with them and they'd come and offer me a biscuit or a crisp or something and then tell me something else which perhaps they hadn't yet had the courage to do in full circle. Or other things: this little boy, who never wrote anything much, would tell me what mattered to him very much which was obviously the birth of little twin brothers. He would talk about them with great feeling and wanted me to share that . . . There was a sort of spontaneous family party feeling about it. They showed me anything they felt like. They quite often brought school work that they liked doing . . .

Being an 'author' might have put Theresa 'at a distance' from them, but Sarah 'certainly never felt like that at all. Maybe because she had brought photographs and things that were personal to her, we were able to realise that she was a person, not just an author . . . She always made us feel at home' . . . Sarah's parents were sympathetic and helpful but she didn't think 'I ever talked about it with them like I would do to Theresa, because it was something very personal to us. It was something special between us all'.

Dawn remembered Theresa 'vividly'. She was 'lovely'. She was a 'sort of teacher' but 'a friend as well. She was always willing to listen. If she disagreed with anything you said, she would never criticize it, just make comments on it, which always seemed to make sense. And she was always willing to help if you had any problem at all. I had expected a rather large lady with glasses, sitting there and saying "that's how it will be", but she was completely the opposite!' Dawn thought that Theresa 'could have been a teacher, but teachers don't usually get that close to the pupils they're dealing with. She was a friend really.' She didn't recall any teachers with whom she had had a similar relationship, except in the last two years when she has been doing A levels. Teachers at primary school 'tended to treat you as one of the little children, "get on with it, I've told you what to do". They've got to be on a pedestal to a certain extent, something to look up to and be frightened of, to get the respect'.

The work thus proceeded on a democratic, participatory basis. The project belonged to them all. All identified with it, and invested part of their 'selves', enthusiastically. It was important that all contributed to it as freely and as ably as they could; that they felt it was theirs, not done for teachers or anybody else; that they felt they had a share in control of the process; and that they approved of the products. Peter described how this worked. Theresa would read out what she had written, using the ideas generated the previous week. She would then invite comments and these would be discussed. If necessary, the text would be amended according to their ideas, for she was 'very concerned that the children were happy with the finished product'. She would then invite them to suggest further lines of development, and they would go off in their groups to work up ideas in detail. These discussions became so productive that they were often continued far beyond the session in pupils' homes. Sometimes these ideas were transferred to the blackboard for general discussion. As well as the usefulness of the ideas, there would be debate about the appropriateness of words, sentence construction, the dangers of repetition and so on. In this manner, 'the children themselves were responsible for finalising the collective ideas of the group'. Peter gave the example of

> the section on the Green Man which evolved through just this kind of discussion. It was put together by one of the groups of children. They continued to work on it at home and there was a minor complaint by one of the parents that their child's bedroom had been invaded by about four other children from their child's group and the resultant discussion had been so animated that Dad in the room below couldn't hear his television programme. What we have here is a group of children who, until recently, had spent most evenings watching television, suddenly migrating to that child's bedroom in order to work on a piece of creative writing.

In consequence, the children had a strong sense of ownership and originality. Sarah had no doubt that 'We all felt very much it was our ideas because there were lots of chunks in the book which were almost exactly what we wrote'. She draws the contrast with her present work:

> At the moment, I write something down and I write it because I have to write it because I'm doing A level English. But I would like to think that there comes a stage when I've finished my education that I will be able to write things that are part of me and not part of what people have told me to do . . .

Sarah seems to be saying that when she has finished her formal schooling she can return to more meaningful education such as she experienced with *Rushavenn*. Theresa remarked that 'you can see in the mass of material they produced that they were using their own voice'. When Dawn read the published book for the first time, 'things would lift themselves off the page, and I would think "Oh! I can remember doing that — or somebody doing that". I was surprised how much of it was actually our work, although Theresa had written it. There's an awful lot of our ideas in there'.

For Peter,

> the experiences of the children and of the adults merged to such an extent that it was almost impossible to disentangle the various contributions. There were occasions when I found myself talking about an idea as if it were my own whereas, on reflection, I have realised that the initial suggestion had come from one of the children. I can recollect a number of instances of this kind when the adult members of the group have quite unconsciously and unintentionally appropriated ideas which have stemmed from suggestions made by the children. The adult may have developed the idea, but the original inspiration could be traced back, through a number of stages, to a statement or a word or a phrase which a child had introduced into the discussion, perhaps weeks before. We were all continually feeding off each other's ideas.

The group, therefore, was a particularly productive organic unit, with the children generating and developing ideas, Theresa providing the overall vision, and doing the main coordinating and sustained writing, with Peter facilitating and resourcing. This was an especially efficacious mix in view of the product — a children's book which explores the links been past and present, and between childhood and adulthood. The children experienced the double achievement of creating a contribution of their own, and then of seeing how it made a higher order sense within a larger whole. Stephen spoke of the excitement he felt when Theresa read out the next piece:

> because, although we were very involved, we were isolated from the plot. We didn't sit down at the beginning and say 'the book's going to be about x, y and z and the characters will change in this way'. We were helped to develop character development, and small points in the plot, detailed areas, but the general plot and theme of the book was left almost entirely to Theresa.

Critical Agents

Theresa and Peter were clearly typical critical agents. Theresa did most of the actual writing. From Stephen came this comment about the author's skill:

> Theresa did an awful lot of work on her own on the guts of the story, the actual churning it out. When I first joined I imagined it more to be like us writing the book under the coordination of Theresa's direction, whereas what it was, we were the imaginative impetus for the thing and she took it on further than that. The reams that she turned out freehand on the draft were more than the group sessions produced per Saturday. It would have taken several years to write if we'd considered doing it ourselves and I'm sure it wouldn't have been of any quality because of the modular nature of it. I think the problems of trying to write a novel with a group of 10/11 year-olds producing all of the work would have been insurmountable, because you need someone who is going to be not just a coordinator but who is going to use all these ideas in the right way. Theresa had all the experience to do that. She's very good at doing that.

Peter was the initiator and mainstay of the event. He had laid the groundwork in his school over several years. Now was the time to strike out and attempt something truly adventurous. He assembled the ingredients, nursed the project along, and was largely responsible for the facilitative ethos that developed. He kept things going after the end of the writing, pursued publication chances, negotiated with sponsors, and finally brought off publication internally, and eventually the esteemed prize. Robert Gibson at the launch paid tribute to his 'vision, patience, drive and dedication'. He said that his seemed to be

> a school where the doors open daily on delight, and that his principal preoccupation is precisely the one under the greatest threat today from all points of the compass. I mean the infinitely precious true values of

childhood. If all our headteachers were so devoted or half so imaginative as he is on their behalf, this country's very real educational problems would be solved.

Peter thus provided the initiating and organizational drive. But he was also very involved on the creative side in a collaborative way. Stephen described how Peter often did his own version of tasks they were set within their groups. 'To listen to that, you could really learn from it . . . it was really very good quality'. As for Theresa, she was

a very special person. I'd never met anyone like her before, and in a way not like grandma more of a great aunt, that sort of relationship. I felt very easy around her . . . I think it was a lot to do with her style of writing. As she's written children's books before, she acquired the techniques for writing this one and so as an author she could relate to us as children. But the most important thing was that she made us feel as if we were making a very worthwhile contribution and not that it was a bind every Saturday to have to go all the way to Brixworth, but that every Saturday was important to writing and finishing the book. Towards the end of the project there'd be a sense of urgency to get it finished by a deadline, and as the sworn authors of the little pieces, she made us feel that there were deadlines there as well and there was an excitement about it all. Theresa was perfect for the job.

As an exercise, also, in team-teaching, it was important that the teachers complemented each other. Peter had clearly identified, through her writings, a kindred soul in Theresa, and she had responded. Theresa said 'I already knew and liked Peter — there was a lot of sympathy between us'. But they could still have got in each other's way during the exercise. This was not the case. Theresa had this to say:

Peter is a gentle and unassuming person, though very effective. He always let me have my head. I didn't feel it would work if there were too many grown-ups sitting in on the sessions and putting in ideas. I'd have lost the thread, but it never did really arise at all. Peter never did that. He very much sunk himself into the atmosphere of the story, and of course it was a great help to me that he approved of it as we went along. It made me, like the children, feel that my ideas were worth having.

Stephen, looking on his school career as a whole remarked 'a teacher has got to be so dedicated to his task in order to be a good teacher that they're fairly hard to come by the ones who are going to be good for you'. As Theresa remarked about Peter

I remember when Peter was getting overloaded with administration, his way of relieving his load was to give up ten Saturdays in his year to this. He didn't get paid for it. He just did it out of love . . . When it came to publishing and printing it ourselves that work was absolutely colossal. Peter and I nearly died of it last autumn trying to deal with it while we were both having flu . . .

None of this would have happened therefore, without the initial vision of teacher and author and their dedication to seeing the task through.

Content

The subject matter clearly appealed to the imagination of all concerned. The task itself had attractions. Theresa felt that:

> One learned much faster and much more intensively with the excitement of a thing that was working towards a performance, and, this idea of producing a book at the end, I think, did help the motivation very much.

They were captivated from the beginning. Theresa

> was astounded by the first meeting because I thought this would prob-ably get off to a slow start . . . I'd never written a children's story before with so many characters. I thought 'let's have a biggish spread of char-acters and both sexes so that they can choose one or other that appeals to them.' At that very first session, they pinned on a particular character and then went off in little groups to discuss it and produce it. And we worked that day, as far as I remember, from 9.30 until 4. I was absolutely starv-ing when I went home. Exhausted!

The nature and ambience of the setting of the book, characters and their relationships also had strong appeal. It was not ethereal sentiment, pandering to the 'innocence' of childhood as in the ideology identified by King (1978) and Alexander (1984), but feelings generated in real life about real issues. The place 'Rushavenn' was in fact based on the North Devon home of Theresa's family, burnt down by accident during the war, where she had spent her childhood. She 'wanted to celebrate her lost home, and share it with children'.

> I loved every minute of doing it. But I think a great deal did depend on the fact that I've always had a story to write about that farmhouse which meant so much to me and my own childhood. The way the child Pin cares for it is direct autobiography. For years after it was burnt down in 1942 I could have told you the exact shape of every inch of it inside. It was a very, very strong passion for the place. I think the children picked up the fact that they were entering into something which meant to me whatever makes any writer write anything. So it wasn't quite like setting out to do a project. It was much more like writing the thing I really wanted to write, with the extra stimulus of these wholly sympathetic and delightfully alive companions.

Stephen pointed out that:

> at primary school you are fairly isolated, so to become somebody in your own right at the age of 9, 10, 11, is fairly special. To be able to move away from that isolated small world by writing, by listening to the stories

37

that Theresa and Peter and the group had created, was secret worlds, lost islands, all that sort of thing . . . I think even now I'd still like to open the cupboard and find something in there. So, yes, in that sense of her creating something that we felt we could quite happily expand was definitely quite a big part of it. If it had been a book about a different topic I'm not so sure. If it had been a book about two children spending a holiday with their family travelling through France, it may well have been a very good children's book and might have been a best seller, but as far as getting a group of pupils to actively take part in that, and motivate themselves, I think it would have been a lot harder task.

As for the characters in the story,

they all, one way or another, turned out to be like Theresa. She'd created these characters. If they weren't like her, they were people that you would imagine that she'd like to have around her. They were children you could imagine she would have in her back garden. I'm sure she did it deliberately, put people into your work who you wanted and you think you could relate to as a writer. We definitely felt fairly close to the two main characters and the family especially the 'Time Ghost' family. Because of the fantasy aspect of it everybody wanted to write the part that, during one particular section of the book, one of the characters for the first encounter, the leaves of the tree form into the shape of a face in one of the children's minds and it is one of the ghosts spooking the child and everybody wanted to do that bit because that was the part of the book that was interesting. The children arriving at the house and the wonderful views were very nice. The characters from the past were the most interesting . . . The story's good anyway, but I think the strongest part of the book is the interaction between the children of the present day, who you could very easily see as yourself, and the characters from the past, who were obviously Theresa's children. So relationships between the present and the past were interesting.

Stephen's favourite character was Fady:

mainly because of the way we came up with his name. He left his old cloth in the window of his tailor shop and it faded in the sunshine. He made one suit a year. The rest of the time the cloth would sit in the window fading, so everyone would call him Fady. That quite tickled me that did, so I think that's what captured me.

'Drawing out'

'It was lovely to have nobody who didn't want to be there, and that's the main thing that makes it unlike school'. (Theresa)

The teaching philosophy was to lead out rather than force in, light candles rather than fill empty vessels, educate rather than instruct. Three prominent aspects of this approach were stimulation, encouragement and example.

Stimulation

After years of 'patterned responses', ideas do not just come. They have to be stimulated and fostered. One way of doing this was by providing 'props'. On Theresa's first visit, she took a hat-box containing some of her treasured mementos:

> I had a mass of photographs of the farm as it was before it was burnt and sketches by my grandmother who was good with her pencil. There were some little drawings of the outhouses and so on, so I think the children got a very strong visual sense of the place. My mother was very good at photographs. They had a kind of poetry to them these things I had of the place and it wasn't the kind of house that the children knew. It wasn't familiar to them. I don't think any of them had been in that kind of old farmhouse. That fascinated them. I think it would all children . . . It has a magic for children . . .

Other things included a book which she had made at school; a 2d story-book and a Victorian manual of etiquette for young ladies. Peter thought this a very effective teaching strategy:

> At that time the children were making their own books in school, and when they saw that Theresa had made a very similar book when she was at school and they saw the date — 1940 something — ancient history to these children, they were fascinated. They suddenly realized that whilst, on the one hand, they had looked upon people of Theresa's generation as a race apart, as soon as they saw her books they began to understand that there was continuity in life. Consequently, they were able to relate much more closely to Theresa, and they began to identify more and more areas of common ground. Moreover, when Theresa was talking about the photographs of a very elderly lady whom she had known when she was young they began to realise that there was common ground between that lady and Theresa, between Theresa and their parents, and between Theresa and themselves. They began to see a variety of new links between generations which they hadn't previously understood. These were to become important themes.

This served them well when it came to developing characters within the story. Sarah agreed that this was helpful:

> If you had a picture of a little girl and you say, 'What do you think? What does she remind you of? What do you do with her?' I found it very easy to respond to.

On another occasion the children were asked to take in a special possession that they would keep if they had to surrender everything else, and to say something publicly to the others about why they valued it. This gave them a sense of personal identification, and practice in speaking to the group on a subject near and dear to them. Since the personal value of these items was appreciated by the others, it also promoted the sense of togetherness. Stephen reported that there were games, collections of things like rubbers, and 'china dolls'. One girl took her 'battered old teddy bear', 'Fiercy'. Among the more intriguing items was a carved sandstone head that Andrew had found in his garden. 'Everyone was fascinated, of course, and we developed on that and that was written into the book' (Stephen).

Another girl, Peter recalled, was rather reticent, but eventually said the thing she would most want to preserve would be her friendship with another girl in the group:

> Now once she'd said it she was much better and she began to talk about their shared experiences. They'd been on holiday with their parents together. There were common interests and other things like that. Subsequently, the two girls worked as a pair on pieces of writing and it seemed to me that, from that point of time, there was far more cohesion to their contributions. Up till then they had been producing joint pieces of work where you could actually pick out the individual components. But after that session, they began talking to each other more about their work, so that in time you had great difficulty in saying which piece belonged to which girl.

> Another girl brought along a little glass horse from a glass merry-go-round and she said how much that merry-go-round had meant to her. This invoked in the group memories of fairs which they had visited, and this, in turn, gave rise to a lot of evocative discussion. In fact, the glass merry-go-round element was introduced into the Rushavenn story.

One of the boys enjoyed drawing cartoons and wanted to preserve his collection. He had been reading some Greek Legends, and he had created a 'Greek gnome' character with a Greek name.

> He started talking about that and he and his partner went away afterwards and wrote a little piece about Greek gnomes, combining the Germanic and classical mythology all in one, and that, too, was introduced into the Rushavenn story. So by talking about cartoon drawings which he'd produced, he evoked an idea which was appropriate to the developing story of Rushavenn, and it was seen to be appropriate by the rest of the group and they seized upon it. It was not the originator of the idea who suggested that it ought to be included in the story. The rest of the children seized upon it because they had begun to see relevance beyond their own production.

The aim was to stimulate ideas freely and engage in a kind of brain-storming. Stephen described it as a 'think-tank':

> At the end of the session she'd have this incredible amount of ideas and thoughts that we'd had around the characters. Then she would take them home with her and turn them into the next chapter of the story. We'd start each session by her reading to us what she'd done so far and then we'd talk about that, and then we talked about new ideas that led from that.

Encouragement

At the core of Theresa's thought was the creative potential of the human being:

> I'm sure that what excited them was the instinctive creativeness that I think all human beings have, whether they're cooking or whatever they're doing. I think it is natural to human beings to create and life stultifies them if it isn't allowed expression in some way or another . . . I wanted to help discover for each of them the kind of interior pressure that makes you want to create. And so I didn't want to criticize. I felt that you get a lot of that as you're growing up anyhow . . . I preferred not to correct their work and I know one or two of the girls rather wished I would say what was good and wasn't good in their own work, but it wasn't really what I was after. I think that people can only be creative when they feel encouragement, when they feel the thing they're trying to do is wanted by an audience or recipient somewhere. What I wanted was to help discover for each of them the kind of interior pressure that makes you want to create. I wanted each to feel like an artist, to feel that they could do what an artist does . . . I had a very strong instinct not to revise. Normally I'm a compulsive reviser. I think that it's a bit purple-patchy, goes over the top rather in description sometimes. I deliberately didn't prune that in my own writing because I remember when I was a child taking off into description and I think it was one of the liberating things when a child finds they can write descriptively. It's very important not to say you're over-doing this because the freedom to express something poetical finds its way out like that at first, and their own sense of self-criticism or other people will certainly prune it later on.

Stephen reported that:

> As a person I'm fairly relaxed about talking publicly anyway but to be given a chance to do it and to be appreciated for it is something different. You're OK if you don't mind talking or reading in the classroom, but when you're actually praised for saying something that makes you feel special. She'd say 'that's a good idea', or 'just hold on a minute' . . .

Peter describes Theresa's technique:

> Theresa's function was like that of an expert seamstress making a patchwork quilt. If we regard the children's product of those sessions as being the individual coloured squares of that quilt then Theresa took various pieces and arranged them and sewed them together in such a way that the resultant coverlet was not only aesthetically pleasing, but held together in all its parts. In any narrative there has to be continuity of language and of structure and it was this element that Theresa, through her long experience as a writer, was able to bring to the story. This was not always directly related to the Rushavenn story. If any child felt like penning a poem or a piece of prose, about anything which stimulated their imagination, Theresa always went out of her way to give the child encouragement, by showing that she was interested, not only in work having a

direct bearing on the developing Rushavenn story, but that because she was interested in them as people and the kind of experiences which were important to them, she wanted to see whatever they wanted to show her. These pieces of writing were collected together in a large brown envelope and sent to Theresa at regular intervals. In this way Theresa was able to demonstrate that other events in the child's life were important and could contribute to the Rushavenn experience. She would sometimes come back to a particular child and say, 'Well, you know that poem which you wrote, don't you think that it might fit in nicely in the middle of this chapter? Go and have a think about that. Perhaps you might like to talk it over with your partner?' A little while later the child might come back and say, 'Yes, we think it would fit in well there, but I think that we are going to have to change the last line, otherwise it isn't really in keeping with the rest of the story. This is our idea for a new ending to the poem'. Thus that piece, was written not for *Rushavenn* but for the *child*.

Example
Peter emphasized the importance of the adult setting an example:

> In our discussion sessions we had to initially help the children to realise the importance of listening to other people's viewpoints. The means by which we achieved that was to demonstrate to them, at a very early stage, that instead of being the didactic persons that they'd become so used to, we were actually sitting back in our chairs and listening intently to what they had to say. We endeavoured to show a real appreciation of their ideas and initiatives — not in a condescending or patronizing manner, but with true sincerity. This could not have been achieved if we had not honestly valued their contributions. We were also at some pains to demonstrate that their suggestions would be assimilated into the text. Gradually, the children became aware that not only were Theresa, Jonothan and myself listening carefully to what they had to say, we were making use of their proposals in a most practical way. Thus they came to realise that if we set so much store by their viewpoints it was equally important that they had a similar respect for the views expressed by other members of the group. As time went by individual children began to be far more sensitive to the thoughts and feelings of their peers and the adults with whom they regularly came into contact during these sessions. This inter-group empathy was somehow achieved — by what means I am not at all certain — without it being taught, at least by conventional teaching strategies. It was certainly not through an articulation of ideas, but through the manner in which we operated and the environment in which we worked.

Conclusion

Rushavenn has achieved international fame. Peter has been invited to give talks in a variety of places — what he calls 'the evangelism side of the project'. Brixworth has had a large number of visitors, from home and abroad. It is something of a showpiece event. It is certainly an archetypical critical event. It yielded exceptional achievement, for both pupils and teachers. It 'opened doors', provided opportunities for outstanding advances and breakthroughs, gave inspiration. All worked very hard, creating time where none existed before, and the project was conducted in a spirit of great fun and excitement. For Peter and Theresa, in their separate ways, it fulfilled a life time's dream. In addition, it confirmed Peter's educational philosophy, so often, throughout his career and life, under siege. Prominent among its features were the constructivist theory of learning; the 'scaffolding' provided for the pupils until their knowledge and skills were strong enough to stand on their own; the democratic mode of operating; the emphasis on 'context' and 'real' and holistic learning, that is, learning involving all the self and all the senses. There was a strong sense of 'communitas', all members of the group, teachers included, stepping aside from their roles and status in normal life, and developing a special 'family feel' within the group which has been sustained over the years. The collectivity worked as one, and was greater than the sum of its parts.

The structure is also there from conception to celebration, with a productive mix of structure and programming on the one side, and freedom and adventure on the other. A distinctive feature of this critical event is the way in which adults' and children' work, perspectives, ideas and abilities combined to produce the finished product. Children were given their heads to generate ideas, which they then fashioned within their groups to meet a limited objective. Theresa then coordinated their contributions within the grand design — which only she could do. At its heart were two critical agents — Peter and Theresa — with the vision, flair, energy, organizing, teaching and writing skills, love of children and of literature, and faith in their beliefs to carry it off to the applause of the educational and literary world. Further, they were doing it, not for career, but for 'life' because it was important to them within the context of their own lives. They illustrate how at times, even if only rarely, given certain favourable conjunctures of circumstances, they can *make* opportunities available, instead of waiting for them to be presented. *Rushavenn Time*, now adorning many a library shelf, and the young people who participated in its production, are testimony to their achievement.

Notes

1 To those in the project I was known as 'the other Peter Woods'.
2 This all took place, of course, before the 1988 Education Reform Act which instituted a National Curriculum and National Assessment.

Chapter 3

Filming a Village Life:
Community Education in Action

In 1989 the children of Class 4 at Laxfield Primary School in Suffolk, under the inspiration of their teacher, Melanie Pike, made a film about their village. It took three terms to plan and make, and the investment of much 'spare' time on the part of both teacher and pupils. It was a resounding success in the eyes of the teachers, pupils, parents, and villagers involved. It also won first prize for primary schools in the 'Suffolk Schools Community Awards' for 1989. These awards were established in 1988 by Charles Freeman, a teacher and author, with the support of Suffolk County Council Education Department, for studies which 'aim to focus upon some issue of local relevance and interest the community in which the children live, with the object of strengthening links between school and community'.

The film was a notable achievement. It showed a level of skill and a sensitivity remarkable for 8-year-olds. It bore the hallmark of artistry in several respects. Above all, and this is what impressed people most, it captured the spirit of village life, celebrating the delights of consociation in its various forms and at various ages. It also surprised the villagers, not only for the children's abilities, but for the extent of information it contained. No matter how long people had lived in the village, or how extensive their activities, they all discovered something new.

The film was distinctive for its scope and contrasts. It was set in the context of a poem composed by the children and narrated by two of them, based on Shakespeare's 'All the World's a Stage', and reflecting on the passage of life from birth to death. The structure then followed this sequence, examining clubs and societies from the Toddlers' Group (for the youngest) to the Shamrock Club (for the oldest). There was dog-grooming at the WI, a ceilidh at the school (in aid of the Parent-Teachers Association), a show at the Horticultural Society, drama and choir groups, youth activities, football, bowls, and so on. However, while recognizing the passage of time, and the particular needs of particular age and sex groups, the film forged links between them, nowhere better illustrated than in the shots of the young interviewing the old. Moreover, the portrayal was no straight listing of clubs. There were imaginative juxtapositions and arresting and highly effective cuts. The main text was interspersed with scenes of the village, the villagers and intriguing rural views. There was great variety, not only of content, but of presentation. A full range of camera shots were employed — close-ups, middle and long etc., sweeps, zooms, individual and group — with steady hand and an eye for lighting and composition. On the audio side, as well as announcements to camera and interviews, there was a generous input of 'vox pop' and *cinéma verité* and a number of songs from 'My Old Man said follow the Band' from a jolly bunch in one of the village pubs, 'The Low House', to 'Early One Morning' sung by one of the adult choirs. These audio inputs were skilfully used with the film coverage.

The film is basically a celebration of humanity. There are affectionate portrayals of individuals, if only a brief glance at some of them, humour and warmth in some of the things people say and in banter and repartee within the groups, and, above all, delight in people meeting and being together. 'I love it, I wouldn't miss it for anything' and 'you meet people and can have a chat all afternoon' were typical comments from participants. The film captures people's commitments, dedication, enjoyment, and public-spiritedness. Mrs Bullock, for example, had run the Shamrock Club for older people for twenty-three years. Mr Thompson of the Bowls Club, told how they had worked their green up to Suffolk County Competition standard, laying four inches of fly ash on solid clay, followed by six inches of top soil, then an inch of sand on which they 'sew the grass seed four times in different directions'. As he speaks, we see people in action on the green, and gain a glimpse of the cups and shields won by the club. The film was thus also a mine of information, including insights into 'behind the scenes' discussion and activity, giving it a tone of real investigative journalism. It depicted a culture that they recognized and identified with, and that was important and necessary to them. They were proud of its history, illustrated again by the impressive village museum, and regarded the video as an important contribution to the local folklore.

How, then, does this qualify as a critical event? What did the children, and others, gain from this experience, educationally? What teaching methods were employed to 'bring it off'? And what resources and conditions were required? To answer these questions I spent two concentrated days in the village, visiting the school, interviewing Melanie, the teacher centrally involved, the children concerned and members of the community mainly in their homes. Prior to my visit, I had seen the film and examined a range of documents and children's work associated with the project. Two years later I returned for a day to gather more long-term perspectives on the project from Melanie, Mr Gosling, the Headteacher and some of the children, now attending secondary schools in the area.

An Educational Experience — Pupils

There were four broad areas of pupil learning and development: information about the village and appreciation of community life; skills of communication and relating; 'mediacy', including camera skills, skills of composition and a sense of artistry, and critical appreciation of television and video; and personal and social development. I shall examine each in turn.

The Village and the Community

The main part of the exercise was for the children to find out more about the community in which they lived, to develop skills in information retrieval and presentation, and for the village in general to have a useful product that would serve the purpose of enhancing community integration. It added a new dimension to the school curriculum without being at variance with it. Melanie saw it as

> very important for children to get out into their community. It's like putting a frame round a painting in a way — pointing at something. You have that amount of power as a teacher in a school to focus child's attention. Life may be happening around them all the time but their attention isn't focused . . . even though they've been in their local shop many times or they've seen some old boy ride up the road on a bike. In this project their attention was focused in a different way.

The pupils surprised themselves by what they discovered about the village. They found out a great deal about the nature of social life in Laxfield and how it was structured. Samantha and Ellen, 'didn't know there was half the adult clubs that there were'. Andrew 'hardly knew anything about it before'; and Ellie, even though she lived in the village, 'used to think that most of the clubs are for children, but there were just as many adults' clubs as childrens'. Abi 'learnt a lot about it because I didn't realise Laxfield was so big and it had so many clubs and everything because I don't live here'. Katie was 'really surprised at some of the things and how many people went'. Before, Cassandra 'didn't think there was really too much to do in Laxfield', and Caroline 'knew some of the clubs like the Youth Club and things that I went to, but not much apart from that'. They were equally surprised by what went on within them. Abi said 'We didn't know at the Shamrock, the over-sixties club, that they used to play whist. We thought that they used to just sit down, eating and drinking cups of coffee and knit and everything'. She was surprised to find also 'two old ladies making this really big blanket and one was knitting all the squares and the other was sewing them together.' Jane 'didn't know her gran went to this club'.

They also learnt a great deal about the history of the village. Melanie reported how one little girl, for example, wanted to take George Fisher to the field he was talking about and film him there.

> We managed to persuade him to come and talk. We went to two places where the horticultural show had been held and he also showed us the old disused railway line. He told us about the day it closed and how he took a party of school children on the last trip on the train, so that she learnt a tremendous amount about our village really in the process of trying to make a tiny little piece of video film. It lasted only a few minutes in the end but she followed it all through herself and decided what she wanted to go in and what was relevant.

As well as experiencing the range of activities, they also met a cross-section of people in the village from very young to old, and from a variety of occupations. The Vicar, Canon Doctor Marchant, noted this function:

> It gets them more used to dealing with adults. They've had a rare old spread of adults in different situations here and seeing them, doing their activities in different sorts of ways. That widens the children's activities,

which they've gone into and taken up, like the dramatic activity or the playground and so on, but quite a lot of the other things are adult activities that they would never get a window into in the ordinary way and therefore that widens their outlook on what actually adults do and are interested in. Children by and large know their parents and their teachers and that's their adult world to a large extent.

In terms of 'subject' there was a strong 'RE' aim 'to present to children a view of human cooperation and interaction, where materialistic values are unimportant, and therefore to deepen their concept of 'community'. Melanie felt something had been achieved here, if only for a brief moment — 'It's a powerful culture we live in'. She could rightly claim, however, that she had to some degree practised the art of community education, which is to provide those involved with 'a rich and varied experience of the interhuman' (Wright, 1971).

Researching and Communicating Skills

Melanie hoped that they 'learnt some of the processes of research, enquiry and putting a product together, therefore some of the feelings of doing something creative, of making something worthwhile'. Interviewing was an important part of the work, and, as with research, there are two main skill areas involved: negotiating access; and acquiring valid and interesting information.

While some aspects of access, like entry to the clubs was non-problematic, others, like persuading people to take part called for special efforts. Elaine Nason, for example, 'didn't particularly like being interviewed'. She wouldn't have minded just being filmed, like 'putting out the stuff at the Horticultural Show, and not having to talk'. But she was 'very impressed with the way the children handled it'. She was 'surprised by the children', not realizing 'they could manage so well, that they'd got it in them to interview people so successfully, and to put something like that together'. Gerald Nason also 'didn't like being interviewed'. He felt 'distinctly uncomfortable. Looking straight into a camera answering questions is a bit daunting. I was much happier getting on with something'. For Gerald, it was the exposure of his whole self on video, and 'being urged to look at the camera' that was discomforting. Melanie remarked that 'it put the children in a really horribly powerful position, questioning adults.' This 'turning of the tables' was an interesting twist in this project, and another way in which ages and their associated statuses were transcended.

The fact that they had to adjust to people of other ages was also an early difficulty. Cheryl found it 'alright interviewing the older children, but the little ones, sometimes you couldn't hear them because they were speaking so quiet and then they mumbled and then they stuttered in the middle.' When they first approached them 'they didn't really know what you were on about and they just burst out crying'. With the old people, there were problems with some of hearing and understanding. Joanna was talking to one woman who 'took the microphone off her and was talking through it, and she couldn't get it back.' Another old woman, asked if she minded being interviewed, said 'Oh, I don't mind if I do', and then just walked off, clearly having misheard or misunderstood the question.

The adults were impressed with the children's interviewing skills. George

Fisher, retired headteacher of the village school, thought they were 'very good', and that 'they asked questions which were very sensible indeed'. They had to talk to a range of people from the elderly right down to the playgroup, but 'the choice of the interviewer was very good really . . . they had the adaptability of putting the right question. They were only simple questions but the tone was quite attractive for an answer . . . They weren't reading [the questions] off a list. There were those that had good conversational powers . . . It was put over in a way that you got a sensible answer'.

Gerald Nason thought Jessica (covering the Playgroup) 'a natural interviewer'. Melanie agreed, reporting that 'she gets all tongue-tied normally but she really achieves some contact when interviewing'. Elaine thought Jo also 'very good at handling old people'. Mr High was also very impressed with the 'little girl' (Joanna) who interviewed him. Mr Bracewell remarked on their ability to put people at their ease. Despite the initial discomforture of some, 'it was particularly nice that no-one was conscious of the fact that the camera was there. They all behaved in a natural way, even the ones who were being deliberately filmed. or speaking'. He knew some, including himself, who felt a bit uncomfortable about being interviewed on film, but 'the whole thing became such a part of the school life that they all became a bit blasé about it'.

Considerable interpersonal skills therefore were needed to persuade some people to take part. What did they do?

Ellie   You tell them how good it is, and you're only going to do
          a few questions.
Andrew   You say it's not going to be anything big and it's something
          to help the school.
Samantha And you beg, 'Please! Please!' I did that when we had to do
          it with some women (in the Body Conditioning Group) who
          were going to go home. We had to say it's not going to be
          on television, nobody's going to watch it, and all this. We
          had to tell little white lies.

However, they were mindful of the ethics of the situation. There were a few mumbles in the Body Conditioning Class, with one woman 'about to walk out because she didn't want to be filmed', and another not attending that session. As Melanie herself admitted, 'I wouldn't have been caught in my leotard in front of that camera.' But any embarrassment was minimized. They filmed one woman 'doing a funny exercise in body conditioning and sticking her legs up in the air' and had to ask her whether they could put that on or not. They did the same when they were filming a woman showing the WI how to groom a dog, and she told them 'you'll have to mind my big bottom, it always gets in the way when you're grooming dogs'. Abi had felt that it should be included because 'she knew we were filming, so if she didn't want it to be on she wouldn't have said it really'. Katie, on the other hand, thought she might not have realized what she said, so 'they better phone up and ask her'.

Launching and conducting the interviews also called for skill. They found it 'quite hard to interview little children', and advised putting them at their ease by telling them 'there's nothing to be afraid of really'. It was also important to ask clear questions. Jessica, for example, had asked one little boy 'what do you like best', instead of saying 'what do you like doing best', so he said 'eggs', to every-one's amusement. Ben said, 'You have to have a page of right questions, like, if it's for a toddler, say "What's your favourite paint colour?", not "What's your favourite engine inside a motorbike?", or something.' Katie said, 'You're not allowed to say anything that makes them shy, because they just don't know what it means. If you say something like how long's your club been going, then they won't know anything about that. You just have to asked them what they like best and things'. In this way they learned to match their approach to the age and abilities of their interviewees.

Melanie thought Ellie was a surprisingly successful interviewer . . . 'She had the technique and just seemed to draw out all their information very well'. She was 'relaxed' and 'talked to them very confidently and made them all talk quite well.' While she had questions planned — they had written them down before-hand — she never actually referred to her notes, and the interview flowed natu-rally. She got some nice comments, like the woman at the Shamrock Club who 'always gives the "Milky Way" to her grandchildren when she wins at bingo', and the one who 'just loves helping'. Ellie is used to talking to old people as she sees her grandad every night and her nan 'every weekend' and her other nan 'every other weekend'. Melanie also thought Cassandra 'asked some brilliant questions' in The Body Conditioning Club, especially when the ones that she had prepared with Samantha ran out. Sometimes, as Ben noted, 'You have to have a mental list of emergency questions to ask if all the questions you've written down are the wrong kind of questions to ask for whoever you're interviewing'. The prepared ques-tions here work as a framework and as 'a way in', allowing flexibility to follow interesting lines as they arise. The skill comes in when the interviewer recognizes these opportunities and capitalizes on them as well as classifying other points. Thus most of Cassandra's questions occurred to her as she was talking to people, improvising on the spot. One of her strengths was that she did not regard it as a formal school exercise. She was interested in what they were saying and really wanted to know more about it.

The children's awareness of the requirements of interviewing and their devel-opment as budding researchers was evident from their comments. Samantha pointed to the need for questions appropriate to the person being interviewed, and for thinking of follow-up questions while they were talking. Andrew agreed, noting that your prepared questions were not always the best ones, and 'you think of more things when you are there'. Ellen remarked that 'suddenly a good one comes up in your head and you ask it', though none of them underestimated the difficulty of doing this. Had they improved? Ellen certainly thought so, contrast-ing her stilted and aided interviewing at the beginning (interviewing 'Nigel at the Youth Club') with her more fluent and independent performance at the bowls club at the end.

Mediacy

By 'mediacy' I mean one's understanding of the media, how information is se-lected, compiled, packaged and transmitted. It includes knowledge of some of the technical aspects of production; some familiarity with video skills and some of the problems of its use; some understanding of the nature of the product and the particular qualities of the medium, for example, the use of the visual image and the effective immediacy of the communication; some critical appreciation of the artistic elements, and some awareness of the power and control aspects. Advances were made here in respect of camera work, both technical aspects of how to use it and the artistic conceptualization of the audiovisual product; appreciation of the power of the medium; and more general elements of artistry.

Camera Skills
They discovered through experience how to use a camera and what it could do. I asked them for advice and was told

— to remember to turn it on. This is a basic lesson all of us have to learn. Katie 'kept thinking I was going to pull it off and break it or drop it, and I didn't know what to press when I wanted a close-up or a distance one. I couldn't get my hand round it.' When Jane recorded someone she forgot to 'put the sound up on the microphone and had to do it all over again'.
— if filming outside, take care if it is windy as you can't hear what the person's saying. Use a windshield on the microphone.
— don't shine it at the light or windows, don't clash with the sun, or lights.
— imagine what the picture is going to look like. Draw pictures and write about what you are going to shoot. Katie kept getting peoples' feet in at first, and Abi 'the floor and the ceiling'. They learnt about different kinds of shots — stationary, short, medium, long and how to shoot them. They also learned to compose. Anna described how, in the Art Club, 'They were drawing daffodils and one person had the picture here on the table and the daffodils were over on somebody else's table. We stood behind that person and we got the picture and the daffodils in from the person's table'. They had acquired the knack of imagining themselves in, and viewing from, different positions. Samantha demonstrated this when speculating on what 'might have been'. For example, 'All Saints church could have been filmed. We could have seen more of it. Or we could have seen a proper view of Laxfield from the top of the church tower. You could see all of Laxfield from up there, all the village, rooftops . . .'
— watch where you're putting your hands, because if you knock the wrong switch you might completely wipe the tape sometimes, because there's loads of switches.
— leave it ten seconds before and after filming (this is the 'cut-in' time).
— use the tripod where you can to secure a steady film (Samantha said it was hard in the Body Conditioning Group because 'they kept moving around everywhere and you had to keep up with them').
— be unobtrusive. For example, when they filmed a play the Drama Club did, Ben didn't 'think anyone saw the camera because it was such a dark area'.
— be prepared for the unexpected. Planning is important, but sometimes good things happen that were not anticipated. Also accidents are part of life. Things would be too contrived without them. Thus Andrew

thought that 'Some accidents make it seem better, because otherwise you don't think people are human. Accidents have got to happen if you're human', as when Jackie Wren dropped her tape case while they were recording. Another example was while filming the PTA, they 'got a few people in the film that we didn't know were going to be there, and they were important people'.

The children frequently picked up how to do something in advance of instruction or guidance. Anna related how, while filming the Fellowship of Youth, they had shot the 'Twister' game. They wanted to get that in, but they also wanted a song that was sung. They found eventually that they could match the two, keeping the soundtrack going but putting the pictures of different activities on while they were singing. That, in turn, called for judicious selection of pictures. By the time Anna and Louise got to the Art Class section they had 'got the editing down to a fine art'.

The Power of the Medium
To what extent did they acquire any critical appreciation of the medium of film? Melanie thought there were two aims here: 'to provide some small antidote of awareness to most children's unlimited, uncritical TV consumption (again a response to the time we live in); and to understand the power of the image maker and the problems of bias and truth'. Her own feeling was to be dubious of much advance on either of these though 'hopefully by decision-making of this kind an awareness grows that those behind the TV are also real people. So maybe the basis is laid for later critical awareness?' In conversation, Melanie said:

> I would hope that they discovered how much influence you can have on what people see. I wouldn't state it very highly, but getting towards the beginning of an understanding of the power the media have, that they are choosing things for what reasons and why, how they have presented a certain image of the village and not another. We discussed it because we were presenting a happy image. They were naturally wanting the fun bits, the happy bits, the warm bits, the bit where somebody hugs somebody else and leaving all the boring bits out. Maybe there was more information in them but they didn't want them in. We played various games where they were film makers and I was the head of the BBC. I was saying, 'Right, today we need some new programmes and I want people to come up with some ideas and we'll decide which are the best'. So quite a bit of time was spent thinking about planning new programmes and what they were going to be about. So we did talk a bit about the medium in a roundabout sort of way.

Some were able to discriminate between the uses of different media. Andrew, for example, distinguished among different uses for film, photographs and writing. Ellen pointed to how the poem was enhanced by the background view of the village. Andrew thought the film very effective in capturing relationships between the generations, as when it showed a child and a woman dancing together. They got to know through their own experience something of the nature of the medium that can be generalized to other uses, such as television. Ellen now appreciated the kind of work, effort and time that went into film production. Andrew said he had become more critical of certain television programmes.

Elements of Artistry

The children also experienced some development in their artistic appreciation. We have seen this to some extent in visual and audio form, in their sense of composition in a camera shot and in their ear for the major phrase that 'speaks volumes'. There is also a sense in which the compilation of the video as a whole was a work of art, involving skills of discriminating, selecting and organizing. They had to build up the film and the various parts within it, establishing the setting of a certain sequence of ideas, appropriate beginnings and endings, and compiling little stories, complete in themselves, but linked in a major theme. It was a kind of structure applying to quite a few artistic forms, including writing a story or composing a poem. The poem formed one element of the structure, and this related art form helped to give shape, and a sense of progress and development through the review of social life. The difference here, overall, was in having a surfeit of material and, as Melanie reported, 'sorting it into an order and deciding which were the best bits . . . was quite testing, but interesting'.

Tolstoy has defined the activity of art as 'to evoke in oneself a feeling one has once experienced, and having evoked it in oneself, then, by means of movements, lines, colours, sounds or forms expressed in words, so to transmit that feeling that others may experience the same feeling'. Clark (1987, p. 62) has suggested that 'one of the objectives of the community educator . . . is to help those concerned validate the experience of others and be able to empathise with them'. The subtle blend of words, pictures and music, the close attention to content and concern for its interest and validity, the emphasis on the 'natural', and filming things as they are, an eye for the telling shot and an ear for the interesting comment, all ensured that the culture of village life was faithfully evoked in not only a mental way, but also affective and aesthetic.

Gerald and Elaine, for example, felt the children captured the essence of activities. Gerald pointed out that in the Art group, they had 'lost all the boring talking and got people drawing'. Elaine felt they had captured 'the whole chaotic hurly-burly atmosphere of the playgroup'. She also thought the Horticultural Society 'came over very well, with its almost reverent atmosphere'; and she liked the beginning, 'with the poem over the top of the visual images; then homing in on various people in the village carrying out their normal activities, like coming out of shops. That was a lovely feeling that part'.

Personal and Social Development

Qualities of character were tested and developed, notably confidence, humility, curiosity, initiative, motivation, satisfaction, perseverance and patience. Melanie hoped they learnt that they 'can ask somebody a question and find something out; that they should never be afraid to ask anybody anything, because I want their curiosity to be alerted'. This is all part of a general growth in confidence, in this case to be able to find things out if they wished to, hence to have their curiosity satisfied which in turn would promote more motivation. She spoke of one girl of 9 years of age as a case in point who 'thought out her responsibility very well and was enormously interested in it, and showed a lot of curiosity in planning'.

> She was quite young at the time when she was doing it but she's capable
> of great patient, quiet involvement. She's the sort of child that will work
> on painting until it's perfect — not particularly fast but with terrific
> concentration.

They talked to people more than normally, took initiatives, used their own ideas and asked questions. Melanie hoped that 'they have felt extended' in the way she wanted them to feel, and that 'they have made a little more effort to think in ways which they might not otherwise have done'. Some discovered the limits of their capabilities, like one girl, who is 'normally so full of herself' found that she had forgotten to put a crucial knob on. Melanie thought 'this was a fascinating moment because she discovered that she was fallible, that other people were expecting things of her and she could let someone down. She learnt a lot just in that moment'. This is a commentary, too, on the group interaction that took place, on the increased opportunity to relate together on 'something that at the end of the day matters and is going to be seen by others, which means they've got to contribute properly and interact effectively'.

Some children revealed qualities not previously known about or suspected. The most notable example for Melanie was Ellie, who seemed to 'come out' during the project. It clearly appeared to inspire her, so much so that she was thinking about taking up filming in a college career. Melanie could not think of any other experience of Ellie in class to suggest that she would be good at that sort of thing, and didn't think those sort of opportunities came up in the ordinary course of events.

> It's a way of relating with people that came out and the way she got
> involved in her project. The way she just took an active role always in
> wanting to know what we were going to do next.

Making an hour's film requires many more hours of filming (eighteen hours of videotape in this instance), and much planning, discussing, selecting and creative link work. Much of the filming was done out of school hours. The task required dedication, perseverance and patience. In deciding which bits to film, and then which to edit, Caroline said, 'It went on a bit. We just had to keep watching it and watching it and watching it'.

Some of them, like Matthew, did very nice presentation shots first time, but others 'took half an hour because we had to keep doing it again and again because people weren't saying the words right'. Cheryl remembered about the poem that introduced the video — 'We had to keep going again and again because we kept getting it wrong and we didn't speak up loud enough, and then we said it wrong'. Cassandra reported that there was so much footage of the Body Conditioning Club that they 'were up till the middle of the night trying to get it all in, because they didn't stop until about ten o'clock at night'.

Ellen and her colleagues who did the Drama Club did 'the tape and the things after it, and then realized that it was too long and it needed more music in it. So we had to go all the way back and do the Drama Club again, and cut things out and put more music in it and do the things afterwards again'. Ellen did the 'Youth Club', and they had to do that several times, 'because there was cars coming down . . . and I sneezed in the middle of it. We had to get it just perfect so the wind wasn't blowing or the cars weren't coming.' They realized the high standard that was required and had the qualities of character to sustain the level of self-discipline necessary.

Ben remarked that you needed patience to handle the equipment, for example, 'to get the camera up'. Andrew said that 'Samantha's mum, when we were filming the swimming pool bit, kept forgetting everything we asked her, so we had to keep going over it and filming it again and again. Then we found the microphone was switched off!'

Inevitably in such a project there were times of boredom, where it was more a matter of 'perspiration' than 'inspiration'. Ellen remarked that 'It got really boring watching it through and through'; and Samantha, similarly,

> We had about an hour of Body Conditioning Class and we had to look all through it, all through dinner and that . . . because we had to pick out bits we wanted Mrs Pike to edit . . . We had to miss things like PE and television programmes just to do this edit. That took nearly a whole afternoon just to edit two minutes of it.

Ellen agreed:

> Pick the best pictures, that was really boring, so people were asking Mrs Pike 'Oh, you can do it all, I don't care which bits are edited.' But we had to sit and choose our parts and sometimes it was really difficult and boring.

There was a valuable lesson here for the children, that is that creative work cannot be all fun and excitement; and that if they are to feel that the final product is theirs, they must go through the consolidation and follow-up procedures as well as front the more glamorous aspects of the activity. Melanie's view was that:

> I don't think it's a bad thing for them to discover that some parts of the job are boring but that the end result is rewarding. It doesn't have to be all fun and exciting at school. I don't think it can be but I think that end results should be rewarding enough and exciting enough and some of the bits along the way fun too.

The children made the point that it was worth it in the end. Ellen, for example, enjoyed it, though there were times 'you got really tired of it and you thought "Oh, I wish we'd never done this", but in the long run it was fun.' Andrew felt that some found some of the preparation work boring but 'when we started filming people enjoyed it more.' Samantha, concluded that, in spite of 'really boring' moments, 'it was worth it'. Ellen remarked on the excitement they felt when they saw the first bit of the video, 'and we wanted to see it again and again'.

There was ample testimony to fun and to a sense of achievement to counter any boredom. Jane thought 'Drama Camp' was 'brilliant'. She wasn't quite sure why, she 'just liked it. We done all different things.' In some groups they actually did participant observation, as in the 'Fellowship of Youth' Andrew reported they 'were actually allowed to join in some of the games. I thought that was fun doing that club'. In general it was the human touches that appealed most. There were all the funny bits like those about 'eggs' and 'bottoms', and the humorous things people say like Rosie when she said 'and this is the old boys' school where the old boys used to go to school'.

Samantha reported another incident:

> Her husband was the one at the end of the song who was mowing the grass. We asked him (if he minded being filmed) and he goes, 'Oh, I shall go and get ready'. He was going to go and put all his best clothes on and then his wife, Florence, Mrs White, came home and she goes, 'Oh, what's happening?' and he goes, 'I'm being interviewed. Now go away, you're ruining it, you're not supposed to be here!' So she went in the house and looked out of the kitchen window and he went in the house and shooed her off. It was really funny.

How far did the fact that it was entered for a competition inspire them? In a way, winning the competition might have seemed an end in itself, suppressing other potential educational gains. Andrew felt, 'we wanted to win at the beginning, but in the end it turned out that it was just something we wanted to do.' Ellen agreed: 'We just enjoyed doing it. We wanted to win so we done all our neatest work. Then in the end we decided, we just enjoyed doing it, so we didn't mind where we came'. In other words it sparked them off, but it wasn't everything. It was nice to win the prize but it was not really important. Jessica thought 'The most important bit was doing the film' and Suzanne agreed that it was 'just the enjoyment of doing it'. Louise wasn't even aware that they were entering for a competition until they were halfway through.

Others' Development

Melanie

Melanie felt that she herself had experienced development, possibly to a greater and more relevant (to her teaching) extent than she would have done through attending any in-service course. Melanie is a part-time teacher with a holistic vision. At the time, she was teaching two days a week, with main responsibility for art on one day, but she also did poetry, maths and English. But

> to be honest, I really only like teaching when I feel that you're attacking some kind of deep creative motivation in a child . . . That's the way you've got to go, to break through to motivation really. That's the way I like to work, but it's got to be with the whole curriculum in mind . . . I don't think it feels very satisfying to teach just a little bit of the time unless you're working on something worthwhile, because you can go in and out again and feel like you're babysitting or something . . . I have had people of different ages and walks of life come in to talk to various classes in the past in order to provoke questioning and response. The video project focused all those things I've wanted to do before.

This therefore was her brand of education in action at maximum effect. Seeing what the children could achieve confirmed her faith in the general principles, boosted her own confidence, and brought considerable intrinsic rewards (Lortie, 1975; Nias, 1989a). As with her painting, the inspiration is intuitional:

> You do it for the state of mind that you are in when you're doing it, when you're making something, so you're feeling you're putting out energies and you're testing what you're doing against your own standards, your own intuition of quality, whatever it is you believe in. You know, every mark you make goes up against what you think. It's something to do with being in touch with yourself.

As the project works out, therefore, so does confirmation of one's beliefs and instincts. A. Hargreaves (1991b, p. 251) asserts that 'all teaching is a constructive trade-off between ideal purposes and practical realities'. This may be true, but one might equally argue that the more closely the practical realities serve the ideal purposes, and the more completely these are realized, the purer the teacher's sense of accomplishment.

She also refined her pedagogical and technical skill. Much of this development was self-motivated and self-acquired.

> I didn't know anything about it when I started. I got some books out of the library and talked to a couple of people — one friend who runs a film company, another who teaches media studies in an art school. They actually came for about an hour each into the school and spent some time talking to children about the different length shots and so on. We tried to absorb as much background as we could . . . I hadn't been on any courses. I got some books out of Norwich library which I took a few notes from: *Videos for Beginners* or something like that, and *Documentary Techniques*. A lot of it was a bit over the top and unnecessary, but I managed to sieve through and get the basics of the techniques.

With hands-on experience, they advanced beyond the book and found better and more efficient ways of doing things. They speeded up the process of 'logging' for instance, instead of counting how many seconds each shot was, developing a much quicker version of working. Melanie had learnt lessons from the experience, and another time, or in similar instances, would try, for example, to ensure that 'all the children were really happy with the part that they had', since that is so important for motivation. She would encourage them to use less film. So much was taken up with learning how to use it, and this suggested that there should be an experimental stage before filming began in earnest. Melanie also discovered a great deal about editing. This was a new area for her involving 'a new way of thinking, which I hadn't tackled before — how to tell a story in a nutshell', and she felt that 'she got better at it'. When she started, she didn't know how she was going to edit it. She just thought 'something would happen — and it did.' She was given access to an edit suite in Lowestoft, albeit some thirty-five miles away.

Again, the 'hands-on' direct involvement was seen as far more effective than what was available to her in courses:

> I know there are courses now but in fact I didn't particularly want to go on one. I wanted to find out what I needed to know for myself really.

I found out about these courses after we'd started and I think I'd got to the stage where I didn't want to give up the time on them. It's not that difficult . . . You only learn by doing, don't you? There was a certain element of the courses which were 'doing', but I would only have had part share in the edit machine during the evening. It was a lot better to go and edit something for hours on end, that was the way to find out. On the first day I was terrified by all those buttons and things but there was a technician who was very helpful. He just explained how they worked. It was surprisingly easy. I really think the children could have done it — and I would have liked them to. What we really need is an edit suite in Laxfield.

It was an adventure for her as well as the children, and she found the intricacies of filming and editing 'absolutely fascinating'.

Further, that's the only sort of teaching I like really, that is when you're working on something which is creative, where there's going to be something good at the end, and it goes on longer than the children might otherwise go on but hopefully they see the point of that involvement and effort, so that it's all worth it.

Melanie has become regarded as something of an expert in the production of educational videos, and has been asked by her LEA to talk to other teachers about her experiences.

Members of the Community

A feature of community education is that *all* members of the community benefit, not just schoolchildren (Martin, 1987). Collectively, according to Canon Doctor Marchant, such activity has a binding and integrating function:

When I came here, after I'd been here three or four years, I knew everybody. I knew their cousins, their sisters, their aunts, their problems. I don't today, and the old folk of Laxfield they say 'I can go up the street today and I see people I do not know' and it is an offence to them. Therefore, anything you can do to draw people together and get them known to each other is a very good job, and of course schools do it. You have to send your child to school so if you're a youngish person coming here you get drawn into a school community and get to know others.

Louise Pratt, who runs the Drama Club which the children filmed, also commented on this integrating function:

Well, I thought it was a very, very valuable thing to do. It will be a very nice record for us later . . . The thing is it's all about community and my club is all about the community too, it's essentially a community activity. I run summer camps for them, I run trips for them as a sort of cohesive process. It's a kind of drawing together and I think the film did the same thing for them. It meant that they were all involved in something which came together as an end product, a very satisfying way for them, and the club is the same. We do shows and they have the feeling of working together to produce something. Lots and lots of people do lots and lots of things and nearly all of them are good and have a quality because they're drawing people together to produce something. That in itself is a very good thing but it's particularly satisfactory if at the end of the day that thing stands up outside its own community and I think this video does that. It's created a lot of interest.

Charles Freeman referred to feedback into the community as a key criterion in making the award:

The original guide-lines were that there had to be some activity in the community, an actual *activity*, and there had to be some reflection on those activities in the sense that you had to feel that the children had actually learnt something and thought about it. We then looked at the third criteria — what feedback into the community was there. Were they just going into it, coming back to the classrooms and that was the end of it when they'd written something out and handed it in, or did they actually have some result they went back into the community with.

The delight of people was not simply at a project well done, but one of unique properties that carried elements of excellence and surprise. It had a value, therefore, over and above the educational one. It had historical and archive worth. Ellen remarked that 'If we still live in Laxfield, it would have changed, and we can show our children what it was like when we were younger'. If they moved, they would be able to remember what the village they lived in as children was like. Isobel Dunn echoed this view when she said 'I think it's a lovely thing to have to keep, because in years to come of course the village will change a lot and it will be nice to look back on that . . . You can actually see yourself as part of the activity, and there's a lot of people's children on there as well'. It roused a sense of pride in people. Isobel Dunn said it showed 'there is a real lot going on in the village life, a lot more than people think. People think that it's only towns that have these facilities'.

The reactions of members of the community to the quality of the product speak for themselves. Isobel Dunn said, 'Although they'd interviewed me and asked a lot of questions for the youth club one, I didn't think they'd got it together as good as that. I thought they done really well'. Isobel works at the school, has five children who all attended the school, and went there herself as a child, so 'knows a lot about Laxfield'. She reported that 'everybody who saw the video, all friends and that have come round to see it, have all said "I didn't realize there was so much went on in Laxfield"', that's all you keep hearing from anybody . . . The community is quite a strong one really, everyone seems to pull together in the village, getting things done'. Isobel thought all the clubs were well and fairly represented, and gave people a good feel of what went on in them, as well as providing a lot of basic information about times, subscriptions, membership and so on. She considered it a motivational force, 'because some people very often are too scared to go along. Like WI and British Legion, sometimes you think that's for old people but that's not. Seeing things like that you realise'.

Mr Bracewell (the choirmaster) thought it was 'great. I thought it was a lot of fun really and very well put together, too, and not actually having much to do with it other than just being filmed, I thought it was extremely good . . . educationally it was good for the kids, too. They learnt a lot about village life. It's good publicity for all the village activities. I'm trying to get kids going myself on the cricket club and I think it's important that the kids get involved with things, just from the point of view of the future of the village . . .'

Colin Emeny, builder, parent and school governor, thought it was 'Brilliant, absolutely brilliant. You probably know there are a lot of people who moved in and some of the locals call them "foreigners". I'm a local. I've been here all my life. I speak to other locals and they think it's remarkable . . . If a professional film company had done it then obviously it would have been more professional, but as children it was tremendous. They covered literally everything and showed it as it is.' He was surprised by the quality of it, 'the camera work, and the sound, and the way Mel arranged it and what she picked out and so on.' He thought 'the older generation thought it was fantastic, they really thought it was something'. He was impressed by the relationships between the young children and the older people. 'This was something else in their lives and somebody was caring about them, and was involving them, not pushing them aside.' He thought 'the beauty of it would come out over the years . . . I'm thrilled with it to be honest with you'.

George Fisher, retired headteacher, thought the children 'met a lot of people and it was an experience that would come back to them in later life, very definitely'. For the village it was good, 'because this was the community right from the very young up to the elderly, finishing with the old boy in the garden using his flymo . . . It's an interesting record of what is happening at the present day and that's the valuable record'.

Elaine Nason thought it was going to be very useful in the village museum. Gerald Nason thought that 'The main thing that came over about it was that it made Laxfield seem such a nice place to live.' In a way, all recognized that it was romanticized to some extent. The children had chosen 'the funny bits', had avoided embarrassing or upsetting people, and it was 'very gentle'. On the other hand, nothing was falsified. It was a *real* slice of village life. And Gerald remarked that 'their poem at the end about dying was very realistic and down to earth.' Melanie pointed out that some were unable to finish their poem, but others 'did it with great emotion, like Cheryl, because her granny died recently and she was able to write about it . . .' Gerald and Elaine thought the film reflected an aspect of Laxfield that they knew, and it 'had certainly gone down well in the village'. They mentioned one villager in particular, 'an old chap with the horticultural society. He's great, it made the show for him, didn't it, the fact that he was filmed and he's never been before. He actually came out of his house in the evening to go and see the video up at the school, which is unheard of . . . He tells everybody about it, and told the judges at the last show, ' "you ought to buy the video".' Elaine and Gerald are active villagers, but even they discovered new things. Elaine, for example, 'had never penetrated into the WI before'. She'd 'no idea what went on at one of their meetings'.

Mary, the School Secretary, and featured in the video as a bell-ringer, thought 'it was an excellent project. Just from the historical point of view, it's a marvellous thing to have for the village. I don't think it could have been bettered really.' She also thought it a reasonable representation of life in the village. Melanie had done 'an enormous amount of looking into what should be put on it and I don't think she missed anything. We have a busy village, and that was a busy video, wasn't it?'

Chris Chambers, 76 years old, a widower, who has lived in Laxfield all his life and now resides in sheltered accommodation, was interviewed in the Shamrock Club. He enjoyed being interviewed and he enjoyed 'the watching of it', and he reckoned 'they done it very, very well as regards doing the whole village and the different organizations they did. It was a wonderful job'. He thought it was 'very good for the village'. He had shown the video around to his family. It had been to Felixstowe (where friends had ordered one for themselves) and shortly would be going to Yorkshire. He would 'like to have had one done, say, seventy years ago, so that you could compare them both together. I mean what difference I can see in my life, how the village has changed'. He was impressed by the children, because some 'wouldn't have give the time for it, would they, not like them ones did'.

Mr High, retired mole- rat- and rabbit-catcher and agricultural worker, and now a leading light of the Horticultural Society was similarly impressed. He thought the video was 'very good, and the children done it well'. A lot of people told him he was 'a star', but he didn't know whether he was. The girl who interviewed him, Jo Welch, 'done it well' and the two judges at the Show also said how well she did it. The video gave a good picture of the show, and was very informative about other things. He didn't know, for example, that there were so many clubs, like the Camera Club; that so many people had entered for the show, and he had known little about the 'youngsters' activities'. There were also some surprising details about individuals. He didn't realize, for example, that Mrs Nason had been 'our secretary for twenty-three years'; what Mrs Pratt did in drama; and Mrs Cox, 'they shew you her a-bowling,' and 'they shew you the football club what I used to belong to for thirty years'. They had been thorough: 'They went everywhere — into shops, bell-ringing, footballers, the over-60s a-playin' o' bingo. They didn't miss much out in the village'.

Canon Doctor Marchant (who is Chair of the Governors at the School) thought it was

> a reasonable cross-section of what goes on here. Obviously there's not everything on it, but there's a fair amount because we are a very lively community . . . They've done very well in picking out salient features.

Teaching Methods

The teaching methods employed on this project are within the 'Personal Enquiry' and 'Negotiated Learning' mould (see Chapter 1). There is the prominent emphasis on child orientation, relevance, cross-curricular application, qualities of mind, self-motivation and self-discipline, democratic discussion and debate. There is the concern to awaken confidence, establish control, encourage curiosity, inspire thought. This is not allowed to find its own level, for part of the teacher's role is to raise standards, to bring about a recognition in the children of the possible quality of work that might be produced. Pride in what is their own work will help ensure the application necessary to achieve the required rigour. The approach was expressed in the Laxfield project in the following ways.

Firm, but Flexible Structure

Clearly the project had to be one that would inspire the children, and had to be organized in such a way that optimized the emergence of the desired products. Melanie's plan incorporated these principles. There were two broad stages. In the first, 'research' stage, the children discussed and prepared questions for research- ing the clubs, completed graphs, and made up project folders of notes on all the groups. In the second, 'operations' stage, they planned the 'treatment', made up 'storyboards' consisting of drawings and notes in preparation for filming, planned presentation announcements, completed logging sheets (deciding order and tim- ing of filming), and prepared poems, letters (to the clubs), posters (advertising the public showing) and a design for the video cover.

This gave a clear structure to the project, but allowed room for flexibility. For example, the storyboard was only a first plan for initial guidance based on their research. They 'didn't really know what was going to be there until they arrived, so they couldn't really keep to their storyboards, but it gave them a general idea'. It also rehearsed the process of compiling a piece of film with them. As Melanie said, echoing a point made earlier by the children, 'there's always the happy accident, and to have the camera running at the point when something good happens is a great bonus really. You've got those lovely moments, which if you keep very tightly to a couple of seconds of this and a couple of seconds of that, you miss'. This illustrates the happy conjuncture of structure and flexibility, planning and serendipity. The arrangement had a logical sequence, contained a variety of instruments which exercised their creative abilities, writing, speaking, discussing, observational and listening powers, presented opportunities to all to excel both individually and in groups, and enabled the entire enterprise to be 'child-oriented'.

Child-Oriented

Melanie uses a constructivist approach which places the child at the centre of the learning process, but uses some direction and instruction (for example, over how to use a camera). The teacher provides the structure (as above); and there will be 'assisted work'. The level of the assistance will vary from task to task and from pupil to pupil depending on need. The teacher is the judge of that need. Some- times pressure of time, numbers and resources forces the teacher to cut corners and give 'heavier' assistance than he or she would wish, for child creativity needs time and space in which to work. But this was not a problem on this project — apart from the editing suite, which perhaps proves the point. Even there, however, the children briefed Melanie on their preferences, and she kept to them as far as possible. Melanie was insistent that as much of the planning, filming and editing as possible should be conceived and done by the children, and that they should follow through the process from beginning to end. Of course, 'some of the children were better than others, more curious, they knew what they wanted to discover and what they wanted to put across'.

They began by 'working out questions which came from them, and we talked about questions, and they wrote out lists of questions that would be useful'. They spent a long time on that. She often does it in fact, because she thinks 'it's a fundamental aspect of teaching about "finding out about your world" '. Then, it was necessary for the questions to have a real direction and to receive real answers, so she selected people 'who would give interesting answers'. These adults, like her, acted as facilitators or catalysts for the child. The child asked questions, and the older person's responses then took the discussion and inquiry into new areas.

The children 'found' their roles in the enterprise:

> They all took turns filming. Every child learnt how to use the camera, but it naturally sorted itself out in that some did more interviewing, others did more perhaps of the announcements . . . others would hide behind the camera. So they, to some extent, fell into certain roles.

The approach is marked by a belief in children's abilities. Melanie expresses that here in talking about their initiative in the preparations:

> I wanted them to make the decisions because I thought that it was important for them to be able to put things in a logical story order. We talked about having an introductory shot, a general shot, which showed where you were or what the subject was that you are talking about. We talked about close-ups and long shots and medium shots and we looked at videos and noticed how long various shots were and we decided how many seconds of what we needed, in what order. So they really did look at it quite closely and again it depended on the child how much I was helping them, and how much they were completely feeling that they were in charge of the situation and sometimes I didn't have to make any suggestions at all. It's surprising how filmically literate they are. They watch a lot of television and they seem to know a lot more about how to edit things together than you think they would do, because the processes are not difficult.

It was this aspect in the end that won the school the Community Award. Several schools seemed to meet the general criteria, but according to Charles Freeman, in some, 'the amount of actual involvement of the children was relatively limited, although the final result was very good, but it had been very carefully orchestrated by the teachers. I felt that in this one the children had to give more'.

Democratic Procedures

Constructivism requires a certain kind of relationship between teacher and children and among the children. Taken to excess, child-centredness can breed individualism and separateness. But the project was as much about collective endeavour as individual progress. From an early stage, therefore, it was established that they would proceed democratically. Thus, power and control resided to some extent in the group. Clearly the teacher had an institutional position and certain responsibilities which required an overseeing role. But it was used here as far as possible to encourage discussion, considering the pros and cons, and respecting and reflecting on the views of others. The group — sometimes the whole class, sometimes the smaller team — take the decisions, but not before they had been thoroughly considered and debated. Melanie describes how it worked:

> The personal feelings of the children often appeared and in a partnership one would say, 'Oh, I really like that bit'. In the Toddlers Group section where the baby fell over and Jessica said 'Oh no, don't put that in, I look such a wally'. So then you have a little discussion between the two children involved about whether it should go in or not. Maybe other people also gave their opinions. There were lots of those kind of discussions where they'd have to decide whether things should go in or not.

Another example was the poem. They all wrote one, then read them out to the class. The class was to decide which one to use, but several of them proved to have merit. Someone then suggested they compose a group poem drawing on all the examples, and they voted for that. Another decision was about the order of clubs as they appeared on the film, as noted earlier. Melanie wanted them to 'feel involved'. She acknowledged her inevitable 'steering influence', but then 'we were all learning as we went along'. She herself 'would make great cock-ups, like not pressing a certain button when using the camera in the early stages', so she allowed them to shoot a lot of film which left space for experiment. The children themselves confirmed their involvement in the decision-making. They were free to ask what questions they wanted, and had been encouraged to produce lots of ideas, many of which were used. They all felt that the film was theirs, collectively produced and owned.

The children reported a big discussion they had had about the ending. The film ended on a sad note, with death, and the wistful last line of the poem 'I wish granny were here'. When they recorded this, someone had burst out laughing fractionally after this last line. Some, like Cheryl and Anna, thought it would be good to keep the laugh on, because it would cheer people up after the sad bit. 'They'd look back on all their younger days when they were all having fun and they will have remembered that and be happy for it'. Others like Cassandra were opposed to the laugh as being inappropriate and cheapening. Abi pointed out that 'if an old lady had just lost her husband, she could get upset when people laugh about it. In the end, they were about 'half-and-half', so asked the Headteacher, Mr Gosling, to decide. Teacher decision therefore won the day at the end of this one, but only as a casting vote. Was it the *right* decision? Certainly keeping it in would have suited the general tone of the film. On the other hand none of the adults had commented on the ending. It did not appear to take anything away from their general feeling of elation at the whole film.

As I talked with a group about this, and they rehearsed the arguments, new ideas began to emerge. Matthew suggested a formula for retaining the laugh, but separating it from the preceding subject of death by an imaginative cut. Melanie herself 'thought perhaps we should have left the giggling sound to be going on while the credits were being shown . . .' Had there been time, this kind of solution, which would have satisfied everybody and would have enhanced the film, would no doubt have been arrived at. Unfortunately, time is not on the side of democratic procedures.

Resources

What are the factors and conditions that helped promote this project? Again, these show a combination of a supportive context, personal vision, drive and inspiration, and contributions from critical others.

The Context

The School
The ethos of the school, its relationship with the community, and the support of the headteacher were crucial elements. The children all spoke very highly of the school. Jessica, Suzanne and Rosie said that 'it was a very good fund-raising school, with fairs and auctions and all kinds of things'. They had raised money for a swimming pool, and recently for a 'bubble cover'. It was well supported by people in the village with a strong PTA. It was also 'good for learning' and they would recommend it to others. It had lots of equipment, and there were a lot of activities, many of them after school, like cookery, chess, football and athletic clubs, and discos. They were currently in the middle of a conker competition.

The adults were similarly complimentary. Isobel Dunn 'loved' her school days there. She thought it a very 'friendly and open' school. Louise Pratt thought that 'this particular school is very community aware'. She had lived in the village since 1971. Her husband was a local farmer. Her children had been to the school, and she had taught children there, who were now parents of children there. She had seen the school change a lot. It 'had varying elements'. She thought it had 'a poorish period, not academically but community related. It goes up and down, but at the moment it's very strong'. The school, in fact, was a strong focal point for the community and one of its main integrating features, as Louise pointed out, 'We have no industry really, and the youth club comes and goes'.

Canon Doctor Marchant agreed with this:

> It's very difficult to think what a village community is today, because it's very varied in work and interests, and one of the big activities is the school itself. The school and the friends and the playgroup and their parents are part and parcel of one and the same thing, because families overlap between the two, and therefore they're one of the big community activities in the place.

This was not a matter of the school on one side assembling a document about the community on the other. It was more a case of part of the community assembling a document about itself as part of the community.

The Headteacher

The Headteacher's role was crucial, both in helping to establish the kind of ethos and managerial style in the school from which the project emerged, and in his support and encouragement during its planning and operation. Melanie found him 'wonderfully supportive'. Doug Gosling, in fact, had suggested the project, but then gave her a free rein, allowing variations in the timetable to fit particular children in with particular activities at particular times, keeping the rest of the school quiet while they were filming inside, welcoming people at the two open viewing evenings, and, above all, in his general attitude, which Melanie thought 'brilliant'.

The School and the Head were also held in high regard by the villagers. Louise Pratt thought that 'the headmaster (Mr Gosling) is brilliant at integrating the community with the school. I mean he really is excellent and that was all very helpful'. Mr Bracewell's views were typical:

I think it's a very positive school anyway. We're delighted with the school really and the headmaster's great fun. The kids all love him . . . They think he's wonderful and so do we really. He just does so much. He gets all the community involved in the school. I'm always walking in there and having a chat with someone or other. The headmaster helps me an awful lot with other things. The choir wasn't a school thing, it was my own thing, we just used the school and the headmaster helped me organise it.

The Community

The community itself was a helpful factor. Not only was it something worth studying in itself, containing some rich material and some surprising features, but because of the revealing spirit and the sense of association there was an identification with the project. It was a collaborative venture, and this had an enabling influence.

Isobel Dunn thought 'the community quite a strong one really. Everyone seems to pull together in the village, getting things done'. Melanie commented,

We're lucky too, that in a village like this there is a tremendous amount going on. I can imagine trying to do a community project somewhere that doesn't have a great sense of community. The inner city of Birmingham, for example, must have one, but I don't know how you'd start. You'd have to find it. You'd have to really go and look for it. It's so obvious here, it's all around you.

Among villages, Laxfield is probably quite distinctive. Mr Bracewell observed that 'this is a very lively village. We've a lot of things going on here, but there are some villages where virtually nothing goes on'. Canon Doctor Marchant agreed with this, and pointed out the extent of the community's interest in the school. Mary, the School Secretary, thought 'a very welcoming community with lots going on . . . There always seems to be something happening the whole time, a very active village. It's a very pleasant village to live in.' Mary pointed out that in past years they had won the award for 'best kept village', and 'everybody was involved in cleaning up the village — I mean everybody, old age pensioners, children, all sorts of folks and everything'.

A film on village life can take one or more of a number of themes. On another occasion, for example, the Vicar thought that 'work' and occupations might be examined. But as he noted, many of the people who lived in the village did not work there, as they did in times past, and Mary thought that 'really the social side is the most important thing', that concentrates the community and 'makes friendships'. The chosen content of the video, therefore, was a rich resource.

Critical Agent

Melanie was the driving force behind the project. She orchestrated the planning and execution, organized the resources, gave unstintingly of her own time and energy, insisted on high standards and pushed everything through to the final outcome. She would claim it was the children's achievement, but such an enterprise makes a high demand on teacher skills, knowledge, and dedication. She had to know her own and the children's abilities and realize their potential. She had to be ambitious and be prepared to encourage children to the limit, which in turn requires a realistic conception of the 'limit', neither under- nor over-shooting. She needed pedagogical skills and good relationships with the children to take them with her for the full distance. She had to inform herself, making herself knowledgeable about all aspects of the project, many of them new to her, and needed entrepreneurial skills to find equipment, persuade people and hold everything together.

There was general recognition of her contribution. Colin Emeny, commenting on the amount of information discovered, said:

> They went to tremendous lengths to find out. This is all down to Mel really, because I mean she probed and asked and so on, and wheedled her way in, into a changing room, a football match, and all sorts of things . . . and all of it was done in Mel's time. She photographed me on Sunday morning, coming up getting the Sunday paper. You're always going to get an occasional teacher like that, who loves doing it, and they'll give up the time to do it. I'm not sure it's fair . . . I think the prize was important, but I still think Mel would have done it without the prize because I know what she's like.

At all points, the exercise called for something extra, far above the call of normal duty. For the villagers, the climax was the showing of the film on a large screen at the school. Chris Chambers remarked how he 'went up to the school that night, and on that big screen, you know it was wonderful to see that'. Where did they get such a screen? Melanie 'went to Lowestoft and tracked down a large video screen and carried it back in the car. It only just got in!'

The pupils supported these points. Ellen thought 'Mrs Pike done well, because I'd never been able to spend all that time doing it. She done really well . . . and she came in three days a week when she was only supposed to come two and she didn't get paid for the third day. She went to Lowestoft and had to pay for the petrol. She done all the work, she took us out. She helped us when she wasn't actually supposed to be in. She wasn't paid for all the extra time.' Samantha agreed that 'Mrs Pike used to come in quite a few other times', and 'nearly every day to edit'.

Melanie pointed out the advantages of being a part-time teacher, feeling that it would be difficult for a full-time teacher to find time to explore and experiment as she had done:

> I was certainly at liberty to spend that time as I was not teaching at the school full time. There was a bit of me left over for it. I had 'left-over brain' to spare, if you like.

She had other things to do, notably preparing paintings for an exhibition in Germany, and domestic affairs, but 'could afford to give up an evening or Saturday morning'. She probably could not have done it if teaching full-time — 'you're so exhausted and pressured that your planning genius tends to go underground'.

Critical Others

These are people who, while not centrally involved in the project, had a significant impact on proceedings. The Head would come into this category, as would Charles Freeman, the founder of the awards. Speaking of the 'Suffolk School's Community Award' Scheme, founded by Charles, Melanie noted that it was a kind of spark that set things off:

> The Headmaster showed me a leaflet which came with the post and said, 'Oh this look's good, doesn't it' and I really thought it did look good. I thought about it a bit and I think we just started with interviews really on a certain theme. Then quite quickly the idea of the video came and we just went on from there. I don't suppose we would have done it in that way if it hadn't been for the award scheme really.

Chris Garnett was 'a very helpful adviser' who, among other things, 'pointed' Melanie 'in the direction of an edit suite that's available for teachers' which she didn't know about, and which he encouraged her to use.' Charles also spoke of 'the enormous amount of field work', encouragement and general facilitation done by Chris Garnett, whose time was the only input made by the LEA to the scheme.

It is typical of a community education project that it draws on the knowledge and expertise of members of the community. Again relevance and motivation count for a great deal here, for these services are freely given (in all senses). They also add to the sense of integration of the project. Both Melanie and the children gained here from the inputs of two parents: Ben's mother, who taught media studies at Lowestoft College of Art, and Rosie's dad, who runs a film company, doing things like making advertising and road safety films for the LEA. Both of these went into school to talk to Melanie and the children. Rosie's dad helped with the storyboards and encouraged them to think filmically, like envisaging the picture which expresses the idea. He expanded their perspective on opening shots, drawing attention to a range of possibilities other than the obvious, like focusing on a dancer's feet rather than simply having a view of a room; and varying one's approach to the village hall, which, as a popular venue for several of the activities, figured prominently in the film. He also persuaded Melanie not to go for a soundtrack to superimpose on the film later, but to use the sounds and interviews that came with the film. She was glad of that advice as it worked well, and she would not have had time for a sound-track anyway. He also helped with editing the initial sequence, suggesting that here, in the reciting of the poem, it was the spoken word that was important and a sequence of pictures to illustrate it — as they were considering — might be distracting. They agreed with that. Ben's mother, Sarah Burns went in one day with a film her students had made, and talked about distance and timing of shots. Louise Pratt, who runs the drama club also made a valuable contribution. Ellen described how she helped them with speaking. 'If we done it quietly she made us do it again. We had to keep doing it till we done it right, and then it sounded alright on the video'. She helped Samantha with timing, making her stay in position for about five seconds after an announcement, instead of 'dashing off' as she was tempted to do.

Conclusion

Two lines of criticism of the project might be advanced. One argument is that the project was too advanced, another that it was not advanced enough. According to the former, one person opined:

> I think to some extent the vista that an adult has of community life is far, far different from that of a child. I don't think one realises the slow de-velopment of a child's brain and awareness of what is going on. It's just a happy time up to a certain age, then it becomes a bit more serious and I think adults look at it in a far deeper way and don't understand what a child really thinks and can understand. One of the problems I think with a large number of teachers today is that they don't understand how difficult it is to learn. Learning is not easy for the majority of children and I think to some extent we've gone too far in teaching children the ad-vances which adults have made.

This view, then, is sceptical of ambitious projects of this nature, what they achieve, what children actually learn, and how that feeds into the general curriculum. While it rightly stresses the importance of evaluation and long-term gains (against short-term fun and chimerical learning), essentially it is derived from a Piagetian theory of learning which sees children's development proceeding in fairly clearly demarcated stages. This is fundamentally opposed to the social constructivism espoused by Melanie. Here, the ways in which children think and learn are strongly influenced by the social transaction and discourse within which it takes place. A great deal, therefore, depends on the context, cooperation, 'scaffolding' and 'handover' (see Chapter 1). These processes seem well illustrated here in instances for example, of learning camera techniques, interviewing and communication skills, researching material, composition. Even more importantly, perhaps, is the development of those personal skills and attributes that equip the child to take advantage of 'handover', such as confidence, curiosity, motivation, enthusiasm, pride, respect for quality. In keeping with the application of this theory to children, Melanie applies it also to herself. She learns in the same way, as is clear from her philosophy of 'learning by doing', her finding out about the technicalities of filming, and of organizing a project of this size and complexity. It is also important for her motivation, self-esteem and morale as a teacher.

The second line of general criticism might be that, regardless of the constructivist theory, the children were nonetheless locked within the perspectives that they had brought to the project. Thus they wanted the 'happy' and 'funny' bits. The sun was always shining, people smiling, they had no hardships and deprivations, nor trials and struggles of everyday life. It might be argued that it was a romanticized image, therefore, that was produced, building up a picture of 'olde worlde Englishness' that is enclosed, and of less relevance than formerly in the real modern world. There is an element of truth in this, and in some ways an opportunity might have been lost. We know that young children are quite capable of abstract reasoning, and of conceptualizing major social issues (Short and Carrington, 1987; Lee and Lee, 1987). Perhaps, therefore, there could have been an element of critique. Did these groups cater for everybody in the village? At a basic level, for example, I was told by some that there was little for teenagers. But on a wider scale than this, some examination of work trends and their relationship to village life, compared to the village of the older people's memory, could have presented a basis for a study of historical trends. Alternatively, a comparison with an inner-city area would have made a basis for a consideration of social groupings and their relationship to socio-economic trends. An investigation of how people spend their time in the village would have yielded interesting information which could have been broken down in a number of ways, for example, age, gender, occupation, 'foreigner' or 'native' and so on, thus providing a useful basis for conceptual broadening.

However, choices have to be made. The 'scaffolding' has to be constructed around a building that is already partly there, and the teacher has to make judgments about that. Once 'handover' has occurred, more construction work can then take place, so that some of that historical and comparative work mentioned above might be a logical extension of the project to be undertaken in the classroom in the usual way. Further, nobody disputes that the film portrayed only an aspect of the life of the village, but it was an important aspect in the view of all concerned, and one that was faithfully and skilfully presented.

The central function of the film seemed to be an integrating one, thus serving one of the generally recognized aims of community education (D. Hargreaves, 1982; Martin, 1987; Pring, 1987). It was a celebration of life in the village in which all shared. It gave them a feeling of pride and reinforced their sense of belonging. This was their village, and they were part of it. Though it was only a small village, they had not realized what life went on beneath the surface. There is, possibly however, a danger in this. O'Hagan (1987) has noted the ideological basis of some forms of community education which seek to 're-establish cohesion within a disintegrating society' and are 'frankly aimed at minimizing interpersonal conflict by social engineering', rather than through the institutions of society. This, I think, would be reading too much into, and expecting too much from, this project. It also under-rates the community as a social unit and the various ways it can help meet the needs of its members. The film gave a strong sense of coherence both within the village as a social world and in its typical 'cradle to the grave' perspective as associated with Henry Morris. The villagers' delight with the video was in large part a celebration of how it encapsulated and articulated a sense of collective autonomy, and for individuals a feeling of being in control of one's own life in important private areas. If a study of work patterns were to throw up a different and more variable picture, at least here there is a sense of one's 'substantial self' being sustained (Ball, 1972; Nias, 1989a). This is important for the feeling of coherence in one's own life, and for the promotion and achievement of personal aims. The film, therefore, was integrating for self, as well as for community. It was also unifying for the team, and for creating a special relationship among teachers and pupils. Melanie spoke of generating a 'better and different kind of relationship than the normal teaching creates'. This was because

> They did feel it was meaningful, and if you create a situation which is of value for someone else there's a level of appreciation in that, and a sense of having worked together over something as well, just to share in the ideas and the energies. So I do feel closer to those particular children . . .

Also, the democratic basis, the fact that the teacher was learning with them, all helped them 'to feel on the same level, and get on better'.

There is another way in which the activity helped to pull things together. D. Hargreaves (1991) has referred to the need for 'coherence' in the curriculum, both in the sense of content and experience. Content coherence calls for integration of knowledge and skills both within and between subjects. Experiential coherence refers to the everyday routine world of the classroom. Summarizing John Holt (1964), he says that children 'stand amid a bomb-site of disconnected bricks and fragments'. The Laxfield Community Project constructed a unified product from a large number of disparate elements, informed by several areas of the curriculum and grounded in the pupils' experience. It contributed to pupil's knowledge, understanding and skills in history, geography, mathematics, English, art, music, technology and RE. It promoted the cross-curricular themes identified by the National Curriculum Council (1989) of 'education for citizenship' and 'environmental education'. Further, it helped lay a basis for work at the secondary level. Already they had applied the benefits to, for example, interviewing people (projects in English), writing up reports, camera craft (in PSE), and group work. It also lay down a standard, both in terms of process and product. There had been 'a vast improvement in their abilities all the way through' (Ben), and for Louise, this experience, compared to her other educational achievements, 'definitely stands out on top'. Projects of this nature, therefore, well-planned and rigorously executed, have much to offer the National Curriculum. As Melanie remarked, 'Life is an integrated thing. It's rather a nonsense to put it into compartments'.

It would be in keeping with the underlying philosophy to allow the pupils the final word. Two and a half years after the event, the pupils, now aged 12–13 and at secondary schools, had lost none of their enthusiasm for the experience. They itemized the gains — using a camera, film and TV appreciation and critique, researching the groups, filming them, learning about village life and social activities, 'how to ask definite questions, not a lot of mumble jumble', sharing knowledge with others, learning to work as a group, making something that 'you will keep for years', the feeling that you have achieved something worthwhile, done something for the whole community of Laxfield, and for children going to the school who would benefit from the new equipment bought with the prize money, 'sticking at something over a long period, even when it got boring and annoying, and seeing it through to the end.' Louise said 'it was definitely more interesting (than more formal work) and it's a very good way of learning'. She, 'personally finds it a lot easier to learn when you do it practically'. Joanna felt it 'brought out a bit more of adventure in the work we're doing rather than just sitting in the classroom'. Andrew felt that at times you learn more from each other than from the teacher. Ben said, 'it was practical and fun, and everybody enjoys it'.

They were able to compare the experience on a wider basis. In some of their more recent creative work, it was 'more the teacher, and not so much of you'. If you think you're doing something wrong but she doesn't like it, then you have to change it to how she wants it'. They were 'more in charge' of the video project. They 'made up the ideas', with 'the teacher there to help us along'. They preferred it that way. They would resent a wholesale return to 'traditional' teaching. Joanna felt that 'the people who want to change it are just stupid, because they've never actually done it so they don't know what it's like . . . If they say practical work doesn't help you, well they don't know'. Louise said, 'They should come and find out for themselves'.

Chapter 4

The Chippindale Venture:
Real Learning in the Making

The Chippindale Venture is an environmental design project involving school-children working with teachers, architects and planners and designing new buildings on actual sites in and around Winchester. The project is dedicated to the memory of Frank Chippindale, ex-head of the architectural faculty at Leeds University, who had retired to Winchester and who died in 1988. Some of his colleagues on the Urban Studies Committee, a subcommittee of the Winchester Preservation Trust, developed the idea. This was to involve children and their teachers from two primary schools, ten architects drawn from nine practices, and a number of planning officers. They were to go through all the proper processes of consider-ing, designing, and submitting plans for a new Heritage Centre. The work was to culminate in a special day when the City Council Planning Committee would consider the plans submitted.

The broad aim was to heighten the children's awareness of the environment and interest in and concern for the local community, and to develop their design-ing skills. In amongst those was a host of other possibilities, including working together and with real professionals in the area, experiencing the real process from inception to conclusion, developing their power of communication and decision-making. There were potential gains, too, for the architects. Frank Chippindale had been keen on architects going out into the community and meeting people, and relating the built environment to their concerns. Going into schools would expand their horizons, and develop the educational side of their role.

The schools involved were Western Primary and All Saints Community Primary School. Debbie Kerr, Head of Western, and Pam Turner, Deputy Head at All Saints, took responsibility for their schools' contribution. The two schools presented a considerable contrast. Western has a high proportion of children from middle-class homes, with professional parents. All Saints has a large catchment area and has 'a lot of children with learning problems and language and social difficulties' (Pam). While all forty of the fourth year children (10–11 years old) at Western took part, eight from All Saints were chosen, on the grounds of 'ability really' — those Pam thought able to cope. Six of the children were 'a good average', and the other two she thought had hidden talents which might be brought out by the project.

Shortly after the Planning Committee's meeting marking the official end of the project, I spent two days in Winchester interviewing teachers, pupils, architects and planners, visiting the schools, the main architects' offices, and the

Teachers' Centre, where there was an exhibition of the work. The main informants, whose comments figure prominently in this review, were the two central teachers, Debbie Kerr and Pam Turner, Joy Williams, Head of the Teachers' Centre, Dot Browning, the Coordinator of the Project, Philip Turner, Assistant County Planning Officer for the environment, and Nigel Green, Planning Officer, of the Winchester City Planning Department. The interviews ranged in length from two hours to half an hour. The two teachers centrally involved had both prepared a record and evaluation of the project as it had proceeded in their schools, and these were made available to me, as were examples of the children's work from inception to completion.

The task given to the children was to design a new Visitors' Information Heritage centre on a site in front of the Law Courts to certain specifications. Some planning ideas were provided. The children were given ideas on 'Things to Look For', and briefed on materials. A visitor to the exhibition of work at The Castle would have seen displays of the work of all the teams. Catching the eye were the designs themselves — pyramids, domes, mushrooms, octagonals, glass cylinders, and even a castle. Accompanying them were the group's description and explanation, a list of the materials to be used, and a brief comment from the Planning Committee. The standard of design, the use of imagination, the awareness of constraints, were all considered to have been of a high order. A local journal, for example, reported that Planning Officer, Mr Chris Williams, thought Team H's contribution 'quite radical, because it did away with the Hampshire rose and courtyard'. The Committee was 'impressed with its relaxed simplicity and attention to detail which enable local craftsmen to show off their skill'. Teams J and K also received praise for their 'revolutionary ideas'. Team J offered an octagonal building 'tailor-made for the disabled because of its lifts to all floors'; while Team K produced a 'construction of stucco and wood with a glass cylinder on stilts feature in which a lift would operate to provide views at all levels'. Team G's 'floodlights enhancing a pyramidal roof and oriel windows' attracted attention. Other teams received similar commendations. A member of the Planning Committee said that he was 'amazed at the depth of knowledge some of them had shown, and their enthusiasm'. The general feeling of great success was such that the Trust Chairman declared that they would seek to repeat the project with a different age group the following year.

The results, then, justified some people's expectations, and far exceeded others. However, in educational terms, it was the effects on the children and the processes that produced them that were important. What educational benefit exactly had the children (and others) derived from this exercise? What were the teaching methods and educational principles that produced that benefit? What resources did teachers have at their disposal?

Children's Gains

Motivation and Confidence

Overheard at the exhibition:

> 'Amazing inventiveness';
> 'Architecture should shock';
> 'Quite a good idea that'.

The general standard of the work produced and the level of skill and imagination shown by the children surprised almost everyone. The teachers, though, knew their children's ability as did Joy Williams. She knew that:

> several people said 'Don't you think that is going to intimidate the young?' And I said, 'No, not in the least, children always come up to that expectation. That doesn't worry them at all. It's adults that get worried about going into other things'.

She was impressed with the variety of schemes. She expected much more similarity, but, 'Some had split-levels, some had tiles, some were flat and all sorts of different ways of doing things'.
Debbie was

> very aware of the ability that these children have, that we treat them like adults and they just do rise to the occasion like adults. I think this is what surprised the architects so much. They thought they would be dealing with children, with children's ways and children's problems. And they were of course, but what I think was a big surprise to them was that you can talk to these children as adults and reason with them, and explain. They've got opinions too and they are as valid as anybody's, if they can justify them and they could.

Some children showed surprising talent. Debbie said:

> One child in particular came back with some super work that he'd done at home. It was his work, I'm pretty certain, and he obviously got this really highly developed spatial awareness that you will see on his drawings that nobody had ever spotted before. He really latched onto this and this is something that he could shine at. Yesterday he came up to me and said 'Do you think we'll ever get a chance to make models of our designs?' He is still interested. He's very average child, and both the teachers who have been involved with him here were surprised at the ability and interest that he showed . . . This is exactly what this child needed. He's not a confident boy. He's a very worried child and he loved this project. He thrived on it and got a lot of attention because he came in with his lovely work and everybody praised it up to the hilt because it was quite exceptional for him. It was lovely to see him shine.

This boy said himself that it was 'much more exciting' than normal school. 'It was very enjoyable'. It wasn't just fun, however, 'but did make you feel as if you could do things better'.
For her children, Pam

> had great confidence that they would rise to it. There was one girl they were a bit timid about. She herself was nervous. She thought that she couldn't do it and she was pleased that she did, and confident now that she did do it and that's great.

The planners and architects were surprised at the children's abilities. Nigel Green reported how

the first school I went to they were clearly on top of it. I was surprised. One of the things that did surprise me was the children were thinking of the whole process. They talked on what planning was all about, what planning would expect. They were taking it one step further, how they would present it. They were looking at it as a complete process. I was thinking it was better to take it step by step.

Children acquired a range of attributes that predisposed them toward learning. They felt a sense of excitement and inspiration, and many discovered new-found confidence. The architects at All Saints thought the children were a little inhibited at first, and perhaps 'too influenced by adults', trying to suggest things that 'we would like', lacking confidence and 'wanting us to do everything for them'. Part of the problem was that 'they couldn't understand the plans, what a plan was and what an elevation was', but in the second week they achieved a breakthrough.

One architect said:

They definitely made progress. I felt really quite happy at the end of that session where they actually understood it. You could tell they understood it, because they could actually draw it. Without prompting from me they had a plan and they could put things in that room and they could understand it.

Debbie thought:

They sensed that they were involved in something quite unusual. Although we do have exciting topics at schools, it doesn't very often involve any outside agencies and people who they felt were important. It was important to them to have a real architect coming into work with them. They liked the idea of the day out at the Castle to present their work and they were going to have a meal. They were far more concerned with the little things that appeal to children than the larger aspects really.

For Pam, the confidence of the children was clearly shown on Presentation Day:

It was a very professional day for the children. They were not considered as children once. They were treated as adults, as professionals really. It was a very demanding day, the morning particularly when they had to sell their plans to their planners. It was very high powered, and the children responded magnificently working with all these adults. It was good to see the confidence of the children and their ability to do so. I am sure that when I was at school I would have been intimidated by it. They weren't intimidated by it at all. They had a job to do and they were confident that what they had done was what they wanted to do. They had a good plan and it would sell well and they were able to put that over to all the various people who asked them. Some of them had to actually alter their plans on the day and they were able to cope with all that. It was great that day, they thoroughly enjoyed the approach.

Philip Turner also remarked on their 'amazing confidence' and their ability to talk to adults on their own level. One of the reasons for this was the range of opportunities that had been presented. Philip mentioned

the children who do have a difficulty, dyslexic children, for example . . . quite amazed how they can tackle a point and do it really skillfully so they can handle spatial things and drawing when they find it difficult to write and read. Here is a skill where they can shine and all the other people say 'My gosh! He's good at this! Wow!'

Pam Turner gave the example of one of her pupils:

One of the boys is quite talented artistically, but he's a bit wild. It's clear to me that he could achieve far more than he does achieve. He has great potential. He showed that during this project, and it gave him a chance to do it and to excel because the children regarded him as the best artist.

Team-Work and Social Development

If individual confidence grew, so did social skills and awareness. Since the children worked in teams of four or five, they had to develop ways of working together which optimized both their own and others' inputs. They also had to relate to architects, planners, other adults and teachers, as well as to each other. It was a valuable exercise in cooperative endeavour, and in learning to make the best use of range of talents for the common good.

Debbie commented:

The children working in groups highlighted the need for them to be able to work together and solve problems together and come up with strategies for making decisions. If you've got to get one design from five children, there's lot of negotiating that has to go on within a group to decide on a final design that five children are going to all be happy with.

Pam Turner thought they worked better as teams rather than individuals

because their ideas bounced off each other. They got more enjoyment out of it. Doing it as an individual is quite insular, and they wouldn't have got all the 'spinoffs' that they obviously did . . . They shared out their jobs. If something really artistic was required then Chas would do it. If it needed more articulate writing, then Gemma would do it. So they pooled their abilities.

As David also remarked, 'If you were on your own you would have to think of all the stuff yourself, but with other people you can help each other out.' One team asked about the advantages of working as a team replied:

Child 1   You definitely improve your arguing skills!

Child 2   If you're on your own, you have to be independent, and if something goes wrong there's no-one to stand there and say 'Oh, never mind, it went wrong, we can all just fix that'. You have to fix it on your own. So you can rely on other people.

Child 1   And it's not just you making the decisions. If you all get to decide together and if you all do a piece each, then it's just easier to do really.

They all thought the product was better for having been produced by a team. One boy said his mother had wanted to identify his contribution and looked for his name on those bits, but 'I said to her that we're doing it as a team, you know, and she sort of looked at me . . .' Asked if they could identify their own bits, or whether they felt they all contributed to even those bits that each one of them did, they felt that the latter was the case. When they first started off they didn't work as a team — 'that was one of the big mistakes'. There was 'fighting and arguing', and one girl used to jam her pencil down really hard into her book to annoy everybody. But eventually they 'knew it had to be a joint effort, so we couldn't have all our own way. We'd have to hear what other people wanted as well'.

By and large, too, they seem to have got over the problem of certain individuals dominating the group. Quieter ones were brought out, louder ones toned down. Two of the architects commented:

Architect 1   Some of them were quieter, but you found that if you actually specifically spoke to them, then the response would come. They needed to be approached directly, whereas others would just voice their opinion at any moment and try to play the role of the team leader . . . They were all different, and all had a contribution to make. Some were deeper thinking. Some were much more flamboyant in their thoughts.

Architect 2   They argued about details, but amazingly enough they were very democratic.

Architect 1   Yes, everything had to be agreed by all before it was written down.

Debbie and Joy pointed to the useful role of the architect and teacher as arbiters on occasions. Joy thought there were a 'whole lot of interpersonal skills that the children had to use which they may not have used very much before'. Debbie said there were different levels of input, but that was to be expected. However, 'that is where the architect came in as the outsider and was able to gel the group together and help in that respect'. The class teacher would also offer encouragement to reticent children, 'making them sit down and saying "come on, I want that done by you . . ."'

Language and Communication

Much of the collaboration depended on language development and communicating with a variety of others. These were prominent features of the exercise. There was a great deal of specialist language, which the children had to learn and understand. Joy Williams on one of her visits to Western, was 'most impressed by the level of the discussion and the language that was being used. She thought 'the vocabulary was great . . . Listening to the children on the day, they were using a lot of the right words, and they knew what they were on about'.

Pam Turner commented on the extent to which they had internalized these understandings:

> The children that have done the Chippindale work you could feel this vocabulary coming out. You could feel their way of looking at things coming out, not just through anybody trying to bring it out, but simply because it was part of them and these things spill over.

She thought the project was worth it for the language work alone — 'working with professionals from another area, the small group, the discussion that was involved, sharing somebody else's expertise, the development of vocabulary . . .'

An architect explained the importance of the vocabulary:

> It's like writing. You have to have your vocabulary of words to begin with and I think design is the same. You need a vocabulary of images or exposure which is what you work with. Initially they'd been surrounded by the traditional buildings of Winchester, and maybe that's what came out. Yet once you start showing them different ideas, that's when they start thinking and their imagination starts to work, which is lovely to see.

She thought 'They were just amazing actually. This is when you listen to them communicate and they actually have taken in quite a bit, more than you realise about the project and the issues involved'.

> One group had oriel windows in their building. The HMI asked them could they explain what an oriel window was, and they could! And what was the difference between an oriel window and a bay window, at which point I coughed and spluttered, but the children knew! It's that kind of thing. The word 'elevation', for example, they are all using that very confidently. They know exactly what a side elevation and front elevation is. A lot of adults don't really understand that.

Philip Turner also agreed that

> the vocabulary is very important indeed. In a way there had to be a preparation for that before the children actually meet with the designer. They did it by exploring the school buildings and looking at them and being taught about what the buildings were made of and what they thought of them and a critical appraisal of the school buildings and the

buildings in the locality. They began to talk about things like the roof and bricks and materials, and they began to have to describe things where a roof overhangs a wall, for example, without knowing the term is 'eaves'. Later on when the architect started talking about the eaves and then explaining what that is, the children have a notion of what it is because they have actually looked at a building and tried to find a word for it.

When he came to talk to them later (at Presentation stage) he found they had incorporated the language within their own discourse fairly readily. Moreover,

> it wasn't just terms that they might have heard from their parents, like 'doubleglazing', which everybody uses. There were all sorts of other terms, for example, they talked about glazing rather than glass in the windows. In fact, they talked about all the windows with great confidence . . .

With acquisition of language went new conceptual understanding and growth of ideas. The two architects at All Saints noticed the rapid development of the children, their initial ignorance of many concepts, but some quite startling breakthroughs as conceptual and terminological grasp began to inform their vision.

Designing and Planning

'They make such breakthroughs because they don't yet know it can't be done!' (Lawson, 1990, p. 113).

Phillips (1980) remarks that there are 'designerly' ways of knowing. This project illustrates some of the properties involved, and how they might be engendered. Jonathan thought 'it was a good idea because you can understand what architects do, and it gives you a chance to design your own building'. Another pupil said she now understood 'what it's really like designing a building. Some people think it's going to be easy — all you have to do is draw a building — but it's very hard'. Another agreed, comparing his brother's toy 'architecture-set' thing which came with 'straightedged and angled' things, which make him think it was easy — 'but now I know what it's like'. What was difficult about it?

> Well, the designing. That's one of the most difficultest bits, and getting all the stuff what you want to get. You've got to take a long time thinking about it . . . I thought you just designed the size of the room and the height, but actually you have to design where the furniture and everything has to go.

Zoë and Melinda also described their first uncertain efforts, and Zoë agreed that designing a building had its difficulties:

Zoë   Me and Melinda had pieces of rough paper with really weird designs.

Melinda   It took us about three-quarters of an hour to come up with one decent idea.

What made it hard work, primarily, was sheer intellectual effort. As Dewey (1934) wrote,

> to think effectively in terms of relations of qualities is as severe a demand upon thought as to think in terms of symbols, verbal and mathematical. Indeed, since words are easily manipulated in mechanical ways, the production of a work of genuine art probably demands more intelligence than does most of the so-called thinking that goes on among those who pride themselves on being 'intellectuals'.

The children learnt 'how hard it was to be an architect', and how frustrating it was to keep doing drawings again, 'because a lot of the measurements weren't right'. Thus they experienced the free-flowing of creativity and the discipline of getting things right within the constraints of the site and its own rationale.

Several at Western said they had learnt about scaling. One child had done mapping with the Scouts for which you need 'a lot of scale work', and 'I never really understood it until I started this'. An architect explained the initial problems:

> At that age they do have problems grasping scale. They went out in the playground and actually plotted the area out of the floor space so that they could try to come to terms with the actual size of the building. When they first produced a plan, they had everything in it including the kitchen sink. It was such a mammoth building . . .

They had refined their tracing skills. Like architects, they made liberal use of tracing paper. If you altered the drawing itself 'it would ruin the picture . . . and with tracing, we could take bits from it and add bits . . . and you can just turn the tracing paper up and show people how it started off.' Drawing skills in general improved. One said she learnt 'an easier way of colouring things'. A most noted advance was in their grasp of three dimensions. Gemma, for example,

> didn't used to be that good at drawing 3-D drawings. I just used to draw it straight from the front like that one. Now I've been working with the architects I've learnt how to do 3-D drawings.

Robert also had 'learnt how to do 3-D drawings, so you can see the side as well, and doing birds'-eye views and pictures'.

This was one of the things that so impressed Nigel Green:

> The first thing that hit me right from the first time I went into the school was the three dimensional quality of the schemes. I was expecting them to draw a house but very two dimensional. In fact some of them had got, for 10-year-olds, quite sophisticated perspectives.

An architect saw the progress of ideas when 'the three-dimensional began to show . . . and they've understood the fact that there's a group of buildings which they're putting their building into rather than it just being isolated'. She found that 'they do have some lovely ideas, for example, there's a list of activities which they've thought of to attract people to the site. She thought that, in general, children as young as 8 or 9 were already inhibited, and beginning to be 'moulded by society as a whole':

> You know, the square building with the door in the centre. Even when it was their idea to create this dome shape we were stuck with the door in the middle and square corners within it. It's when you get them to question these things, to use space in a better way, and to see everything doesn't revolve around a corridor and to think about the building in a wider frame, that is exciting. The overall standard of the schemes I thought was very good. They were far higher than I was anticipating.

Nigel was surprised at how they had used the space and levels, which is not easy to do. He was also surprised that they actually tried to think of how the buildings themselves would be used.

> When I went into the schools one of the boys was saying 'I've got a younger sister and if I wanted to come along to see this with my Mum, we'd want to put my sister in a crèche so that we could enjoy the building'. So he was designing a crèche in his building and they were thinking on that level.

Nigel thought that some of the schemes were buildable, and that some plans would have been passed, thought they might have 'raised a few eyebrows'. Some of them were 'sufficiently well thought out to have stood a chance of being developed into a workable scheme'.

Philip Turner had had previous experience of working with young children, and had found the level of participation and motivation 'amazing'. With regard to this particular project, he said:

> I think the architects were pretty astounded at some of the results. Looking at some of these early designs, that one (pointing to one that was not actually pursued) is quite extraordinary for a 10–11 year old, to have got to that stage with the concept of a building of that kind and to be able to draw it in that way almost entirely on his own.

His own judgment on the final designs was:

> Very good, they were by and large full of pretty free ideas. The ideas had been modified to suit some kind of reality but they were still very strong ideas and concepts and that was good to see. They had not been brought down to something that had to meet a cost limit. They had still got their character. It was quite clear that the children were more at home with ideas which were modern rather than oldie worldie. Even the castle itself was actually post-modern when you looked at it in detail. It was fascinating.

The Environment

'They were quite well aware of the environmental issues here — "We mustn't kill the worms and the ants!"'

The whole exercise was intended to raise awareness and improve understanding of the urban environment. Philip Turner said that Frank Chippindale had been very keen to

> use the city as an educational experience and he was particularly good at acting as educator and just walking round and opening their eyes . . . just the very simple thing, walk round Winchester's precinct and look above the shop fronts for a change, see what's up there, and it is very revealing. The amount of art and social history and the economics that you can gain from just looking up there is quite extraordinary.

The architects felt that it had opened up the children's minds:

> I think probably before this they maybe didn't look at buildings or think about buildings the way they might do from now on. They have begun to think, 'Well, what is a building, what does it do, what happens inside it', that it has a site and that it relates to other parts of the site. I think it has developed an awareness.

Debbie pointed to the relationship between people and the environment, how decisions change the environment for future generations, and how they affect other people. The children had become very aware of the needs of disabled people, for example, and 'whether cobbles would be a suitable surface for people in wheelchairs'. The project had also raised awareness of their local environment. Many had not known, for example, about the 'big Hampshire rose' on the site, nor had they been into the Great Hall. Many children 'are not aware of how much history there is under their feet here in Winchester'.

The children proved keen conservationists. This was a prominent issue in the planning, and was brought home to them in the reception of the proposals on the final day. For example, they had to take care that the timber they were planning to use was not going to constitute a demand on the rain forests.

Nigel Green found the children's views and analysis of the town 'very interesting, as they had gone out and looked at the town.' One of the things he found particularly interesting 'as you come down into town from that end, there is a row of Regency houses, bow-fronted, to my mind lovely houses, but they thought they were appalling!' Nigel did not demean their views, but took them seriously. It forced him to re-examine some of his own assumptions. He also compared his own schooldays, when there was no education about the environment at all.

> Children now are beginning to understand about the environment. I think most 11-year-old children know what the greenhouse effect is, possibly because of what is happening in the Amazon rain forests, but they don't know what is happening to their own direct environment — the decimation of Hampshire woodlands, the decimation of Dorset heath land, rare habitat, just fifteen miles from where they go to school.

As for architecture, his own 11-year-old son, just like him when he was at school, was 'learning music and the names of the famous composers, the great works of literature, art and the great artists — but absolutely nothing about architecture and who the great architects were'. He saw the Chippindale Venture as filling an urgent need in a particularly interesting way.

Others' Development

As a pilot project, not everything went smoothly. Teachers, architects, planners were all approaching this kind of exercise for the first time. They all had much to learn — about their own capabilities as well as those of the children, about each other's roles and jobs, about ways of working together, about management and method, as well as the substantive content of the project itself.

Teachers

For Debbie there was much at stake. As the school that provided most pupils, she might have been seen as the major educator involved. As a recently appointed headteacher, she almost inevitably felt on trial to some degree. There was enormous personal investment in terms of time, work and expertise. She felt that she possibly 'over-managed' things (see 'Teaching Methods'). Here, the 'reflective practitioner' (Schön, 1983) shows the processes of self-evaluation, and how it feeds into future policy and practice:

> But you live and learn. What I would do next time, I would say to the architects I think at the end, 'Well how would you present this? What would you do with this work?' I didn't ask that question and you've got in our work a school presentation and a school display and that's where we weren't really benefiting from the skills that the architects had and the expertise that they brought with them.

The project showed Debbie where previous work at the school was important for building learning skills — the project was not just a creative exercise. The school had been involved in design and technology projects before, so some skills (like scale drawing) were quite well advanced. However, the project also revealed deficiencies:

> Some skills the children had not been used to working with, and there were implications there for our school policies and our school approaches. One thing that did come out was that we didn't deal nearly enough with how to ask questions. When we did the surveys, that was quite a struggle for the children. It was clear to me that there was an element missing in what had gone before at school.

In one respect, therefore, the project was for Debbie a test of school provision in general. It told her where the school was doing well, and in what areas it needed to give more attention. She also gained in other ways, for example:

> I learnt a lot from [her deputy head] and I know he learnt a lot from me. We did learn from each other, and that was one of its greatest values

from my personal point of view, the relationship that I built at the beginning of my first term at the school.

Debbie was also at the time taking a course at King Alfred's College. Joy pointed out that she was able to study the project as part of the course, 'because I don't think anybody had got time to do things in isolation, and if they can be linked in it makes it that much more worthwhile from everybody's point of view'. Debbie's new senior position, the project, her central role in the project, and the course, though a potentially stressful cocktail, combined to confirm her position and to produce a considerable boost to her career.

Pam found the architects refreshing. They caused her to reflect on some of her basic assumptions, some things in her teaching that she had come to accept as routine — like the persistent emphasis on neatness and tidiness.

> The architects that we had were great, and it was interesting to see their concept of the children's work. I found it most useful to be involved in the project because it's nice for me to go and meet other professionals. It is a lonely job teaching and there are things I forget as a teach, like display and the children's presentation of their original ideas. They are very sort of scribbly. Yet the architects didn't seem to worry about the display and other things that I would be concerned about as a teacher. I would have trimmed it and double mounted it. It is refreshing to see somebody else's viewpoint and you think, 'why am I so concerned about their handwriting?' They are absolutely right. It is the ideas which are the key thing. One does a bit in the classroom when one does drafting work but there is still a bit of you which says 'Gosh, if somebody sees that and thinks ' "what awful handwriting and scribbling" '.

I shall return to this point later. Pam said she learnt an immense amount:

> How life goes on in the outside world, other people's approaches. I've learnt all about planning. I had no idea of planning committees. I had no idea that architects had to sell their plans to planners who in turn sold them. I have learnt a lot of factual knowledge plus the sort of social vibes, like how architects go about working and where they work and I very much enjoyed meeting all the people and learning how other people earn their livings. Being in education all my life . . . yes, I've learnt a lot from it. Also I learnt . . . well I knew it really . . . but children do rise to what you ask of them . . .

It also consolidated Pam's educational philosophy, as she thinks 'it is so right to work this way with children.' She had hope for the future as 'so many attainment targets of the national curriculum are actually covered by this way of working,' even though so many unreasonable demands were being placed on them. Teachers and pupils learnt together, especially on a project like this, where it was a matter of 'pooling our ideas, because they knew as much as I did really'.

Joy also felt that she had learnt enormously from the project.

> I've learnt how vulnerable the architects are, and those sort of people when we are talking about children. I've also learnt that anything I say

is taken down as gospel, which is frightening, because that never happens in educational circles. Somebody would say, well have you thought about this or whatever and you get some feedback and you have to clarify your thoughts . . . I learnt a lot, of course, about how architects and planners work, although I still wouldn't be considered to be even an expert on that. I don't know whether it was this project particularly, but certainly working in this particular Committee and with this as its fundamental bit, I've been much more interested in buildings themselves. I always was interested in looking at buildings, but I now look at them in a much clearer way. I have also learnt that I can trust colleagues to do the things efficiently in their own patch.

The Architects and Planners

Just as the teachers were venturing into new areas of design and planning processes, so many of the architects were having their first taste of teaching and relating to groups of primary school children. As Joy Williams remarked:

They had to change their whole thinking. They were very good . . . Whereas we are used to working with the young and we know how these things work, for adults who are doing things in other fields, this is quite a difficult turn-about.

Joy thought 'they got a lot out of it'. They had been detailed by their firms, and were 'very, very worried about what they were expected to do'. Another worry was the technical terms they would have to use, and their ability to communicate with the children. Joy thought:

If it's done again, and the same architects do it, they will be able to take the lead from the children almost automatically, because they had known that it worked before, but when you start from scratch, that's different.

Pam thought they would have learned a lot about current education, and how, perhaps, it has changed since they were at school.

I think it was very good for them to see that education in modern schools is not just sitting down and working on a book and getting your sums right . . . Education is so broad really and the children are so much wider in their capabilities and expertise, and I would like to think that the architects were surprised at how well the children did it.

So the architects will have developed as teachers and as communicators with and understanders of young children. They also refined their teaching techniques. One said:

The one thing I've gained is that, certainly with children of that age, to work with them, you need to work in three dimensions and lots of colours. That's where you start to get results and understanding from them of what they're producing.

Another commented,

> We had to learn a new art. We had to learn how to teach them a subject that was for us to have to deal with. The day-to-day sort of things we talk about. You can't just talk normally to the children. They don't understand the basics of what it's about.

Philip Turner summed up the gains of the planners:

> We actually wanted the elected members of the planning committee to be confronted with children's design work and to say something mature and sensible about it to give it status. So we used the planners as a mouthpiece. Actually, they did their job exceedingly well, and it was good training for them. They got an enormous amount out of it, because they had to discuss with the children in the morning and find out what the designs were about, what the children's objectives were, what they felt they had achieved and the points they wanted to put over. Then, in a very short space of time because there were so many schemes to talk about, they gave a positive assessment on the plus points of the designs and acted as sales persons, if you like . . . So the planners learnt a lot in the sense that it was a challenge for them to talk with the children and then to have to say very positive things in a very succinct way in the afternoon. It was a very strict discipline.

Planners who had been through this process had told him 'Hey! That was absolutely amazing!' They had no idea that children were capable of tackling some of these challenges; and it was refreshing for them to get a whole range of perceptions different from those they would usually receive, 'uncontaminated by bureaucratic thought systems', and which would often cause them to think differently about an approach to designing a neighbourhood, for example. He cited one of his own experiences. He was giving a talk on rural issues to a group of sixth formers. They challenged him on his argument on the subject of the environment versus agricultural productivity:

> They said to me 'You half hinted that you would really like to see some strong planning control over what the farmers do as they are damaging the environment, are you pressing for that?' and I said 'I don't think it's realistic in this political situation' and they said 'That's a cop out!' Now I remembered that and that's actually coloured my approach to the whole subject ever since. What they said to me actually changed my attitude to wrestling with that issue . . . So, we get influenced . . . And it is actually more refreshing than doing some of the other bits of consultation and participation. If you ever go to talk to a Parish Council, you probably come out of it very tired indeed, because you will have heard those comments before and there'd be a lot of 'not in my back yard' about it and there would be a lot of the local government officer coming along to talk to them about man, universe and everything related rather than the future of the New Forest.

Philip also pointed out that planners learnt from working with teachers, both of them 'learning alongside the children'. Though they might be 'experts and specialists' they 'don't have all the answers'. It is not a question of right or wrong in terms of design.

> You negotiate an answer from all those constraints and factors and it's an exploration. So it really is a waste of time if you are just telling people things and making them read about it in books . . . the making of the English landscape is something that you can interpret from the ways of looking at it. You go out there with a simple plan and a little bit of knowledge and you begin to unravel why it is this road went that way, why it is there's a kink there because of some previous building or event and how things were before. All that's very useful in informing you about how things might happen in the future as well, but it's all an exploration. There is an enormous amount to be learnt by everybody.

By the end of the project it was possible to see an overlapping of roles rather than strict job demarcations. To some extent, teachers were better architects and planners. One architect, in fact, told Debbie that,

> 'You should have been an architect', because I had obviously highlighted the sort of things that they do in their job before they start to design which is to go out and look at the site. They've obviously got to view more critically to design, something that will fit in with it. But I wasn't doing it because I thought that was what an architect did, I was doing it with the children as a general awareness raising exercise so they knew the site, so the time spent on the site was not wasted. They weren't just talking round in an aimless sort of way trying to find out about it.

Architects and planners had also become better teachers, and, not least, more acclimatized to the culture of the school.

Teaching Methods and Approach

First, I give a brief overview of the sequence of events at the two schools. I then select three prominent features of the approaches for more detailed consideration — managing creativity, cooperation and real learning.

The Overall Strategy

Both schools followed a similar strategy with one important difference, as we shall see. There was a preparation and planning stage designed to provide the children with background knowledge and basic skills, and to raise awareness. Both schools had brainstorming sessions on what architects do, and what materials and resources they need when designing buildings, and the factors they have to take into consideration. Both examined buildings and architectural styles in the immediate environs of the school, considering all their features and evaluating them. At

All Saints, they collected pictures of buildings and styles of architecture from magazines, observed Winchester from a renowned vantage point, made sketches of the shape and colours of buildings, noted their feelings. At Western, they considered the notion of the school's heritage through the school log, old photographs and other memorabilia.

Highpoints were the visits to the actual site. Pupils were to work in teams, eight groups of five at Western and two of four at All Saints. The aims of the first visit were to develop pupils' awareness of the surroundings and to absorb the atmosphere of the area. Western pupils, sitting in a circle facing outwards, systematically sketched and made notes of what they saw and felt, and in their groups built up a data bank of textures, shapes, windows and doors, site and space, building styles and ages, each group concentrating on one aspect. They took photographs. This was all collated into a complete display at the school the following day. The All Saints pupils did similar tasks. They also took a 'people count' of the rate of people passing by, complete a 'feelings' chart on how things struck them on such measures as beautiful–ugly and friendly–unfriendly, and compiled a 'streetometer graph' for indices such as litter, sky view, noise, and air-freshness.

Shortly after this came the first visit of architects to the schools. Their aim was to encourage children's creativity, and to assist them in their designs. One explained how he came by his ideas, and what factors influenced him, such as fashion. He said there were no right and wrong answers, and design briefs were there to be negotiated. Debbie said:

> He was hoping that the children would be far less inhibited than they appeared to be by conventional buildings. He talked about some buildings around the world, how, for example, a chain of hamburger restaurants in America actually look like hamburgers. He was suggesting this was an opportunity for the children to let their imaginations run riot.

At Western, the work was closely structured. Each group had been asked to produce three designs based on the brief, working on squared paper. The architects were asked to work with their team, consider the three drawings, consider strengths and weaknesses, decide on the basis of the final design, and give suggestions for the children to follow up. A similar carefully structured programme was suggested for their second visit, with particulars being addressed, such as internal layout, features of external design and elevations. By now the building material samples had arrived to much excitement, heightening the sense of reality.

A planning officer, Nigel Green, had also visited the two schools. Up to then, the pupils had only considered the effect a new Heritage Centre would have on surrounding buildings, but now they had to combine these with the possible effects on Winchester itself. Pupils' accounts told how Nigel explained that the Heritage Centre had to be in a place that had light and shade, and should not be in the way of another building's light. People should be able to get to it easily. He also talked about the history of Winchester and some current developments that were going to increase the already considerable traffic problems of the city. Another range of considerations was thus added to the task.

Much the same process occurred at All Saints, the crucial difference being that Pam chose not to structure the two architects' work because she 'didn't want to inhibit them'. She 'knew little of how they worked anyway, so gave them practically a free rein'. They reviewed the children's work, discussed the wide variety of buildings possible, and experimented in drawing various shapes, particularly hexagons, H shapes and circular shapes. They gave advice, and made suggestions on the pupils' designs. One accompanied his group to the site for a second visit helping them to envisage where to place their building and considering accessibility on three levels. They decided eventually not to channel the children's creative ideas into the confines of a scaled drawing. To add to the reality still further, the architects arranged for the children to visit their offices, where they used the photocopying and workroom facilities to refine their plans, and the architects did the boards and mounting for the presentation.

The main difference between the two schools was that the work at Western for all participants was more structured and firmly related to the brief, whereas that at All Saints was more free-ranging. The implications of this will be considered in the next section.

Managing Creativity

The difference reflects the point that the distribution of time and input into the divergent and convergent phases of creative activity varies in accordance with constraints and resources. At All Saints, a more unstructured approach was an easier option for them with only eight children and two architects involved (compared to forty and eight at Western). In each school, however, there was a productive tension between structure and freedom, between provided tasks and pupil self-initiated products, between imposing skills on pupils and giving them liberty to do things in their own way — classic dilemmas in the teaching of art and design (Schools Council, 1974), and in art generally (Wolff, 1981). At Western there was a need for more structure — there were higher numbers and more was at risk. The architects admitted that they were 'very nervous' and worried about whether they could handle the children ('We were terrified', one confirmed). Their suspicion of groups of children persisted through to the presentation day. Debbie was asked to do the introductory speech, because, someone told her, 'we thought you would be the only one who could stop the children talking'. One of the architects said 'But the children are very quiet, aren't they?' and they kept saying 'Aren't the children good?' The skills of class management and familiarity with school culture are not gained in a day. Dot Browning also pointed out that

> it's important to have a lot of background and the structuring of the time that Western did was essential because architects are clearly not used to working so tightly within that sort of time scale. But they would probably prefer to have been slightly freer, particularly with the way of displaying the schemes.

She thought that now the architects had had this experience they knew what was expected of them, and could be given more freedom and flexibility in any repeat of the project.

Philip Turner pointed out that architects need some structure and discipline in any case. You cannot design on a blank sheet of paper, because you have no constraints and no brief. 'The more that you load the constraints and the requirements of the brief, the more complex the task, the more exciting it becomes and the more likely it is that you get something which is notable'. A second point is that you can never meet all the objectives, so you have to prioritize, 'throwing some out' perhaps, 'negotiating our way through until we get a set of objectives which suits us, and the concept and ideal that we've got.' In this process the actual specifications might change. 'When you start to get out of the blinkered thinking then you start to get something which is very exciting'.

This 'creative tension' produced between structure and freedom is not independent of context. There were differences between the two schools, and different demands of different stages. All seemed to appreciate the programming at Western, but next time round, they would have internalized much of the structuring and been more confident in their own instincts. Debbie felt that ideally the teachers should manage the educational side and the architects be given a free rein on the drawing side. The advantages of this were evident when the final results were seen. Debbie said that Western, working to strict parameters and using squared paper, 'ended up doing a lot of fairly rectangular drawings ... 'The All Saints' children came up with some far more exotic looking buildings, spaceship-type things'.

The two architects at All Saints commented on another aspect of school style. This was the almost obsessive concern for neatness, (mentioned by Pam earlier) and how this can potentially obscure the really creative moments:

Architect 1   The funny thing was when we started on these documents they were drawing on them frantically and in amongst the drawing were some interesting sketches and doodles and just general stuff, basically what we would produce when we are doing sketch design.

Architect 2   They came up with a lot of ideas. The teacher got very upset by these drawings because they were not neat drawings. But to us that is the best, the sketches, the ideas. The drawings can produce the ideas for adults to understand, but the sketches to me said a lot more and we tried to use those in our final presentations ... We were trying to get shot of any preconceived ideas and say 'look we want to just let the kids draw and get some advance here,' and when they were drawing it try and encourage them.

This recalls John Ruskin's remark that 'if a child has a talent for drawing, it will be continually scrawling on what paper it can get, and be allowed to do so at its own free will' (quoted in Read, 1966, p. 261). There is a tension here between the need at times to scribble, doodle, sketch, experiment, be fanciful in order to conceive, give body to, and capture the idea, and the more dominant pervading value in schools of neatness and precision. The key seems to be in a healthy balance between the two, but it seems fairly evident that the ideas must come first. You can then put these into action in design. The debate here reflects the universal dilemma in the encouragement of the proliferation of ideas of the need for 1) a framework both to guide and stimulate their production and 2) freedom and flexibility for the mind to explore broad pastures. The two schools provide useful contrasting experiences to inform later projects.

Structuring, however, whether it comes before or after the 'brainstorming' has another purpose, which is to provide progression and integration. At both schools, in their different ways, the various techniques employed complemented one another, the creative aspects were followed up with consolidation, and planning ensured that creative thought was directed toward the most profitable and necessary areas. The project made great demands on teacher skills of orchestration. They had to encourage, direct and inspire the children; maintain excitement, but ensure educationally worthwhile products; structure the enterprise; control behaviour; and guide the architects and planners in maximizing their input. It would have been easy in such an ambitious project with so many participants for it to get out of hand. The teachers, however, maintained centrifugal cohesion among the various elements, and cumulative development throughout.

Cooperation

The scheme could not have worked without a high degree of cooperation among and within all the groups concerned. Yet there was a high risk of culture, role and personal conflicts, given the range and number of professionals and people involved, any traditional strains that might be present in teacher–pupil relationships, and the complexity and novelty of the scheme with ill-defined roles and responsibilities. So how were relationships established and roles identified?

One prominent method was through discussion. One of the architects referred to this, pointing out that this was not apparent to observers on the presentation day. The pinboards may have looked 'terrific', but there was a lot more went into it, and it would still have been a valuable exercise without that. It was this activity of brainstorming, pooling thoughts, putting them together, weighing up the points for and against, seeking solutions to problems, discovering the nature and value of personal input into group creativity and the dialectic between them, and relating to different categories of people — one's peers, teachers, architects and planners, parents, members of the Planning Committee — wherein lay the strength of the process.

The relationship between architect and children seemed particularly productive. Joy said:

> They were absolutely thrilled to bits with their own particular architect. If there was going to be any competition it was 'my architect's better than your architect.' That's where the competition was coming, if there was any.

Debbie	Again, in the evaluations I did with the children, quite a lot of them said the bit they liked best was getting to know their architect, 'I liked it when my architect came in, and she helped us to sort out the problems'.
Joy	I know from lots of experience that youngsters get an enormous amount out of working with experts who they wouldn't otherwise come into contact with, whether it's a thatcher, or somebody digging the road up or an architect. They get a different perspective of what's happening. The language is different,

the vocabulary is different, the end product is different. It widens their horizons.

Similarly, the children from All Saints reported good relations with the architects:

Child 1 They weren't sort of bossy. They weren't always going on at us that we'd got to get it finished, and it was quite fun working with them.

Child 2 He helped us know what sort of job he did, and all the things you have to think about before you build.

Child 3 He was the one who thought of having a hexagonal building, and then we decided to have half down the bottom and half at the top.

Pam Turner also found her two architects refreshing.

They were delightfully laid back and casual about it all. They didn't say 'We've got to get all this done by Friday'. They were, 'We'll get it done, don't worry!' It was lovely. It was quite nice working with them. I'm sure you get architects who equally flap and panic, but our two were totally unpressured and unworried.

They also treated the children as equals as did the planner. Pam said 'The two we had were so ready to accept the children at a professional level and were not in any way patronizing, and that was great'. We have already seen that Debbie also quickly established firm working relationships with the architects.

Real Learning

Although they were engaged in a hypothetical exercise — none of the designs were ever going to be built — there was a strong air of reality about the project. The *relevance* criterion essential for creative work (Woods, 1990a) is being largely met. Although it might in some respects seem similar to the 'cold science' identified by Atkinson (1975), the extent the organizers went to in order to reproduce verisimilitude was uncommon to say the least.

The location of the work, opened up the city to them in several different ways, showing the whole point of the heritage centre, people working within the city, the buildings of the city, and siting education within the city rather than the school. Philip Turner remarked that the project dissolved boundaries between school and city, and 'it has this holistic character that people could constantly put more of their whole selves into'. As Debbie put it:

It was real to the children. It was a real problem and real people involved in it. Although it was a hypothetical building, the context was very real. There was a real site, and there was a possibility that something might be built there. There was a real need. We looked at the Heritage Centre that exists at present, and, well, — you should see it! Winchester needs a Heritage Centre. So it was a real site, it was a real need, real people involved. It had a real context for them, and that did, I think, give it some meaning.

The children supported this notion. To Laura, to begin with it seemed 'a very weird idea', because 'we'd never done anything like it before'. Asked what was different about it, they commented:

Angharad   It was for real. It's like being a proper architect and working with them.
Zoë   When the architects actually came in, it gave us an idea of what they feel like. And when our planner did it, he didn't say all we wanted him to say.
Melinda   He was being a proper planner, how they were with architects.
Laura   So we know what the architect feels like when the planner doesn't say all that you want him to say.

The All Saints children had a bonus for, as Pam explained:

Our architect said that 'what we would really like to do is take the children into our office and let them work in our office, because we have got our photocopier, and we've got our this and our that; and we would finally like to do the boards and mounting in our office to give the children the experience of working in an architect's office'. So they did, and thoroughly enjoyed it . . . The equipment was especially useful for them . . . for cutting up materials for the display they had these very sharp knives to get the things right, using the real tools. The architects came in originally and gave the children an architect's rubber and a pen each. It was quite a thick felt tip pen and they felt obliged to use this pen because it was an architect's pen and the tracing paper image too. Architects are very, very into tracing paper. When they want to alter a design, they don't draw it out again they merely stick their bit of tracing paper on the top and alter the bits they want. All the way of working for the children was a bonus for them because it was a different way of going about things and was very good.

There were periodic injections of 'reality'. Thus, large amounts of the designing had to be done in classrooms, but the basic work was enlivened by visits to the site, visits to the schools by architects and planners, the prospect of the final planning committee day, and the delivery of material. For example, Debbie thought the latter was a 'turning point':

At the time the children were getting a bit fed up with working in two dimensions on paper. They needed a model, but there wasn't time for that, but they needed something tangible. And Dot Browning came in with some actual materials that could be used, including a lot of samples of rather attractive glass, and their eyes lit up when they saw them. here was something they could handle, it suddenly began to look real. We were talking about real materials, and they could choose colours. That was a turning-point.

Joy pointed to the value of visiting the site. On the site is an Elizabeth Frink sculpture, 'Horse and rider', and there's the 'Hampshire Hog', and

> several of the children mentioned sculpture, and because they'd been there and seen it, it had influenced the way they actually thought.

This emphasis on reality has another connotation, which is not to encourage unreal expectations in children. Philip Turner pointed out that you could become involved with children in planning and design choices, and they could get to a point where they realized there were challenges and problems in the environment. It was important, he thought, that they were given an opportunity to act and devise realistic solutions. The worst thing, in his opinion, was to take children out of their environment, confront them with a topical problem like litter, ask them to devise solutions, getting them all motivated towards them, and then find impracticalities getting in the way of achieving them.

On the presentation day, the teachers were worried that the planners would not take it seriously enough, or that they would perhaps be a little condescending, but 'they weren't at all. They were super'. Joy said:

> They took it all very seriously. They used the proper language — 'My clients this, my clients that'. It was fascinating. It was hilarious.

Pam said the planners were

> so ready to accept the children at a professional level and were not in any way patronizing, and that was great . . . It was a very professional day for the children. They were treated as professional. It was very high powered, and the children responded magnificently working with all these adults.

Nor did the planners shrink from criticizing. Some concessions were made to youthfulness (architects often being 'torn to pieces'!), but the Planning Committee nonetheless made their points, such as 'I'm a little concerned that in this area of flint and brick or whatever, you are introducing a bright orange concrete building'.

These real parameters produced 'real learning' in which the children had a large measure of control and ownership of the product. Though they had received help, the work was theirs. The ideas, the designs and the constructions were theirs. Furthermore there was a sense of group, rather than individual ownership. The plans were sophisticated and to a large extent practicable. Yet Joy

> was delighted that the work, when it went up, actually looked like children's work. In some children's exhibitions you can see where the teachers or somebody else has been doing the work. This was so obviously children's work. How it was written, the way it was written, and everything else was real children's work, and that was very important.

Pam Turner respected her architects for letting so much of the children's work come through, and for not imposing their own superior knowledge and skills. The children did all the lettering, mounting and displays themselves, with adult advice, but the children *did* it. She thought that must have been hard for the architects when they were in 'this competitive situation with eight other architects'. But they had all discussed it and had agreed that 'it was useless adults doing the children's work'.

The teams that I spoke to all described their schemes to me eagerly and in great detail. They were able to answer critical questions of design, arrangement, space, relationship with other adjacent buildings, materials. They were also able to recount the genesis and development of an idea, showing the interaction between individuals and group. They were all very appreciative. One group, asked what they thought of it as an educational project, said:

Child 1   Well, to be honest parrot-fashion teaching is so boring for everyone. It's boring for the teachers as well, I think, and everyone gets fed with it in the end.
Child 2   At school sometimes you only get the same things repeated time and time again, and you never do anything like this, so I think most schools should do this.
Child 3   I think every school should change to this style.

Resources

To hold such a project together and to bring it off successfully requires a number of supports. Most of these are evident from what has been said, but I shall summarize them here.

Critical Agents

The man whose name was given to the project, Frank Chippindale, was its inspiration, and also exerted some influence upon the resolution and dedication of all concerned. A Heritage Centre had been his dream. Not only the aim, but the means would have delighted him, and it seemed, in a way that his character pervaded the proceedings. One young architect, an ex-student of his, said:

He would have approved wholeheartedly of this. He was a very humane, likeable man . . . He regarded people very highly, and thought that architecture was not here to create a monument, but was a product of the people to serve them and be used by them.

Dot said:

He was very keen on the environment, children, education and he really strove to make all the people aware of their surroundings. He was not afraid to say what he didn't like about a form of new building. He admired good design and he criticized openly what he thought was totally the opposite. He started up the Urban Studies Committee in the Preservation Trust and that was active for many years. He organized lunchtime lectures, he produced pamphlets which were able to show good design in the streets. He would take a street in Winchester and he'd write about the buildings, be they old or new and the history and how it had evolved. He took a lot of school trips around the Heritage Centre, but he also took them on guided walks round Winchester.

Keith Leaman, of the same firm of architects, whom Frank had persuaded to join the Urban Studies Committee, took over the chair after Frank. An informal 'planning group' consisting of Keith, Dot Browning, Philip Turner, Nigel Green and Joy Williams gradually evolved the idea of the project. The nurturing of the idea was thus a group effort, and clearly there had to be accord on a number of principles — the purpose of architecture, the importance of education. There also had to be considerable personal investment. Much of the project, for example, was organized in people's spare time.

There was, therefore, an infrastructure of groups and individuals among whom the idea of the project developed. The support of the local Authorities was also fairly crucial, as Dot explains:

> I think the project only actually took place, not only because you had an architect and a teacher from the Teachers' Centre, but you also had two planners from both the Authorities. If one had not had the backing from the Authorities by having someone on the Committee, I don't think it would have taken off in the same way we wanted it to. You wouldn't have had quite so many people backing it.

Nigel agreed:

> It clearly needed to be sold to the Planning Authority because when I first went in and said 'We've got this project where we've got children de-signing a Heritage Centre for the Great Square', their first reaction was 'Can't we do something that is more appropriate?'

With all these different groups, committees, people and different professions and responsibilities, there was a major coordinating task. Dot played a key role here:

> Debbie Dot managed it. Dot did all the hard work. She organized it. She was the person, I felt, who was in charge of the project.
>
> Joy   That's right. And she got the whole thing very, very well thought out, and at our meetings she would keep saying 'Right, I want you to go back to what you were saying to begin with. Let me get this quite clear so I get it straight on the piece of paper' and so on. It was very meticulously done.

The coordinating task was considerable. For architects and planners, no less than teachers, time is at a premium. For their firms, the release of an architect for a number of afternoons is a considerable investment. For the planning group, somebody had to take responsibility for pulling things together into a practicable policy and for negotiating among all the interested groups and people. Dot appears to have done that. Clearly much was owing to her own dedication to the project, drive and abilities. But her own position, almost fortuitously, lent itself to the task. At her firm, she 'handles the publicity side, which is anything from office brochures to how things look. It involves media, selling the firm to magazines, trying to get their work published and so on. It's supposed to be part-time, but it isn't. I have a funny sort of job really.' Perhaps it was important for the project, that there was somebody with 'a funny kind of job' concerned with promotion, liaison and negotiation; somebody not too tightly tied down by professional constraints, whose job, in fact, required a more expansive perspective; somebody who, technically at least, was 'part-time', who, like Melanie in the Laxfield project, had 'left-over' time and 'brain' to spare.

The link between the architects/planners and the teachers was Joy Williams, Head of the Teachers' Centre and member of the Urban Studies Committee. They had decided on a Winchester school for obvious access reasons, but Joy felt that more important was using 'a teacher who actually knows what working outside a classroom is about, motivating children and so on. It's the teacher's attitude that is more important than the children.' She talked to Debbie — they had worked together before and had similar interests in the environment. Thus another link in the chain was forged. These existing relationships were of paramount importance. Could people work together? Did they agree on the basic principles? Could they rely on each other for support? There was clearly that kind of connection among the architects, the members of the planning group, and between Joy and Debbie.

Clearly the teachers bore a considerable responsibility in planning and organizing the work of their pupils and coordinating the teaching. They were experienced teachers who had developed their own personal philosophy of teaching based on constructivist principles, which seemed eminently suitable for this project. It allowed them to strike a balance between direction and freedom, structure and discovery, convergence and divergence. They identified strongly with the cause. They had the personal qualities, not only to help their own pupils along, but to relate openly and constructively with the other professionals involved. They had resolution and flair in tackling and solving new problems and strong vocational and professional commitment, necessary for the extra workload. Debbie observed that there were points where it was

> heavy going. It was hard work for the teacher managing forty children. It was bigger than the normal class group. They were doing practical drawing, discussion, problem-solving activities where you have no room to move and it has to be fairly noisy if you work in groups of five and are discussing and negotiating, and it was hard work, it really was. The constraints of the building and the resources available and the manpower. It was very wearing at times.

Individuals were important, but so, too, was the way they interconnected through their professional relationships. The interrelationship among the architects, planners and Planning Committee was there in their everyday concerns, as was the process from conception to final consideration. So, too, was the liaison and publicity work provided by Dot. Could schools have initiated this? They might, but as Dot pointed out, for certain aspects of the work you had to have fellow-professionals dealing with each other:

> Dot   If you've got someone who is organizing this project and they are asking for architectural funds — say Joy Williams was doing it, and she is writing to the firms of architects (a) she doesn't know the principals or the directors or the people you have got to write to; (b) who is going to say 'Three whole afternoons and a day?' You have to have one professional writing to the other in order to get the backup.
>
> Nigel   That's right. It's the same as we needed the help of someone like Joy who understood the teaching requirements.

It was also noticeable that some of the architects and teachers had a foot in the other camp, so to speak. Thus Joy Williams was a member of the Urban Studies Committee. Philip Turner was Chair of the Royal Town Planning Institute Environmental Education Panel, and Vice-chair of the Civic Trusts Education Group. He already had considerable experience of working with schoolchildren. It was not a matter, therefore, of two different professional groups coming together for the first time. Though some of the architects may have had concerns originally about their ability to manage the children, the previous experience of some in their ranks may have been an aid to morale.

Critical Others: The Architects and Planners

Clearly the contribution made by the architects and planners was considerable. They introduced a new perspective and new skills that challenged some of the schools' methods and routines. They had a liberating effect upon pupils and teachers alike, but at the same time introduced the principles of a new discipline. One described how she found young children quite constrained.

> I had to bring in big, fat, black pens and big bits of white paper to get them actually drawing freely, because they're so used to drawing little tiny detail.

Not being 'responsible' for the children in the same way as the teachers were, either from the point of view of behaviour or structuring and progressing the scheme as a whole, they were free to indulge their art and expertise, and to be bold and expansive while doing a thoroughly professional job. The children pointed to the architects' methods of getting ideas out of them, helping them to combine ideas, providing expert advice. Several said they would not have been able to do it without them, but 'they made us work for it'.

One of the architects illustrates an aspect of their input:

> Initially they came up with an idea of the dome shape and a siting for it. We asked them to question whether that was the right site for it. How would they get access? How would you get in if there was a fire? Where would people park their cars? Then, of course, they'd done some environmental, so that this was all going to be very sensitive, so we asked them to work beyond that. It was a matter of finding out which bits they were interested in contributing and once you hit upon that they would happily go away and do it.

The planners wrote the brief. Nigel Green later visited the schools to explain the genesis and importance of planning, raising specific points about the project. And 'on the day itself, the exercise almost changed from being an architectural exercise to a planning exercise, getting the thing through the Committee.' Philip Turner elaborated on the role of the planner:

I think the planner would have been concerned with the placing of the building and the spaces that were created by that act and the relationship between the proposed building and what was there, the existing spaces and buildings and trees and views, or whatever, and whether it was the sort of use or activity that was appropriate for that particular place. If I were doing an exercise in which planners worked with teams of children, I think it would be more wide ranging. It would be something on the lines of 'find the site' in the first place and assess Winchester as a whole, decide where the main tourist routes are, pedestrians, those in cars, public transport, where the main centres of activity and attraction are or will be. But this one was tailormade for architects to work with children. The site was in broad terms accepted and they were given a challenge to design a building to perform a particular function.

The Schools

Neither Debbie nor Pam would have been able to take part in the project without the support of their schools. Debbie was faced with the prospect of taking an ambitious high-profile enterprise to a new school, where she would have to work with somebody she had not worked with before. Fortunately, he had experience of that kind of work, and they had 'the same educational philosophy'. The rest of the staff were 'sympathetic and flexible', as they needed to be since the project impinged on normal processes. Parents, who might have raised objections ('where is their science, etc.?'), were also supportive, being 'quite used to their children working in this way'.

For All Saints, Pam stressed that the school was the focal point of the community and that they were used to working with people from outside:

The community come and work in the school. We do a lot of work with pre-school children and parents because the school is seen as a sort of centre, the hub of activity. People are in and out all the time. They come here to have their meetings and bring their toddlers or come to various things that go on in the evening. We hope to be an open school sharing our facilities with our clients, people outside, and encourage them to share themselves with us.

The City

The particular urban environment was a huge resource. Debbie feels that

it is such a fascinating city. It is so important. We are so privileged to live here. Of all the cities in England, it's got one of the richest histories. I think we take it for granted.

Winchester, home of King Alfred the Great, was once joint capital of the Kingdom. It has a magnificent Norman cathedral in picturesque surrounds, and many other interesting buildings of note. It is a surprisingly small town, with its sense of history compactly preserved among modern amenities. As with many modern towns there is a major problem with traffic. The need for visual harmony and historical faithfulness in an era of general environmental threat, and issues of access and pollution intermingle to provide a powerful motive-force for an educational project that many feel should command a high priority. Philip Turner spoke about the concept of city as a learning resource:

> That goes very straight to the objectives of the Heritage Centre. You have got something very valuable in the city. It has a lot to offer in terms of experiences in learning to a wide range of people, not just children and not just the people who are visitors, tourists, but also local people. So that's a very strong objective in terms of urban studies centres to use the environment as an outdoor classroom and it's also something which the people of Winchester and other cities and places are also keen on pursuing. It's really field study centre in an urban context.

All thought the site itself important for the study. Dot said:

> The actual site that we had to deal with had been fairly carefully thought out. It was important to have a site which was, certainly for the first pilot, relatively safe for the children to go to. There needed perhaps to be the different buildings around rather than have a totally open site. A site had been suggested for a future year which happens to be an allotment on the outside of town. That's very difficult to give to children because they've not got enough around it, and clearly it appeared to us that they needed the surrounding buildings to actually get them going. A total landscape project, which again is a possibility, would be different because, although you wouldn't perhaps have buildings, you would have different uses of land.

Sponsorship

The project involved considerable cost, much of it 'hidden'. Dot's firm of Plinke, Leaman and Browning made a major input and provided much of the coordination. As Dot pointed out, it was good for publicity, but the educational aims of the project were also well within the philosophy of the firm. Like Chippindale they believe that 'as a profession you are very outward-looking. They've always felt quite strongly that people don't know much about architecture. This is one way of making the links with children fairly early on.' Representatives from the firm had given talks in schools, and they had a lot of students on work experience. Even so, the investment was considerable. As Dot explained, 'It's a very expensive activity for the architects', and there were other costs to her firm in terms of secretaries typing, telephoning and photocopying, and her own time. She found it 'great fun, but time-consuming'.

Dot was successful in persuading a number of firms to sponsor the event, though she feels that there is a quid pro quo. These are not charitable organizations, and some no doubt became involved with a view to the publicity opportunities the project afforded. The funds they provided were nonetheless essential for materials, equipment, photocopying, publicity, and the financing of the exhibition on Presentation Day, and nothing was lost by the publicity afforded to the firms.

Conclusion

This was a typical critical event. Notable advances were made in pupil and teacher learning and development, and in that of architects and planners. It was a considerable boost for the teachers' personal educational philosophies. It was also critical for Winchester, being a 'first' for the city — a breakthrough in environmental education. A working party of the Environmental Board (1979) of the Department of the Environment recommended that 'Urban environmental education should help people perceive, understand, analyse, and finally improve their built environment' (p. 1). The Chippindale Project is an illustration of one way in which that might be done. Debbie recorded that it

> has given the children a glimpse of the real world by bringing them into direct contact with their own environment and provided them with the knowledge that as the future generation they are responsible for it. We hope that our children will become active agents of change rather than passive recipients of it.

Nigel Green reported that awareness of the environment had been raised generally. For example, there had been a number of approaches to the Planning Department to give talks in schools, and one school, where buildings are going up around them, had requested help with a project which 'shows the children how things get built, why they get built, and the process of building. So the children won't just be sitting in their classrooms watching houses go up, they will know what the process is'. Thus there was a ripple of activity out from the event. There was also a long-term effect. Since this particular pilot, Ventures II and III have taken place, and the project seems well-set to continue for the foreseeable future. The idea was a real brainchild, born out of the death of a remarkable architect-educator, among a group of people keen to carry on his life's work. It captured the imagination of a whole range of people, and was sustained by inspired dedication among the promoters. It helped induce a feeling of 'communitas' among them, sharing the underlying values in promoting the environment and the educational aims; and being part of a pioneering venture that might break new boundaries. Philip Turner said that the architects and planners had had a debriefing, discussing the value of the project, 'whether boys and girls responded equally, can we do it again . . . let's keep the network going, and this was good. We liked doing it and got a buzz out of it. We would like to do it again and go a bit further'. In some respects they were playing a game, though it was one with real and serious purpose. It was a game in that they were sublimated from their everyday concerns, all had their parts to play, and by certain rules. That sublimation freed them from roles and statuses. They could act the parts that those roles and statuses prescribed, but also engage in strong personal accord as if they did not exist.

The structure of the project also takes a fairly typical line for critical events from inception to celebration, with the interaction between structure and freedom, 'romance' and 'precision', in between. Most teachers would agree with this recipe. The art lies in getting the right mix of ingredients at the right time and in the right context. There was much discussion about this as the participants reflected back on the event, particularly in making comparisons between the two schools and their different approaches to the project, one more structured and programmed in the early stages, the other more open and divergent. Both, however, laid strong emphasis on 'personal enquiry', 'negotiation' and cooperation in their teaching methods, and provide good examples of teacher's facilitatory roles.

It has to be said that not all would recognize the special nature of the event, and this might be either because the notion of 'special' connotes exclusivity or elitism or because most of what goes on in most schools is regarded as 'special'. Pam Turner, for example, thought that in essence, it was nothing out of the ordinary.

> There was a lot of external professional input into it and no way doing it within the school would we have got a planning committee to sit down and the children wouldn't have had those experiences, but the basic work is what is going on in schools anyway. It isn't really anything all that fantastic apart from the input. If you are doing a project on building you bustle round and get your adults to come in and talk about what they knew about building. You bring in people anyway in normal school projects and if it's convenient you take the children out anyway to the planning offices or something like that.

Critical events, therefore, have to be seen within the context of particular sets of ongoing activities, their definition depending in part on the contrast; and from the perspectives of particular people who might vary in their experiences, notwithstanding the collective nature of the event. Like any such event, this one was not above criticism. However, the main agents were reflective practitioners who provided their own critique. Thus Debbie was concerned that she had over-planned and over-structured, used squared paper, not allowed time for the construction of models. Having two schools, especially when selected by different criteria, was thought by several to be a mistake since it inevitably engendered a note of comparison and competition which was inimical to the aims of the project. However, while this might have been a matter of some discomfort at the time, it has had an analytic advantage in helping to inform future ventures.

There was general agreement that there had been too much to cope with and not enough time. Debbie felt that it needed a full term rather than a half. Pam thought the timing was wrong, that it would have been better in the summer rather than autumn term, when you would know the children better and could make preparations accordingly — an important point about situating the event to optimum effect within normal procedures. A similar point applied to the timing of the Presentation Day — the last day before a school holiday. Some thought there should have been space for de-briefing before the holiday, thus facilitating exit from the project and re-entry into normal school. These points, like several other matters of detail, could be attended to in future projects.

Another point for consideration is the selectivity of the exercise. How can the benefits be spread among the broader range of pupils? Pam feels that most pupils at All Saints 'could not have coped with it, and would have just been disheartened and discouraged because they wouldn't have the skill'. She would have liked

> a much broader based project where one group could do this and the other groups do connected work according to their abilities.

There is a danger, however, that two different curricula might operate, involving basic skills for the less able, and opportunities to engage in creative work for those seen as 'more able' (Tickle, 1983). There is evidence within Venture I that some children have surprising abilities, that sometimes were not even suspected by their teachers, but were brought out and operationalized by the particular circumstances of the project. It would be good for the opportunity, in some form, to be available to all. Herein, perhaps, lies the major challenge for the Chippindale organizers.

Chapter 5

The Magic of Godspell:
the Educational Significance
of a Dramatic Event

The Roade Godspell 1988–9

In September 1988, Roade Comprehensive School in Northamptonshire began rehearsals for the rock musical 'Godspell'. Five performances were given at the school in December 1988. It was seen by selectors for the National Student Drama Festival, and chosen by them as one of the twenty-two entries (from seventy-five applicants) to the thirty-fourth festival. When it appeared in Cambridge in March/April 1989, it won a top award. Following this, BBC Northampton asked the school to give a performance to the general public in Northampton to launch their BBC Children in Need appeal. This final show was given to a full and enthusiastic house in October, 1989.

'Godspell' basically is a 'pop' version of St Matthew's Gospel, featuring Jesus and his disciples, with the parables as script and a rock music score. The religious message is carried through to Christ's crucifixion and resurrection. God sends his son to earth. His teaching prepares people to enter the Kingdom of Heaven. Then He is betrayed, crucified and resurrected. By so doing, He saves the world. In the Roade version, directed by Sally Mackey, Head of Expressive Arts at the school, Jesus is a young boy, who, half asleep, discovers disused toys under dust sheets and shut away in cupboards in an attic nursery. His aim is to give the toys the 'garden' — the outside world. By encouraging them to share in the telling of stories — the parables — he guides them towards taking responsibility for that world. The toys gradually come to recognize that their mentor will have to leave them. Finally betrayed, the boy knows that only through this betrayal can they all leave their shelter. His resurrection, however, leaves them with hope and ensures the eternity of the message.

At all points, the production won high praise. The County English and Drama Inspector wrote: 'I have never seen a better school production.' Alex Renton in *The Independent* admired it for 'finding a brilliant balance between style and content, and holding it for two heart-lifting hours'. He praised 'the remarkable flair' of the direction, and noted that the cast 'acted, sang and danced the schmaltz with overwhelming enthusiasm'. Robert Hewison in *The Sunday Times* spoke of 'the sheer delight it produced in performers and audience alike', and was impressed with 'the detail and the individual touches that flourished within the community'. Glen Walford, one of the judges spoke of the 'joy, love and commitment of the company and their marvellous ability to portray childlike adults'. *Noises Off*, the daily Festival newspaper, applauded 'a brilliant interpretation!' But it was something more than this. It was an educational event. It was also an event in the lives of the participants, and, in view of its character and development, a critical event of some magnitude. I was concerned, therefore, to discover the meaning of the event to the participants; what was 'educational' about it; and why it was so special.

Sally Mackey kindly made available her file of director's notes, scripts, reviews, radio discussions, audio-cassettes and videos of rehearsals and performances, and letters and poems sent to her from members of the cast. I had several conversations with Sally, most of them taped and transcribed. I also had interviews ranging in time from one hour to fifteen minutes (times varying in accordance with the stringencies of the school timetable) with Ian Willison, Head of Roade Comprehensive School, Lesley Fielding, Musical Director, and nineteen members of the cast and orchestra. I consider first the students' educational gains. I go on to discuss the teachers' sense of development. Finally, I examine the 'magic ingredients' that went into the making of the play.

Student Gains

Personal Development

The participants felt they made great strides in personal development during the ten-month period. Many achieved a quantum leap in some respect or other in ways they had never imagined possible. Many felt they were new persons as a consequence.

Discovery of Self

Sara, chief ballerina, was the oldest student in the cast. She started at Roade in the third year, and felt that she 'never belonged there properly, not having formed the friendships that most of them had'. At first feeling awkward and misplaced, not even feeling part of the school, she underwent a transformation:

> It was such an important year for me. I had my A levels throughout that year. I don't know how I managed to do this as well because it was so intense and it literally dominated the whole year of my life . . . It has affected me so much . . . I was not going through that good a stage at school because I didn't feel that I fitted in and I wanted something more. I then decided to go for the school play because of being involved in A level drama I thought I'd better. I walked in there and I sat amid all these kids that I'd never seen before and I saw them as young children. I just thought, 'What am I doing here? I am 18 years of age and I do not want this sort of thing!' And I got up to go and Sally said, 'If you're thinking of going you can sit down now.' Then gradually we started, and if I hadn't have stayed there I don't know what sort of a person I would be now. I feel I've gained so much from this . . . I'm now helping to direct Oedipus with Sally . . .

Matthew felt that it had been a maturing experience:

I'm more calm and rational. I mean, I don't sort of leap around and go 'Okay, Okay, Darling!' all the time. I never did then, but I wasn't far off it. If I wasn't careful I could have turned into a real pretentious obnoxious git.

The band also developed as people, developing their expertise and becoming eminently reliable. Lesley reported:

In rehearsals sometime Richard would play the fool a little bit with Owen . . ., though he's grown up enormously in the last six months. But on the night he was there, and he was concentrating and it was brilliant, so I'd never worry about him being silly. He was mature enough really to know — 'I've got to concentrate, don't miss my cue . . .'

In aiding self-expression, drama is not purely self-indulgent. Godspell was performed both for the actors themselves, and for the audience. The actors had to see themselves as others saw them. This encouraged reflectivity, aided their 'taking the role of the other' (Mead, 1934), helped establish their 'selves' on a broader basis. Ian reported, 'being up on stage makes you see yourself as others would see you. You have to think about what you are doing from the audience's point of view, because you want them to see the play the best way possible'.

In the Head's opinion:

Their lives have been directly influenced in a most positive way by it, and that's got to be an important part of it. They're better people because of it, and that's great. It's not only eyes being opened, it's their hearts and their very being in fact. Their education would be a soulless experience without something like this.

In his belief, 'it's through the Arts that finally we can begin to rate ourselves as human beings. I believe it to be as crucial as that.' Matthew illustrates the point. He had a limited view of drama beforehand, thinking it was just 'acting' and 'having a good time'.

But I learnt more about myself at Cambridge than about drama itself. I came back and I was a completely different person to how I went. I was much more outgoing. I was not pretentious but more caring.

Creativity

The demands of engaging with the role fostered their creative instincts promoting spontaneity and intuitive powers of improvisation. Here actors have to 'ad lib' to turn to experiences which are not performed and ready-made, but are still buried within them in an unformed stage. In order to mobilize and shape them, they need a transformer and catalyst, a kind of intelligence which operates 'here and now' (Moreno, 1972, p. 138). Speaking of drama as therapy, Moreno states, 'It was an important advance to link spontaneity to creativity, the highest form of intelligence we know of, and to recognize them as the primary forces in human behaviour.'

This, therefore, is of considerable educational import (see also Slade, 1968, and Moreno, 1964, on the importance of spontaneity). This is well expressed by Matthew:

At Derngate, the Jill-in-the Box, Kate, suddenly found a new level. The Jills don't have any character except to be bouncy a bit. Then the very first parable they did, Kate was brilliant. It's little things that make it work. She started to cry when she was imprisoned. She'd never done that before, and you suddenly think — why hadn't anybody thought of doing that before. It looked so good.

The reservoirs of (unsuspected?) talent were fully tapped over the process as a whole, whereas, perhaps, only hints of it came through in earlier performances. Take, for example, Ian G's final performance as seen by Matthew:

I think he just commanded the stage. He developed this charisma that he'd shown flickers of earlier. He hadn't done any bad performances. But he went up to the next level. He allowed much longer time for pauses, and each one paid off. You could just look at him and you could tell that he was feeling what Jesus was feeling, whereas before it wasn't so obvious.

Ian G. tries to explain:

It sort of arose spontaneously from the actual doing of what the director told me to do. It was never a conscious decision. If anything ever happened it was in the course of a rehearsal, from the initial impetus that Sally gave like — 'Ian do this, or do that' — then something else would come out. It sort of came out from the inside of me. There I was, doing something, like there was this stamping of feet and things like that, which was never actually scripted or anything. They were just the bare bones and it was up to me to provide the flesh and blood to it . . . You have to involve yourself in (the role), let yourself be consumed by it.

Sara described how she really felt the part. It 'really got to' her and she was 'very, very overwhelmed with it'. The first half is 'great fun', but the second half is 'so serious'. By this time

you've established this role for yourself and just get caught up in it. You'd look around and no one would have a normal expression on their face. They would all have a toy expression. I remember just standing as a Pharisee. Someone stands behind me on a box and we were supposed to be genuinely quite wicked and we were accusing the young child representing Jesus of everything under the sun, and Jesus himself had got so into it. The look on his face, no one would ever appreciate it, the audience, because they would never be able to see his eyes. He was so angry with us, and I remember being genuinely frightened.

Matthew also conveys some of this intensity of involvement in his special relationship with the Jesus figure. When he betrays him at the end, he has to hug him.

When I hugged him, I looked back and I looked in his eyes and they looked hurt, sad and upset, and I felt bad . . . I felt 'Oh! What have I done!?' I had to grip myself and say 'Look, you didn't do it, it's in the script' — to stop myself wallowing in pity.

Kevin had to become a teddy bear. He had to resolve being this soft, cuddly warm creature with the macho male image. He plays American Football, and 'when they heard I was a teddy bear, the amount of ribbing I got was unbelievable. But I just took it all in my stride'. Kevin felt the comedy came from 'sparks of inspiration' deriving from their strong identification with their characters.

There wasn't much (comedy) to begin with. It mainly came from ad libs and how people said the words, like when Jo said 'I will pay you back, honest.' And 'It's a secret, shh!' When you get given a part you just take the part of your own soul in the stuff and then you just enlarge it. I took what niceness, what softness, stupidity, friendliness I have inside of me, and I just tried to enlarge that, and eradicate the nasty side of my personality.

He had got all the teddy bears he could find and watched how their bodies moved. He imagined how they used to talk in the past, and that all went into his role. For him, it all came together at the dress rehearsal. Up till then, he had been saying his lines as Kevin Tomlinson, but now

this voice suddenly came along. It was weird, it just came, it's kind of inspirational. I guess it was the wearing of the costume and being on the stage in the nursery. It made me feel more like I was a toy in a nursery. It came from within . . .

Sara thought Kevin

created something incredible. At the beginning it was just a teddy bear, but everyone added something to their character at each performance, and you ended up improvising so much that you could do anything and it would be within your role and it wouldn't look over the top.

Ian G. found the transition to role a fairly natural one. He had to work on it, studying the script in his spare time and thinking 'what could I do here?', but actions always arose spontaneously. New things happened with each performance. He gave these examples:

At Derngate — just the way Kevin said — 'Blessed are the Poor in Spirit' — I put my hands on the side of his face, round his ears like this — a sort of comforting gesture. I've never done that before. And there was one other night, where Kevin says — 'When was it we saw you hungry and gave you food', for some reason, I don't know why, I just put my hand on his head or on his shoulder. Then there are times when you pronounce the words slightly differently . . .

Ian also related how he had learnt to improvise, making a virtue of almost forgetting a song, or when a cane fell to pieces pretending that it was meant to happen. 'Doing plays certainly sharpens your thinking under pressure' he said. Improvisation, spontaneity, invention were fostered even during the one interval in the play. While the audience broke up for refreshments and a stretch, the cast remained on stage acting out little improvising scenarios of their own. Jo, the baby doll invented 'Fergus the flea' who appeared in every performance and went round at the interval frightening people. 'She'd go around and say "Guess what's in my hand", like this, and she had it cupped. Then she'd suddenly go "Boo!" as loud as she could, and throw her hands in your face. Nothing would come out, but you'd jump, it was such a shock. Such an innocent little baby, and it was just brilliant. She'd giggle and run off — brilliant.' (Kevin) Kate rolled Sam's boa into a bundle and pretended it was a pussy cat — 'brilliant'. Kevin wore Adam's hat the wrong way round — 'there were so many other new things each time.' Kevin thought this was allowing you to 'let off steam and have fun' and also to 'increase your understanding of your character'. You were put in situations you would not otherwise be in in the play itself. For example, 'a ballerina will suddenly come up and cuddle you, and she's never done this before in months and months of rehearsals. You react as a teddy bear, and it's really interesting seeing how you react, because it's new and it adds to your character'.

What might have seemed, therefore, to the audience to be rather aimless 'messing-about' in the interval was, in fact, constructive and imaginative behaviour. Moreover the involvement was total — both of each individual member of the cast and of the whole cast. In Martyn's opinion:

> Every single person was actually acting 100% of the time, and some of these really wooden characters were no longer. They somehow got transformed into actors. I think that's what took it out of the ordinary.

It was difficult to part from those characters. Jo Smith, for example, in her baby doll's roomy dress and big side bunches 'absolutely hated her appearance to begin with', and they all 'had a massive giggle about it'. But by the end 'she didn't want to part with her bunches. She just didn't look the same without those ribbons!' (Sara).

Members of the band also put their 'selves' into it, blending their ideas into the music, which, like the play, allowed room for improvisation. Lesley reported that:

> Godspell was completely new to the band, but by the end, very much like the kids on stage, they were putting their own ideas into the music and a lot of it was improvised on top of what was actually written. We just had the basic band parts like the bass guitar part, the drum part, which we didn't even look at. Owen did it all. He couldn't read music anyway. He couldn't read the rhythms well enough to follow the music and I think it would have inhibited his playing. So I said — 'right, listen to the song, what can we do with it?' So it wasn't just taking it. But the drummer — he was absolutely fantastic — the best drummer I've ever known.

At Derngate, he 'played his heart out' — and his fingers too, and they had to put plasters on his hands for protection. Richard, the pianist, also 'improvised with the pieces . . . not actually playing the music note for note . . . but it didn't matter, it was just lovely how he did it. Ben Baynes on bass guitar, again, can't read music, so he improvised too. He just picked the key up, absolutely fantastic, and it was so professional. Michael Daley played lead guitar in the end, and his playing improved . . .'

Michael, for his own part, found it 'fun to do' and felt that he had 'developed a lot and gained a better sense of rhythm and better improvisation.' Before, he had been playing chords all the time. Richard found himself stretched by certain demands, for example, the different times one of the songs was written in. He felt his experience had broadened. He plays the organ, and hadn't played much piano until Godspell. Now he played them both equally.

Confidence

Students acquired new-found confidence. In a letter to Sally, Claire said, 'I had been involved in backstage work for the past two years for I never felt that I was good enough to perform on stage. When Katie persuaded me to audition it was the best decision I could ever have made . . . I doubt that I will ever be quite the same person again . . . I feel as though I am starting to get over that shyness, because if I can perform on stage in front of 1200 people, let's face it, I can do anything'.

Samantha Jane found it

a really brilliant experience. I feel more confident in myself now and it just meant being so close to so many people, I really loved it. Before, I was very loud and blurty, but I didn't really mean anything I said. I was really scatty, but I learned to control that in me during Godspell, because, with being around quite a few older people I had to be more mature and work with my group, and that helped me a lot.

Sally-Ann had had a 'group' part in previous productions but

in Godspell you became more of a main person because you were on stage all the time, and it builds up your confidence a lot to do things. That's why I went in for a lead part for Oedipus (the current production), and I got it this year.

Chris felt that he grew with each performance. At Cambridge I thought:

Oh no, I've got my lines coming up, but at Derngate it didn't bother me. I was going to say them whatever. If they wanted to watch me, they could watch me. I was going to enjoy myself, and I did. I felt it progressed me personally.

Josie thought

you gained so much more from that experience than you ever could from sitting in a classroom . . . You gained more confidence in yourself which obviously makes you more confident in the classroom. Because you felt totally secure and totally part of something, whereas at times when you're in a teacher–pupil situation you don't always. But with that you felt confident about yourself, everyone around you, and good about what you were doing.

Part of this new found confidence was reflected in a heightened sense of control. Johanne at first 'couldn't accept criticism' and thought that she would feel 'totally ridiculous' playing her part of 'baby doll',

> but I now find myself being more laid-back than I was before. I can handle things a bit better because I know I can change to suit situations. I can also accept criticism better, though I might not agree with it . . . I don't think you can do something like theatre and not have a fairly thick skin . . . You have to respect other people's opinions.

More examples of such control follow in the next section.

Emotional Development

> We have failed in helping to drown the emotional powers of many young people, including students, whose development as feeling beings is dwarfed and stunted. (Schiller, 1979, p. 68)

Ross (1978, p. 43) argues that the purpose of self-expression in the arts is 'the elaboration and development of our emotional life, of our capacity to make sense in feeling of the subjective world of feeling, our capacity to feel intelligently, to find our way among feelings by feeling.' Phillips (1982, p. 28) argues that the understanding of our emotions requires a great deal of knowledge, some of it purely factual. She gives the example of fear. To dispel fear or to focus it more clearly we need to find out more about the object of our fear. If we are to acquire control over our emotions we need a real understanding of them at a personal level. We thus discover more about ourselves (Geertz, 1973). Curiously, perhaps, drama offers opportunities for 'real' investigation.

Godspell is a highly emotional play, and taking part in it is a highly emotional experience. The extremes of love, happiness, joy, grief, trust, deceit are all involved. The young actors had not experienced all of these in all their various forms and intensity. Delightful and highly pleasurable at times, at others the play was totally traumatic. As Sara remarked, 'during two hours of performance you've been pulled through every emotion that you could possibly imagine. You have to try to convince yourself that wasn't reality, that was a performance, but you feel it was a reality. That's why we all looked such a mess afterwards. But it was worth it!'

> To be able to summon up such feelings and meaning to this part that you have, and the relations between the characters as well . . . You can sort of click your fingers and it comes up immediately. It's wonderful to have this.

There was plenty of crying, for both joy and sadness. There were times when Tatty Doll Sally and her friends on a trip to France 'burst into song and we all get that wonderful feeling again'. They had gone into a church and seen a 'big picture on the wall, of Jesus on the cross, with Mary Magdelene (Ian and Sam) at His feet. Sam and I were both in tears'. At Cambridge, Claire cried before, during and after the performance. 'My tears were a mixture of sadness though, as well as happiness, for my whole body was filled with so many different emotions'.

Matthew as the Judas figure arguably had the most difficult part in the sense of self-identification with the role. He told how, after the second performance of the play at Roade:

I had a guilt complex. I just couldn't get to sleep. I shouldn't have felt guilty but I did. Once, I openly cried on stage. I never cry, not because I won't, it's just because I can't. Yet it all got so on top, and I felt so good after each number and at the end I felt so bad — the massive emotional outlet when we're all shouting and screaming and wailing at the end. I just broke down — just by watching the others and shouting to them. It was awful.

Sara notes a similar experience during the 'Pharisee scene':

I was made to feel as if I had totally betrayed Jesus. I remember the strong sense of guilt I felt when Ian turned on the three of us Pharisees with his aggressive interpretation of 'Alas for you'. I will always remember the power of his expression as he pointed an accusing finger at us. It genuinely moved me *every* time . . . When the rest of the cast act out an aggressive moment where they stone us in slow motion, I remember experiencing sheer terror, as if I could feel the harm that they were inflicting on us. I think this must have been connected with the real bitterness their faces expressed, so believable, so realistic, you could not help but get so involved and indeed overwhelmed with it all. I would often find myself shaking during the performance. It was almost as if I'd lost touch with reality, could not wake from a dream. I guess that is why the entire cast looked somewhat brainwashed after every performance!

The disaster potential in the piece from these comments is clear, both for the play which could become maudlin and cloyingly sentimental beyond words, and for the individuals involved who could be dragged through emotional turmoil for no reward other than a feeling of neurosis and instability. These, however, are better seen as stages which may have been gone through at some point or other during the ten-month process, but were not terminal in themselves. They are part of the liminal phase of status passages (Glaser and Strauss, 1971), when things are thrown into temporary confusion, before reconstruction leads to a new order. Things eventually worked both within the play and within individuals. How did it happen? In Sally's opinion:

The emotion worked because the kids actually did feel it a lot of the time. I'm not sure whether adults would. Certainly that last night in Cambridge was absolutely incredible. They were howling on stage. They were really difficult to control themselves. It never came away from what it should be, but they were so wrapped up in it, just sobbing their hearts out. It was because it was naturally there, it was them feeling it within their roles that I think we escaped.

Equally, however, the play, the roles, and the manner of production provided a structured framework within which they could experiment and which also helped discipline their emotions. In this sense it provided both opportunity and constraint. This is well illustrated by how, in developing their role, they 'became the part', but also developed the ability to recognize that very process and to de-role; also, by how they developed the art of the actor in 'achieving that absolute contradiction — the control of spontaneity' (Barrault, 1972, p. 31). There are many instances, therefore, of the power of drama to bring people out, and to give them voice and expression.

Ian G. described how he found it difficult to begin with to control his sense of personal anger at certain points in the play. 'I wasn't fully in control of myself because I'd shout and I'd be angry', when obviously a 'certain amount of restraint' was needed. Then, in preparation for Cambridge, a drama expert came to give them some extra coaching. He told him:

> You've got to be angry but compassionate. I'd never read this compassionate side into anger before and when I thought about it, I thought — 'when a teacher is angry with a pupil, he's angry but why is he angry?' He's not doing it to shout at them, is he? He's doing it for a compassionate reason. I thought to myself, 'Yes!' and I went away and this bit came back as 'You must love the Lord your God' . . . It was a scolding, but it was very tender, compassionate and — 'please believe me and listen to what I am saying because it's very, very important'.

Matthew came to terms with his role and developed it in a number of ways over the ten-month period. For example, he related how he had discovered a stance, legs astride, hands behind back, straight back, that once he had it, it always made him feel powerful and in control. He watched a video, listening to his voice, making it deeper in places, and more threatening. Things, he felt, were always improving in this regard. For example, at Derngate, in the middle of Jo's song,

> when I'm talking, and then 'the man they call Judas Iscariot', I got spite into it and that worked much better. It says in the script 'do it dead straight', but if you do, no one can hear a word you're saying. It was the little things that are powerful in it that developed as it went through, like Jo, when she says during her song after I've said my bit, she just says it completely straight, no baby doll voice, but a very adult voice. And this adult voice saying terrible things coming from this little baby's mouth, it's heart-rending!

Chris (Chief Sailor) and Sam (Chief Tatty Doll) also had difficult moments. Sam was a scantily-clad, lascivious siren, a complete contrast from the demure 14-year old in her school uniform with tie slightly askew whom I interviewed.

> The first time I did it I was so embarrassed, I didn't know what to do. The character wasn't that developed and I was still being myself and

feeling shy because I don't wear very much. I just felt really open to the audience, like they could just kind of touch me, and I just felt I didn't know what to do.

Eventually, however,

I just went completely out of that and put my whole self into it . . . I get myself psyched up to being a tatty. I have to think about being really tatty and all the sort of things I would do. I'm sitting there and thinking 'Cor! I wonder what Chris (Chief Sailor) is doing now, and whether he's thinking about me', and things like that.

For his part, Chris also had problems with the lecherous side of his character:

At first, I was very embarrassed with groping Sam, and I found that very difficult to get out of until — well, I don't know what actually happened — but I just forgot that I was groping somebody. It's not me really, but that totally went . . . There's a bit in me that was like that and I tried to bring that bit out in how I acted.

Baby Doll Jo agreed about the development of self:

It's very true actually about working on something you've got inside you. I myself just found it brilliant to be able to turn into this escapist character who was allowed to do what she wanted all the time. It was great not to have to act sensible and grown-up for a while. You totally left the outside behind you when the costumes went on — however silly they felt.

The costumes helped establish the identity (Stone, 1962):

It's not Johanne going on stage, because you've got this white dress and pigtails to hide behind. It seems easier to let yourself go more and become a bit more convincing.

As in other respects, there was no difference between girls and boys here. Matthew said that people were

not too afraid to show affection on stage, like boys not being afraid to sit next to other boys on stage and look friendly, or put their arm round someone.

Sally said that those boys she knew best were really 'not afraid to actually say what they feel, and talk very gently and sensitively about others'. The hugging at the end was a bridge that had to be crossed, as Ian reported:

When we started off there was all this hugging going on — 'Oooh! You're hugging!' . . . And you had to hug Mr Glass, the teacher, who was one of the clowns. You were wary of hugging a teacher. It's not done, is it — the contact, the intimacy? You go on, and you go on, and you get to the performance and it all slots in. You hug, and you don't just hug because it's a direction. You hug because you'll never be seeing these people again. It changed its form from being mechanical to a more compassionate thing.

How real is this character-building? How closely does this working out of role penetrate to the inner psyche? Are these aspects of character simply worn, like the costumes, in a 'theatrical' way. Or, in becoming the part, does the part become part of the person? Sara is enlightening here:

Matthew as Judas did so much. Sometimes you would look over at him — he was the observer in the play — and he would have such a look of contempt on his face. He is very easy going and yet he created such a role. He was very frightening at times. When he actually grabbed Jesus and blew the whistle to take him to put him on the cross, he just looked so angry and his expression was so deep. You know how you see some actors and they're almost mechanical and they have these cliché expressions of shock, horror, anger, all this sort of thing. By the end of Cambridge and indeed Derngate as well we had created a kind of truth in the play. You believed in everything, and by the time Matthew was about to betray Jesus, you could see genuine regret on his fact. It was so genuine, you totally believed him. It wasn't that we were meant to believe him. We actually did believe, and when he took him and put him on the cross, usually he would just blow the whistle and drag him to the back but, by the end of Cambridge, he shouted at the top of his voice 'Get out of my way!' to everybody with such a look. I was so frightened! We just automatically ran away from him because he was so frightening. You get so caught up in it, it's beyond your control and you just go for it. To take part in such an experience it does something to you.

The educational benefits of emotional involvement in acting appear to be twofold. First, drama provides opportunities for a range and depth of emotional expression that has a relevance for real life. Secondly, and almost ironically, it provides experience in searching for truth, and for what is real, for the discovery of genuine, rather than theatrical, emotion. Stanislavski (in Hodgson, 1972) writes:

Truth on the stage is whatever we can believe in with sincerity, whether in ourselves or in our colleagues. Truth cannot be separated from belief, nor belief from truth. They cannot exist without each other and without both of them it is impossible to live your part, or to create anything. Everything that happens on the stage must be convincing to the actor himself, to his associates and to the spectators. It must inspire belief in the possibility, in real life, of emotions analogous to those being experienced on the stage by the actor. Each and every moment must be saturated with a belief in the truthfulness of the emotion felt, and in the action carried out by the actors. (Stanislavski, in Hodgson, 1972, p. 94)

Collingwood (1966) emphasizes the importance of lucidity. It is not sufficient that we produce emotions in ourselves or in an audience without understanding what they are about. The actor's object is

> not to produce a preconceived emotional effect on his audience but, by means of a system of expressions, or language, composed partly of speech and partly of gesture, to explore his own emotions: to discover emotions in himself of which he is unaware, and, by permitting the audience to witness the discovery, enable them to make a similar discovery about themselves. (Collingwood, 1966, p. 47)

Godspell provided the opportunity for trial and error. Because of the extended period of its life, with progressive development in newer and freshly challenging situations, the participants became clearer about their emotions and came closer to the truth than they had ever been before. There was a progressive attention to detail, to the minutiae of interaction. 'Such a concentration is necessary if you are to possess real feelings. You will come to know that in real life also many of the great moments of emotion are signalized by some small, natural movement' (Stanislavski, 1972, p. 98). Heathcote (1972, p. 158) argues that 'it lies in the nature of a man [sic] to at once escape from his own existence and to learn from the events he sees, reads and hears about by sharing the emotions conjured up by the author. We are thereby given fresh acquaintance with mankind. We are offered a further opportunity for insight into human actions and feelings, and some of this which we share is brushed off on to our own lives though we may not fully understand this'.

Godspell provided both a challenge and a discipline. The challenge was to release emotion, to feel, to enter whole-heartedly into the full range of experience offered by the play. The discipline was to 'organize their feelings into some kind of expression' (ibid., p. 160). In order to do this they had to understand what was happening to them. They were not always able to articulate it in words, but then this part of the experience was not a matter of language or cognition. In a sense, therefore, Godspell is an example of the Stanislavskian mode of emotional involvement, entailing an 'act of being' (Marowitz, 1978). The participants are concerned with 'tapping their own reservoirs of emotional memories to find within themselves a sophistication, subtlety or depth of emotional engagement so that in concentrating on the character's actions, a wider, deeper range of emotions may be released'. (Bolton, 1984, p. 119).

The development of identity occurs in the same way as it does through the reading of fiction. Hardy (1977) argues that by examining what we feel about people and events in stories we come to know ourselves and therefore become independent thinkers. Fiction offers some structure, whereby 'the randomness of the world is given some form through which the reader meets possibilities — of other lifestyles, relationships, situations and values.' This is an 'ordering' process, involving a 'genuine, moved interpretation and revision of one's world' (Hayhoe and Parker, 1984). Fry (1985) calls this 'virtual experience'. 'We re-create what has happened so that it becomes a part of our own remembered experience.' However, it may be *more* powerful than real-life experience. Harding (1977, p. 61) says that the reader, by responding emotionally yet with a degree of detachment 'extends and modifies the observer's outlook on life much more than experiencing the events at first hand'.

Social Development–'Communitas'

D.H. Hargreaves (1982, p. 151) complained that 'drama teachers have unwittingly become victims of the cult of individualism', preoccupied with the view that 'drama is concerned with the individuality of individuals, with the uniqueness of each human essence' (Way, 1967). Individualism, however, can get out of hand, and work against the common good, especially if it fails to recognize that personal development takes place within a social context (A. Hargreaves *et al.*, 1988). As Bolton (1984, p. 46) argues, 'drama is a social event, not a solitary experience'. Drama can certainly promote personal development, as we have seen, but it also offers excellent chances for solidarity and corporatism. Godspell provides an outstanding example of what that constitutes.

The state of 'communitas', involves liberation and fulfilment. 'Spontaneous communitas has something magical about it. Subjectively there is a feeling of endless power' (Turner, 1974, p. 127) and a sense of 'oneness with humanity' (Musgrove, 1977, p. 9). Opportunities for this kind of association are rare at school, particularly secondary school. Shipman's (1975, p. 30) point that 'the sixth form of a grammar school rarely deviates from the examination syllabus' still holds. Yeomans (1987, p. 163) states that 'life in secondary schools means that most classes consist of a transient shifting population which meets for a limited period . . . before dispersing in order to re-form with a changed membership in another setting and with another teacher'.

Contrary to this kind of experience, Godspell facilitated the formation of a special group that developed its own internal dynamic and 'communitas'. At first they were suspicious and hesitant. They had to shake off the inhibitions, the defences, the attitudes and protective roles of ordinary school life. They had to enter into the spirit of it, make a self-investment. Once the bridge had been crossed, and as the possibilities began to capture imaginations, then they were ready to reconstruct. There was a levelling process as they came to recognize their common goals and values. The group soon acquired a structure of interdependent roles. Individuals were subservient to the group, but not dominated by it, contributing to it, helping to shape it, and, in turn, being influenced by it. All became totally involved and committed as they created a life together, making new characters, language, voices, gestures, developing a culture peculiarly their own. Free of the constraints and trappings of normal, everyday life, this reconstruction was, in a sense, on a higher plane. The task was to find the truth — how these characters would really feel and behave, how they really would interact together given their characters and situations. The quest took them through nearly every emotion in human sensitivities (as we saw earlier), and cemented the bond between them. The Godspell experience illustrates the following features of 'communitas': the special culture developed by the group and strong affective ties; discovering others; levelling; spontaneous and total mutual support; and its potential contagiousness.

Culture and Caring
Sara expresses the 'life' that they had developed and which was peculiarly theirs:

> You've all got some of this big thing in common that outsiders just don't
> really know about. When we came back from Cambridge we'd been in

this own little world, and we were so full of it. Yet no one could understand and it was so annoying. You had friends back at home who didn't know anything about Godspell, and you wanted to tell them what you'd been through and what it meant to you. And they'd think you are mad. They'd think 'God! These theatrical people!' You want to spread the news and say 'Look what we've been doing!' but you can't.

So solid was the group, that if one out of the forty-seven were missing, it didn't seem right. Thus when Jo Astley missed the final performance, Chris commented:

That felt strange to me . . . Even though I probably didn't say anything to her on the actual performance, I felt there was something missing.

They thus reproduced the sense of belonging to a social whole that Lee (1915) observed about the 'ring game':

We feel and care about the ring itself. There is a sense of personal loss if it gets broken — to have it squashed in on one side gives a sense of impaired personality . . . and we hasten in such case with much squealing, to mend or round it out again. The ring is now a part of us, as we of it . . . It is an extension of ourselves, a new personality; we act now not as individuals, but as the ring; its success is our success, and what hits it hits us. The ring, like the family, is a social whole. (Lee, 1915, p. 139, quoted in Bolton, 1984, p. 29)

Significantly, perhaps, one of the big numbers in the play, 'We Beseech Thee', involved the cast forming a big circle. There were many expressions of camaraderie, love, caring. There was so much contact and closeness between us' (Kevin). And it was genuine — not merely assumed for dramatic purposes.
Sara commented:

If you are told 'pretend you love each other', will you? It doesn't work, you can't do that! That's what we developed through it. At the beginning, in the December run, I just didn't know people enough even though we'd done lots of rehearsals. They were just like other characters in the play. By the time we got to Cambridge I literally adored everybody, and I still do. I've made forty-five friendships that I would never have done without the play.

Chris found the unity 'amazing':

In Oedipus (the play they were working on at the time of interviewing) there's 170 people, and no way am I going to know everybody. But there's fifty people in Godspell, and after a performance, you can just walk by somebody that was in it and smile, and you both know what you're smiling about because there's something between you and it's just special.

Adam also emphasized the community. He did not think the play's success was due to individual performances, excellent thought some may have been,

> but it's really the group, the group in itself, I think, which has brought across the atmosphere . . . and it's the general atmosphere that comes across.

The power of the group draws in the reserved and the sceptical. Sara relates how she feels Adam was caught up in the tide, albeit, perhaps, reluctantly. He had been one of the more sceptical ones.

> And then we were walking on to the Cambridge stage and he turned round and he said 'Let's show them shall we!?' And I just went, 'ADAM! Is this really you talking?' He said 'Let's show we can do it, shall we? Let's show all those students that us school kids can do it!' And just that gave everyone such a morale boost you know. It was wonderful. I think that's what it does to you, it just gives you this strong sense of motivation to succeed.

This illustrates the power of drama to surprise people, both to be surprised by other people, as here, and to be surprised at oneself. In another instance, Martin told how he was 'surprised by Ian Robson' on one of the nights he had to play the part of Chief Clown. He 'took over brilliantly'. Speaking of role-taking, Heathcote (1970, p. 1080) states that 'it may surprise persons by a constant confrontation to them of their own thinking and behaving'. The challenge of repeated public performances intensified the confrontation and heightened the potential for surprise. Surprise continued to arrive, up to and including the final performance.

Discovering Others

Sara expresses how barriers have been broken down, how people have discovered new things about themselves, and how new relationships have been made. These relationships are special, for they are forged, released almost, by the discovery of a new truth and sincerity through the requirements of the framework of the play. The context is provided and general directions given, but in this broad remit, the players make their own relationships spontaneously, feeding off each other in inventive dialogue and gesture. Sara illustrates how this occurred:

> I never knew Sam before this. She was my rival in the play. The two of us conflicted all the time and we actually built up this total hatred on stage: 'Just leave me alone. I can't stand the sight of you!' She's always pestering me and taking the mick and everything. In fact, we got so close just because of the play . . . In the second half it starts to get serious. She comes up to me and looks at me, because she wants me to accept her. She wants us now to stick together and we're not going to be rivals any more because that would probably make matters worse, the fact that Jesus is going to leave us as well. She just looked at me on the stage and I would stand there and I would ignore her for ages. She would be tugging at my tutu trying to get my attention, and then eventually, I'd turn round and

give her this hug ... Every time we see each other now, I say, 'Sam come here', and I give her a hug sort of thing. So when it creates this bond between people, it's got to be special, hasn't it?

Sam said there was one tatty in her group she didn't get on with at the beginning and 'most of the way through',

but then we got used to each other and we had to get on because of the roles we were playing. We developed a friendship, whereas before we didn't have a friendship ... You discovered things about other people. Some people I didn't even know and never spoke to. I thought Sara was a real snob, but I got to know her, and she's really, really, lovely, totally different from what I expected.

Sam found the unity particularly strong where conflict resided for much of the play — in the enmity between the tatties and the ballerinas:

It's a really good feeling because we used to improvise at the time. We had such faith in each other to do what we wanted, and know that she'd respond to me and I'd respond back to her.

The tin soldiers were a disparate group to begin with. Sean and Ivan knew each other quite well, but Martin knew neither of them, and Adam 'found it difficult working with Sean and Ivan to begin with', because as Sally said, 'they're unruly and cynical and witty'. But this was turned to advantage in the development of the group, as the smaller, officious, commander struggled in vain to control his squad. In this way the unruliness became order in one of the funniest groups. Matthew emphasized the 'special' friendships he had made,

especially with girls like Sam-Jane and Josie. We were all friends beforehand, but now we're really good friends. Just through Godspell and through having a common interest for about twelve months, we've become ever such good friends. And I've made more friends through it. Also, when I look back at it I feel warm inside. I don't know why, I just do.

For Johanne, it all began to work and come together,

when the relationships between the actual actors came. We all became very friendly, and I myself made a lot of friends that I didn't know beforehand ... The characterizations just came from those sort of tangents from the actual relationships themselves.

Levelling
The experience was clearly a great leveller. Pupils of different ages, backgrounds, sexes and teachers were all one in cooperative unity. Thus Matthew reported how he had broadened his outlook:

I'll talk to fourth years, which is unheard of being the Lower sixth form. I don't mind being seen talking to them. A couple of the sailors were third years when they did it. My sister was one of the tatty dolls. I was pleased my sister was in it. Normally, I think — 'Oh God! none of my family in it, it's just me.' When we were on stage, we were a company — as if we'd been working together for years and years and years, instead of just twelve months.

Martyn makes the same point from a participating teacher's perspective:

One of the amazing things was that there weren't any barriers of any sort. Before we actually started, amongst the chief toys there was already working a sort of group identity, a sense of togetherness. It wasn't me, a member of staff, plus the pupils . . . It was all teamwork really and it's amazing how creative people were in those situations. I was putting myself into the role and they were putting themselves into the same sort of role and we were just on the same level.

Students also saw teachers differently 'especially Martyn' (Mr Glass). Sally-Ann used to have him for French, and always 'got on with him OK, but since Godspell, tended to get on with him better'. In general, 'it makes you think more of the teachers when they're involved because they become one of the group'. What was it like for Ian D. having a teacher in his group of clowns?

It was quite good really because we didn't think of him as a teacher. We did at the start, but eventually when we got going, he was more like a person to us, just another member of the cast.

This is the classic distinction between teachers, constrained by their role, and what pupils regard as 'proper persons' (Blackie, 1980). Godspell had the power even to transform teachers to persons. It was as if Martyn passed through a magic screen. To Matthew,

he ceased to be a teacher when he got on stage. He was Martyn, Martyn the Clown, not Mr Glass the French teacher, and now it's rubbed off. I mean you can chat to him. You don't sort of say 'Yes Sir', and it's Martyn now . . . There's Sally and Lesley and Martyn, instead of Mrs Mackey, Mrs Fielding and Mr Glass.

Before, members of the cast had different impressions of each other formed by perceptions of institutional roles and barriers, or typifications of people on slender evidence without real knowledge of the person. However they found each other's true selves through the play and through their characters. The general lessons being learnt here were not to judge people too hastily or shallowly, that there may be hidden depths, that communal activity promotes reciprocal development, and that the investment of self in collective endeavour in the pursuit of mutual aims can bring the greatest personal satisfaction.

Mutual Support
'Communitas' is empowering to the individual, who gathers enormous strength from the support of the group. The main thing Sara found was

to have so many people supporting you. I can't call them 'kids' because I don't feel any age difference between them. I know them so well and they're so dear to me. To know that they were all behind me all the time and that I had their support, and I had their friendship. I felt that I could just go for it and do whatever I wanted to do, and I felt such a sense of achievement in so many different senses . . .

As mutual trust and self-confidence developed, so they were encouraged to experiment, to take a risk in the interests of finding what worked best, and what capabilities they possessed. They were secure in the knowledge that they were among friends, who would help to draw the best out of them, and for whom they would do the same in return. They grew, as a unit, together. This rapport even cemented over cracks in the performance, turning mistakes into natural developments in the play. Martin gave two examples, one where Ian G. put his foot through one of the boxes and there was 'a big loud crack'. They just carried on. When they had to use the box later, they improvised. On another occasion when someone forgot some lines, they made it appear natural. 'Everybody goes "Oh, right, yes", and everybody gets into it, realizing he's made a mistake, covering it up and it worked so well'.

Early counter-indications, like a sense of competition, were shown in the end to be unnecessary, even counter-productive. Chris felt:

I was having to keep with everybody else because you see a group and you think 'That's brilliant!' I always felt we were competing with each other but then when we were on the stage it was alright. That competitiveness totally went. It was unity, which was superb.

For Martyn, it was the religious message that was so binding. But for Matthew who is

not in the slightest bit religious, it was slightly hypocritical me being in the piece . . . the strength of Godspell itself wasn't the fact that we were promoting Christianity or any sort of other religion, but that we were showing that people can work together.

They rendered assistance to each other, freely and generously. Kevin said:

The other actors were brilliant. When people are having a hard time they do encourage you. They were saying 'Well, it's okay, don't worry.' Loads of people said that and that really did help me build up my confidence again. In a previous play I was in there was a lot of bitching and people knocking other people to build themselves up. The contrast was amazing to Godspell where everyone was loving and helpful and friendly.

Contagiousness
The audience was part of the community. Responsiveness in an audience is important to any cast. In a play such as this with its young performers, it was particularly important. Rehearsing without an audience after the December run was difficult for Sara, and they lost faith with it a little. But it was recovered with

a warm-up public performance in March, showing that 'it is a play that needs an audience desperately, just to keep the morale up and to convince us that it was funny in places'.

Sean noted:

You get, say, one night an audience that wasn't so involved, whereas the next night you'd get laughs on even the silliest things and that would pep you up even more. So it would be like a circle. You'd get more and they'd laugh more and so on and enjoy it more. If you got an audience that wasn't so receptive to you, then you wouldn't. You'd try even harder but then perhaps mistakes would be made and therefore it wouldn't be so good.

Kevin, too, illustrates the audience's complicity in the generation of humour:

The reaction of the audience, I could really feel it right from the start. They were really willing us on and laughing at the small stuff and it gives you the confidence. You can feel it — the energy that's inside of you and then start ad libbing — it was good fun. For example, when she says 'Oy! teddy bears!' — we're all asleep and we all get up and I go 'Alright Miss Bossy Boots', and then we go to sleep again. Then Jesus says 'Oy! The teddy bears!' and we go 'Not again!' and it just came out — it just came naturally. And the funny thing is you don't know what's so funny about it, but at the time it just is. I think people can analyse it too much.

This indicates that there was more than just response in the audience's re-action to this production. The sense of community included the audience. They became part of the one-ness, embraced by the spirit emanating from the stage. Their reaction was more than appreciation of a good show. The play was a cathar-tic influence upon them (Moreno, 1964). The audience had been 'purged of their personal anxieties and (purified), reassured, revitalized, tranquillized by what seems a dispensing of justice' (Barrault, 1972, p. 25). They identified with characters, felt the emotions, anticipated, prompted, revelled, laughed, grieved. They partici-pated with their whole selves — not just minds, but hearts and feelings. It was one of those rare occasions when there was a mutual recognition of truth, the kind of truth that reflects reality, but comes from being lifted on to 'the plane of imagin-ary life' (Stanislavski, in Hodgson, 1972, p. 93).

Stanislavski (ibid.) draws the contrast with some of his students' 'make-believe truth' which only 'helps you to represent images and passions':

My kind of truth helps to create the images themselves and to stir real passions. The difference between your art and mine is the same as be-tween the two words *seem* and *be*. I must have real truth. You are satis-fied with its appearance. I must have the belief. You are willing to be limited to the confidence your public has in you . . . From your stand-point the spectator is merely an onlooker. For me he involuntarily be-comes a witness of, and a party to, my creative work; he is drawn into the very thick of the life that he sees on the stage, and he believes in it. (Stanislavski, ibid., p. 104)

This is the difference between a good technical performance and an artistic one. It is the spirit that pervaded the operation and inspired actors and audience alike. Kevin's grandad

> was one of the first to stand up and shout 'Encore! More! More!'. He wasn't bothered about what other people were doing. He's a conservative-type person, but he was up there cheering. He'd had a heart attack previously. We thought he was going to have another one — my dad was really worried. Anyway, he was yelling and everything, and afterwards he said he'd never been so moved in forty years of going to the theatre . . .

Ian G. illustrates the kind of effect this had on the participants:

> After 'Prepare You' there was the most massive roar of applause you ever heard. It was amazing, it was so uplifting! At the end of 'Oh Bless the Lord', the little rag dolls' song, there was the most tremendous roar. It lifted me.

Several mentioned what a great thrill it was to give other people so much pleasure. This was a satisfaction they would take with them through life. Kevin especially recalls one dress rehearsal which they opened to about fifty people from a mentally handicapped institution:

> It was a lovely gesture and they really loved it. That was one of my favourite performances, because it was just seeing their happy faces afterwards. They really got into it, though they couldn't understand the jokes much.

The 'Experience of Magic'

> I have broken the invisible barrier,
> I have the key to that door, in reality,
> the sun shines a little brighter, but . . . will I ever
> enter that same, magical world again that lies
> beyond the horizon?
>   (from a poem by Sara)

All drama in a sense is akin to 'magic' when we act out 'as if' situations if only in order to plan them (Heathcote, 1970). It can be a profound aesthetic experience. As Ross (1982, p. 80) writes, such experience,

> occasionally reaches the state of rapture and ecstasy as commonly understood. It always implies some degree of standing outside the merely mundane and the sensing in some degree of something infinite, of the heart's leaping in wonder as expectation and longing are somehow felt to be satisfied — beyond our dreams and hopes.

There was some of this in Godspell, as we have seen, but in addition, for the participants, it had a special magic. The original show portrayed the Jesus figure, performing magical tricks. In the Roade adaptation, Sally felt 'it seemed to work even better in the nursery because he was like some sort of magician figure. They just relied on him to be able to do these things for them'. As Martyn put it:

> When the Jesus figure came into our midst, he had an effect on all types of human beings. He had a magnetic, mystical, magical attraction, and I think that's what happened to us during the play. We became suddenly transformed into the characters that we represented. Jesus had this attraction to us and on us, and we came out of ourselves. We were able to form a relationship with him and have hope for the future which was leading us into the garden.

A sense of 'magic' thus pervaded the whole production. Several spoke of the 'magic' of the experience in the sense of it producing unexpected and startling results, and it never stopped doing so. In consequence, they were continually finding new peaks of excellence. A great deal of time, hard work and emotional energy went into the preparations. But it was great fun. For Matthew, one of the important things about Godspell was that

> it was fun to be in, it was fun to do on stage and I think it was fun to watch. It wasn't just hard slog from Day 1. We didn't sit there for hours talking about the depth of the piece, we tackled it bit by bit and built comic bits into it, enjoyed it, had fun doing it, and then when we performed it, we had fun performing it in the end.

This 'fun' built into ecstatic delight at Cambridge. By this time they had already achieved a great deal, but now,

> it's just like nothing on earth. It's so difficult to explain. You just can't believe that you are there in front of all these people . . . we were out there to prove ourselves. We wanted to prove that kids could put on a piece of drama and that could be recognized as perhaps within the standards of the NSDF. The morale was just incredible. It was like this electric burst as we were just about to go on stage.

Sara said they were caught up in

> the creation of another world — something which others have said is beyond your control and you are carried with it as opposed to creating it yourself. It's so difficult to describe, it's magic. You don't believe the power of the play until you've finished it at the end.

This special feeling was enhanced at the final performance at Derngate by the effect of professional lighting. This made them feel as if they 'belonged to a separate world from the audience. It was so bright and powerful on stage. It was as if everybody glowed, radiated a warmth, a magic'.

As an experience, this came top of most people's list. For Sally-Ann, 'So far it's the best experience I've had at school. It was absolutely amazing to be involved in such a brilliant show.' For Ian D., what he got out of the experience was 'the joy of being on the stage' and 'the fun of all being together'. For Jo, 'It's something you never forget. I mean just to do one school play at the school and then to take it to Cambridge, and then to have it put on at Derngate is just a once-in-a-lifetime chance.' For Ian G., the prevailing memory would be that he had done 'something that's worthwhile'. He could think that 'Whatever you have done of any importance, I've helped to make 1200 people quite happy on a Friday night in October, 1989, and that's a very good feeling.' His lasting impression was being 'overwhelmingly happy round the end, and the Mayor saying "Well done, that was a fantastic performance."' To Johanne, also, people's reactions 'meant so much':

> I think that's going to be hard to leave behind, because you feel you're special then. You feel you've done something for other people and it just feels different. You feel you are able to do it more as somebody else. I was able to do more for other people as the baby doll than I am for me.

For Matthew, as an experience in his school career to date, 'Emotionally it comes top. Mentally, it comes joint top along with my GCSE results' (Matthew achieved nine A's in these). For 'tatty doll' Claire, 'the last fourteen months have been the best months of my life.' She had 'never felt so good before in her life', enjoying herself 'as I could never have imagined possible'. Sally spoke for them all when she said, 'It will always be something that's there, now, that I can recall and feel "That was incredible, and that was a wonderful achievement!"'

Teacher Development

In a letter to the cast after the final performance at Derngate, Sally said:

> I shall quite simply never forget this show. I have also had to come to terms with the fact that there will never be another show like it for me and I shall never be quite the same person again.

With the students, she had entered into the activity 'totally and completely'. There was no distancing, no regarding this as just another school production, or as just a part of her teaching. The powerful emotional bond that developed with the company included her also. At the end of Cambridge she 'couldn't believe that I was never going to see the show again . . . I was in a terrible state'; and after Derngate, there was 'an aching hole'.

This is symptomatic of her own emotional involvement, which had left other legacies:

> It's dominated a whole year of my life. You can't be the same person after that. On this occasion, it's difficult to say exactly how. I feel much more vulnerable in some ways as a person because it opened up whole ranges of emotion that I hadn't experienced to such depth before. It gave me tremendous faith, obviously, in young people. It's given me some wonderful friendships with some of them. It's given me those people to care for and it's made me happier really. It just gave so much more

meaning to life. It was so wonderful to see that on stage and it just made me very, very happy to have thought I'd created that and of course very proud. It's given me much more confidence in myself. There's knock-on effects. Clive Wolfe, the guy who runs the National Students Drama Festival, has now asked me to direct a production in Edinburgh next year. So practically-speaking it's changed my life because it's led to other things and probably will continue to do so. It's given me an insight into what we see at more professional theatres. It's just made me feel more relaxed. It gives you so much hope when you see young people working like that, and you see what they get out of it, and it suddenly makes everything worthwhile . . . I suppose it's the ultimate production for me, the most satisfying. I had the chance to work on something and develop it as fully as is probably humanly possible within the job that we do. I don't think I've learnt to employ many new skills or developed that much as a teacher because of it, except that I feel much more positive about life in general . . . You're constantly striving to get that feeling again in other situations with other productions, in other lessons — and it does seem much more attainable now purely because of my attitude. I'll go into lessons and expect the best. I suppose in that sense the work actually has improved. I never even thought of it like that, but that's probably exactly what's happened, and that's one of the reasons why I'm so pleased with my teaching over the last few months.

This seems to be a kind of ultimate in teachers' experience. It is perfect in its own terms. It reaches heights unthought of in the initial conception, brings out hidden or dormant qualities in the self, and opens up new educational possibilities.

Lesley, the Music Director, said:

I think it brought me closer to the kids, and it also made me more aware of what they could actually do if you give them a chance because often in teaching you direct a lot and you say to the children — 'Oh, here's an idea, do this'. Instead you should say: 'Here's an idea, just go away and see what you can do with it'. In music you can so often direct it and say — 'No, I'm sorry but you've got to play this and nothing else', but I said to them — 'What can we do with this? Michael, can you improvise on these chords?' 'On The Willows' — at the end before Fiona and I come in for the last few bars — it's like a duet between the piano and the lead guitar and Michael listened to the record and got the ideas, but it was his own soul, his own ideas doing that. That's what Godspell's done for me, I think. It brought me closer to the children as well and I'm just amazed what they can do. I feel very, very proud of myself as well as them, that we actually did it, and we did it well and we got the feedback we did. I don't think it's changed me in any way because I just look forward to the next thing. I say, right, that's over, it's lovely, but let's go now onto something else.

The only member of staff in the cast was Martyn, the chief clown. He, too, found the play made quite a difference to his role as teacher. He had been involved in lots of productions in the past but never in something where the same techniques have been used, of getting everyone to contribute in that way, to participate in the choreography of the thing. I've never really been in something where a real sense of identity has been produced in the way it was for this, and when I see some of the kids now walking around the school or even in my lessons, I look at them and I think of them as a clown or ballerina or a raggy doll or something like that. I find it very difficult to forget. It was a very big, very strange, experience really. I don't think I've ever gone through anything like it before.

Martyn here expresses the extent of his own involvement — as total as any of the others — and experiencing similar problems of disengagement. The long-standing effect, he felt, was on the easing of the teacher–pupil relationship. Though there were still demarcation lines, different rules applying in different situations, they had become softened. He gave the example of a relationship in the classroom with one pupil which had been problematic for some time being vastly improved by their working together on Godspell. Summing up his experience, he felt

a sense of great satisfaction in doing something well as a team, realising that something which was bare words in a book actually came to life for other people as well as us. Secondly, you've deepened relationships with other people and once you've gone through that sort of experience, it's something which you can't change. The whole thing was just a fantastic experience. I would say it's the best thing that I've been involved in. I've taken part in other things where I had a larger part to play. There are other things that I've done which I've totally enjoyed, but I think this stands out as the most enjoyable by a long way.

The Magic Ingredients

What were the factors behind the success of this activity? I identified the following:

Content: The Play and its Adaptation

The Script
Even the sternest critics of the play were won over by this interpretation. So the opportunities were there in the original script for the kind of development that won universal acclaim. Some felt the original play was strong. Martyn, for example, disagreed with those who criticized the script, which,

apart from one or two adaptations, is straight from the New Testament. It's verbatim, and in that sense it's what you make it . . . I know our interpretation of it is totally different from any way it had been performed before, but I think there's something fairly gripping in the message that it puts across, whether you think it's syrupy or what . . .

Ian G. also thought it had something to do with the 'teaching of the gospel', people 'always being ready to hear a message of love . . . and if you get yourself completely absorbed in the message in the scriptures and done in the way like Godspell, then that's very listenable to. It will sink in, I suppose, if you're really enjoying yourself and you think to yourself — 'this makes sense'.

So we have the basic, old, enduring, eternal message in a modern, popularizing form that brings it to life. Martin expressed it thus:

> The words are augmented by the music, and to see the teachings, rather than sitting and reading a book about it, and be part of it, which is what Godspell invites you to do, you get into the show and you follow it like a story. Through that it becomes enjoyable and you take in more, and you can actually see what those teachings mean.

He gave the example of Kate Urwin's (Chief Jill-in-the-box) parable: 'When you see that, you think "yeah, that works!" You can see the entire story, you don't just see someone saying "don't be nasty to your brothers or your elders otherwise you'll be reprimanded". You see a lot more than that, and it comes to life almost'.

Kevin agreed:

> I love the messages behind it and the morals and I think it does educate people. You go home and you think about the parables. You're singing the songs or what have you — and then you start thinking about the meaning behind them and listening to the words more . . . It's really funny then going to church and hearing a passage read out. It comes alive in your mind.

The Music

Some members of the cast were not endeared to 1970s music, but they were won over by the score of Godspell, and it obviously had a great deal to do with bringing the story to life, facilitating emotional expression and creating an atmosphere of energy, warmth and celebration. Many of the cast applauded the brilliance of the music. Matthew gives an idea of its range:

> The music is very uplifting in places. The really big numbers, one of them was Kevin's 'We Beseech Thee' and the other one was Laura's 'Oh Bless the Lord', both of those make you feel — 'Yeah! Great! We'll sock it to them!' Then there's the ever mournful 'On the Willows' that brings a lump to your throat. They're all saying goodbye to him — it's sad. Then there is a good funk at the end of Act 1 'Light of the World'. It's not just have a good rock, it makes you want to sit there and tap your feet. Then there's 'All for the Best', which is completely different to all of them. If I had to pick my favourite song, it must be 'By my Side', the one the baby dolls sing, and the clowns' song — 'We Plough the Fields and Scatter'.

Lesley, the Musical Director, said:

> It's one of the very few musicals where most of the songs I could safely say — yes, I love and I'd love to hear them again and love to play them

again . . . They're very repetitive, some of them, like 'Day by Day'. Who on earth could write a song with just two lines in it, and make it work and it just works, especially with the routines and the little bits of acting along with it. And 'Prepare Ye the Way of the Lord' — one line, but it builds up so beautifully with just 'Prepare Ye', the solo, the a cappella at the beginning and then the bass being put in, then the piano and then suddenly — this big explosion on the drum-kit which is absolutely incredible.

The music complemented the message and the characters, and helped convey the various moods of the piece. The songs are markers for the stages of the show, and 'they heighten each moment.' Lesley explains the blend:

We have a parable and then we have the music and it sounds cut and dried, doesn't it? But it's not, because it's so beautifully blended in the show. 'By My Side', for example, has got to come because Jo has just been almost stoned to death. The feeling and the look between her, the chief baby doll, and Ian is amazing. Then suddenly the guitar comes in and it's like magic and the feeling is in that simplicity of the guitar coming in with 'By My Side'. It's lovely.

How had she coped with the emotion, in, for example, the beautiful duet 'On The Willows', in which she was one of the singers? It had come with practice, getting into the play and developing professionalism. Even so,

I must admit I do have a tear sometimes. On the first time we did it at Roade, I couldn't look at them. I had to just put my head away, because you get very choked. You just can't sing if you're choked up, you just blubber into the microphone.

Martyn gives an example of the blend of music and character:

The songs fit in with the characters that are performing the songs. Take my song, for example 'We plough the field and scatter'. It's an old hymn that's given a revamp musically. As I understood the character of the clown, it is someone who outwardly is very extrovert and bubbly and larks around but inside has a very serious side. It was the clown at his most serious at that point, when he's singing that — and to me each character in the play — each doll — represented a type of human being. The soldiers, for example, are very self-opinionated, rather stiff and starchy in their character and find it very difficult to show their emotions. The very naive baby dolls are bubbly and kind and never see double meanings in anything. When Jo sings her song as the chief baby doll, that again fits into the character. Her relationship with Jesus is being explored in the song.

The Interpretation
On the basic framework, Sally constructed her inspired adaptation. She had done the play before at a previous school, using the same concept of the attic nursery

and the groups of toys, but it had been a much simpler version with no development. 'It was literally just a setting and there was no thinking through of the whole meaning behind it'. In the original version there were only ten or twelve people in the cast. For a school production, Sally wanted a bigger cast but wanted to preserve the sense of unity. This was when she 'came up with the idea of groups of toys, and then it just slotted into place'. Jesus' open speech about 'I will make him gardener for his own recreation' gave her the idea of the toys going out into the garden. The 'door' also then became important. Eventually they would pass through this into the garden, but they 'had to be shown the right way to live, and how to take responsibility for the garden'. Sally describes the progression of ideas:

> It took three weeks originally to think of the idea of the nursery. I can remember every day in the car thinking 'I've got to find a format for Godspell', and just running through ideas and eventually I hit on it. Once I hit on the nursery idea, everything followed. I wanted the small toys, I wanted toys and I wanted groups of toys. In the first production we had an action man and a nurse. This time we had a sailor and ballerina, because I was quite determined that it would be more timeless. I needed a tatty doll, that kind of character because of the song 'Turn Back O Man', and there had to be somewhere in the play, a female who was not pure, who was a little bit tarty because there was so much in the script that provokes that and reacts to it and I wanted to build on that. The other toys are all fairly stereotyped, but they have certain characteristics which I wanted to use. The Jill-in-the-Box was purely because I wanted another female role rather than Jack-in-the-Box, and the bounciness I thought worked with the female. The sailor was a case of replacing somebody with the action man characteristics, but I thought the sailor worked much better. And the ballerina, I was so pleased with that this time because you had that meeting. You had the elegance and the beauty which again is another part of human nature, so I was going for the human types but within toys, and that added another dimension — the sort of fairly elegant, slightly snotty but underneath very, very gentle. We had to have just a pure clown who seems to be just for a good time but that his heart can really be touched.

Matthew felt it was all in the interpretation. 'If you did it straight now it would be boring and no one would like it . . . But if you find the interpretation that works for you, and works for the era and the school and the people you've got, I don't think the play will outdate'. The developed interpretation was thus a stroke of genius. It embraced more students, provided for the generation of unity among them, capitalized on the qualities of youth, remained faithful to the basic text, and, above all, provided its own impetus for further multiple individual and sub-group interpretations within the overall plot. In this sense, no two performances were alike, and it was always developing and improving as people got further within their roles. Thus, from a relatively simplistic start, this particular production gradually acquired two distinctive features. One was the amount of detail that it contained. The other was that there were a number of levels within it that different people could react to, from profoundly religious to light-hearted musical, from serious drama to light-hearted, knock-about comedy.

Martyn thought it was considerably enhanced by Sally's production. As it 'unfolded before his eyes', he 'could see all humanity represented by the toys and their characteristics'. Johanne thought that the idea of a nursery and toys gave

> it an almost instantaneous kind of charm. I think a lot of people were quite shocked when they actually found out that it wasn't just children singing songs and that the relationship was actually more important. There was a great feeling of unity and working together, which radiated out.

There were so many opportunities for development, so much of interest going on away from the central line of action. As he views and re-views the video, Matthew studies the characters. Knowing the story backwards he now 'watches the people that aren't directly involved and I find that a lot more interesting to be honest'. Matthew's mum, also, had 'seen it loads of time, and she says, even when she watches the video now, she still sees things she hasn't seen before, and that's the strength of it'.

Emma also thought:

> the cast was developing each time, and also my understanding of the performance, because there's so much in it. I've never once been bored. I've seen it no end of times, but each time I've been totally involved in it. You just see so much more each time you watch it. There's so much going on that you can't take it in all at once.

Kevin saw several 'levels' in the play, providing 'something for everybody'.

> For young children, just the colour and the excitement, the energy, the love and, maybe, the few funny bits if they can understand it. For adults there's looking at the ability of the actors but even they get involved with the show. Then for the really 'dramatist' people it's all in-depth stuff.

The adaptation, and its manifold development within and between the various groups, thus created something unique. Adam thought this took people by surprise,

> especially when we went to Cambridge. There are a lot fewer people in the original version of Godspell, and this was a totally new interpretation. From the moment the curtains opened and everybody was jumping about on stage, it must have hit them just there and that feeling must have lasted with them till the end of the play.

The subtleties and intricacies of behaviour, gesture and look going on all the time among a large cast on stage for the whole time, created at times a sense of gleeful anarchy. The sense of chaos was, perhaps, part of its charm and a source of its energy. But it was an organized chaos, as Josie observes:

> It feels like chaos, especially the first performances, because although you had loads of rehearsals and you do know where you're supposed to go,

you're not entirely sure. You're always conscious that you could crash into someone. But by the later performances, as we did more and more and more, you know where people are going to be and so you're more confident. So you put more into it and it seems really organised. You know exactly where you're going and you can sense where everybody else is going to be.

In short, the adaptation enabled the cast to go through the same process of 're-making' the play, as Protherough (1983) speaks of when readers 're-make' a book:

In these terms, one of the marks of the best fiction for children is that it leaves the readers sufficient room to re-make the book as they read it, bringing to it their own experience of life and of other books, giving characters and incidents a concrete form, filling in what is implied rather than stated, speculating and questioning, judging and sympathising. (Protherough, 1983)

It thus gives both scope and direction to their creative power, and enables them to feel that they have a stake in ownership and control of the play.

Process: Methods of Production

The mode here was to combine firm direction and leadership — necessary because of the large numbers and complications of the production — with democratic-participation. Fairly flexible directions were given, and groups sometimes sent away to work out the details for themselves. This encouraged creativity and spon-taneity, and no doubt contributed to the verve, dynamism, energy and freshness that so impressed the critics. This openness encouraged continual refinement, even during performances. The central principle was that the activity should come from within the cast themselves. It was not specified in the script, nor in the Director's instructions, though she often knew exactly what she wanted them to do. The important thing was that they think about their role, and feel it. The appropriate actions, expressions, nuances, even some improvised language in places, would come once they had become one with their characters and started to live them.

The Director's role, therefore, was not to prescribe, but to facilitate, to pro-vide the opportunities and the framework within which the cast could create their parts and relationships. She gave advice, commented on what worked and what did not, helped to analyse, provided moral support. Sara said that obviously they had a lot of direction from Sally, but they were encouraged to do 'what came natural to us in our parts so that we weren't forcing anything . . . You became so engrossed in it, you almost forgot you were being directed'. Sara gave the exam-ple of the parables:

Sally would say, look I just don't know what to do here, shall we do this, that or the other, have you any other ideas? . . . She then strung all the ideas together so that everyone was happy in what they were doing.

Sally's technique, therefore, having created the characters, was to provide the 'scaffolding'. She did much of the 'blocking' — the cast then worked on the development. So, when they were doing 'Love, love, love', she would say 'I want you to end up here, because you're then going to cross the stage in a diagonal line like that. Now how you get to that position is up to you and your group to work out . . . They were much better at thinking of individual little movements themselves for their toys than I was'. She was available for advice when needed, as when 'the tin soldiers had a bit of a problem. I'd have to go up to them and say, "Try this", but on the whole, they came up with their own little tiny gestures and movements'.

Sally had various techniques for trying to induce the mental and affective attitudes most conducive to creativity. There were many ways in which she did this. There were 'breaking-down-barriers' sessions, which helped to initiate the feeling of 'communitas'. Martyn reported:

> There were games where you had to react to each other and report back to everyone else. For example, one of the techniques was to think of something which is important to you that's happened in the recent past, and tell it to someone else. I could either have opted out totally or joined it totally. I chose the latter course as it happens. And then we had things like — choose one of the people here, in the group, and pick out a quality that you admire and a quality that you dislike about that person and tell everyone else about it. Little things like that.

Other techniques were to get them thinking, improvising, and into character. For example, there was the pre-show warm-up, perhaps a 'fun improvisation'.

> Once I said to them 'Right, I want you as a group to come up with something and to tell the rest of us something that you don't really want anyone to know about you'. So they all went away in huddles to discuss it. The tatty dolls was the one I remember because they all came back and they stood there, flaunting away and they went: 'We don't want anything to know that (whisper) we're virgins!' It was absolutely brilliant.

The students affirmed the productivity of their approach. Josie thought that

> the script reads very dry, but the way Sally was getting us performing it was so different and it gave you such a lot of scope to do virtually whatever you wanted. A lot of it was Sara's ideas but the rest we're putting in as well — just how we think like a ballerina. For example, we'd got the idea of the pigs because the ballerinas were sort of prim and proper and how they wouldn't want to be pigs — so aloof and nose-in-the-air, and then almost sarcastically doing the 'Oink' bit.

Similar methods were employed by the Music Director, and a similar creative but disciplined spirit prevailed among the band. Leslie told how on a couple of occasions Richard came in too quickly on one of the slow numbers:

> He'd look at me, and I'd say — 'Yes, it's too fast', because although I directed it, I didn't want to conduct it as such. I felt that the whole group

was so close they could feel their own tempo anyway. The drums all had eyes on each other, they could keep together without me shouting and waving my arms about.

The model of teaching, therefore, is one that I have described as 'person-centredness in a structured framework' involving 'collaboration and participation' (Grugeon and Woods, 1990). It features active learning and democratic procedures, with the teacher providing firm and supportive leadership. Sally saw her role as creating a situation, devising a structure, and inspiring the participants. If all that went well, the cast could almost 'lead' themselves in working out the detail. But she was there as a guide and consultant on their creative endeavours, and, since the complicated whole needed a central point of integration, the final arbiter.

Critical Agents and Others

Credit has to be given for individual contributions. While success breeds more success, creativity more creativity, uncovering and developing talents in the process, things have to begin somewhere. There has to be vision, inspiration, and professional skill.

The Director

The Director, Sally, provided these qualities, and the cast widely recognized her contribution. The generation of 'communitas' was at the heart of her educational philosophy:

> On the whole what we're aiming for is the relationship within a group where you can work positively, constructively and creatively together, and learn to negotiate, compromise and build . . . You're just building, building, building all the time, building relationships.

At the beginning she had to generate an atmosphere of mutual trust, and motivate them to engage with the project:

> I'll never forget the very first read-through we had, which I just did with the chief toys. It reads so flat. I kept saying to them — 'Look, just have faith, just trust me — I know what I'm doing'. There's a lot of fairly heavy sort of biblical stuff in there that looks very dry and there's some loopy stage directions which didn't mean much to them. Of course we didn't use them at all and I just had to keep saying to them — 'look, we're just reading through, you won't understand what I want to happen here but just have faith'. And they did.

This matter of faith and trust seems the central property. They had to generate it amongst themselves. They had to rely on each other. In order to be creative they had to take risks, put their selves at the mercy of others. This was necessary in order for them and the group to grow. So it was essential from the beginning that the Director, above all, had that trust and faith cultivated among the group. Sara indicates its importance:

We had to get across this message of being so deliriously happy all the time, adoring each other, the sense of fun, the sense of love, connecting us all, being a big unit of people. But at times, when it didn't go right, you had to be shouted at. But because she got it right somewhere along the line everyone accepted anything she said. When she shouted it was for a reason. When she was trying to go over bits, over and over again, people were complaining, but they knew that it was for our own benefit and we would get it right because basically everyone had faith in her from the beginning.

Sara paid tribute also to Sally in the example she set of commitment and energy:

It got ridiculous at times before the December run. She was having re-hearsals at break times, lunch times and after school every single day. She took on so much. I think everyone admired her for that and because of their sense of commitment everyone felt that they owed it to her to be the same and commit themselves and be loyal to the play. We were loyal to her and to the play in the end. She is responsible for bringing it all together and bringing it up to the standard that it is. She may say we have as much part in that as she did because she was only the Director, but obviously she was very important in it all. She's a great Director.

Josie noted Sally's 'dedication':

The first time we did Godspell last Christmas, at least half the cast were down with flu and we weren't at school, but we dragged ourselves into rehearsals. Like the dress rehearsal on the Sunday, most of us were ill. I think that's a lot to do with Sally, the way she commands so much respect from us.

Emma found Sally's direction inspirational:

It was just like an example to us all to show what can be achieved with a piece, with all that time and effort.

The Musical Director

As well as the 'fabulous Mrs Mackey' there was the 'phenomenal Mrs Fielding', the Director of Music. Sara commented:

She has got so much enthusiasm for music and she has such a wonderful talent as far as music is concerned that she inspired us in that direction. Her pure enjoyment . . . it's infectious . . . She trained all the band to-gether . . . Gosh! Thinking back, what she did, she went over and over with us with the songs, the harmonies and everything and, because she has so much inspiration, so much energy for it and she'd sort of bounce up and down when she's teaching you, she just gave that over to us.

What is clear from this is that the Musical Director had the same kind of whole-heartedness, dedication, and commitment of self as the Director, with a special kind of *joie de vivre* in her 'bubbly personality' which informed the music she helped to create and radiated out to the whole company. Equally important, Sally and Lesley appeared not only to complement and lend to each other's strengths, but to be great friends. In an enterprise where unity, togetherness, caring, trust and truth were crucial factors, a measure of these qualities in the initial relationship between the Directors was not amiss.

A 'Critical Other'

Another important part was played by Nick Phillips, Head of Acting at Central School of Speech and Drama and one of the NSDF Committee. Here again, we see the significance of the contribution of an external professional coming in to complement and enhance the work of the school, to keep the spirit and sense of ongoing creativity alive by introducing some fresh techniques following the school performances, in preparation for the forthcoming challenge of the student festival. With his intervention, the play took another step forward. He 'tightened bits up' and 'put a little bit of polish on the numbers — which they needed'. He introduced what they called 'the Nick Phillips finish' involving 'arm movements with a sudden jerk of the hands, or send a paw down, and pronouncing the letters more as well', which all added to the sharpness of it all. Thus he helped them create a grand finish to the big numbers, 'ending the song with such a bang that people think "Oh wow! Sock it to them!" sort of thing. We enjoyed doing that because you really feel a sense of power when you all get the same beat. Again, it's the unity idea as well, all working together'. (Sara)

He saw his own role as 'working on some points of techique concerning the production as a whole, concerning the shape and rhythm of the production. These are things that they could not be expected to know, but which will just help to tighten up certain points of it . . . It's a question of allowing what is there to have its fullest impact, and to allow the criticism at the festival to be for the right reasons.'

What did the students feel he added to the production? Martyn noted that everything 'gelled' after Christmas in the build-up to Cambridge, and that Nick had contributed to that. His intervention helped them 'find the energy we thought we'd lost'. Matthew reported that Nick completely re-choreographed a song he did with Ian ('All for the best'), which they had not got right ('we weren't interacting at all, or involving the people behind us or the audience'). It became 'much more stagey and showy and much stronger'.

Johanne said that Nick 'finished it off', making the show 'a bit more flowing and professional'. He also gave them confidence in the run-up to Cambridge, where they feared they would get 'booed off stage'. Nick helped them squeeze even more enjoyment out of their performance.

Jo said:

> He made us feel good about ourselves. He taught you to enjoy it — like if it's your number — 'Hey! everybody, here I am!' Basically he taught us how to get the best out of it personally.

Nick complemented the team, worked with them, revived flagging spirits, re-injected pace. Coming in with his own brand of expertise and fresh vigour, he revived others so that their own abilities and spirits were restored and primed to go on to even greater things. Nick played the role of 'critical other'. The initial life of the play was conceived to be September–December. The week's performances at the School were the public celebrations that marked the end of the event. Mental processes, affective states, work schedules, stamina levels, were geared to this. After December, it was back to school. Even though they were selected for Cambridge, it was, psychologically, more of a prize for a task completed than an inducement to begin the gruelling work of rehearsals and the draining work of revising and improving all over again. Something else was needed for that, a fresh ingredient that would be a medium for change, re-awaken the zest, enliven and strengthen the unity, and point in the new direction. Once guided, their own energies and abilities carried them forward.

The Participants
As for the contributors themselves, Sally spoke of the 'incredibly talented kids' they had at the school who 'never ceased to amaze her'. As well as being talented, they were such 'nice kids'.

> There's a lack of cynicism about them. All the kids who were at Cambridge, there was an enthusiasm that wasn't present in the older students. That was lovely to see. Not gullibility, just freshness, and ability to enjoy themselves without hang-ups, which was great.

In a way, however, and without wishing to detract from individual accomplishments, this talent and character is exceptional not so much in the sense of it being part of one's individual, unique, personally endowed, make-up and more in the fact that it was unlocked, freed, formulated and given expression by the confluence of factors that produced the Godspell experience. Among these, the school itself, policy and ethos, was of critical importance.

The School: Policy and Ethos

Sally: You couldn't do it just at any school.

Sally found Roade a 'smashing place to teach. It does not have the panache of Crawley or Stantonbury (two of her previous schools), 'but the kids are lovely, mature, sensitive, and not afraid to show it. You don't have to discipline them'.

For creative education to occur, it is necessary for there to be not only opportunities for pupils to learn, but also for teachers to teach (Woods, 1990a). The Head, and the LEA ensured curriculum space, staff, moral support and basic resource. Godspell was constructed totally in extracurricular time, but it built on skills developed in classes in dance, drama and music. When he became Head, Ian made a commitment, not only to retain the Arts in the curriculum at a time when they were under attack, but to strengthen them. He secured resources from the LEA therefore to develop expressive arts within the curriculum, and to make a senior appointment. The LEA, also, through their 'Arts in the Curriculum' initiative, made not only money available, but also the opportunities to work with professionals, such as a professional dance company. The school had a drama studio and an attractive music suite. Now they spent £1,000 on converting a canteen area into a room for dance. Soon, too, the three subjects of dance, drama and music, previously separately timetabled (and 'vulnerable because of that') became integrated, and 'drew upon the strengths of one another'. With talented members of staff who were 'prepared to work all hours', they had large numbers of students enrolling on GCSE courses (over 100 in the fourth year taking Expressive Arts), and had had several major productions year after year.

Ian talks of the money put into the area as an 'investment', one 'which has borne fruit and you actually see it in the children themselves'. He mentioned the previous summer when a group of students had worked for two days with members of the Industrial Society 'simulating the kinds of situations they would encounter in the world of work'. The industrialists said they were 'staggered by the majority of the youngsters, by their confidence, and their ability to get up and speak in front of groups'. Ian saw that as a spin-off from their Expressive Arts experiences.

He is aware of the danger of elitism among drama groups, but feels it does not apply at Roade. Godspell 'reached out and tapped a whole range of youngsters' which went along to 'support their pals', but also because they 'actually enjoy it'. Large numbers of students are drawn into these productions. It was their intention to spread the benefits among as wide a range as possible. They did not seek to get to the NSDF every year — that had come as a pleasant surprise. Rather, it was the groundwork that was important, the day-to-day opportunities to develop interests that they had achieved within curriculum time, for example to do dance as an activity in the lunch-hour or play in the band. It is crucial, he believes, that Expressive Arts should be an opportunity for all students, that it should be a curriculum entitlement. He has been 'massively encouraged' by what has been achieved in a relatively short time-span.

> I look at that area of the curriculum and say 'My God! It's working, it's actually working!' Children are enjoying a range of experiences that go far beyond what we offered in the days of a period of drama, a couple of lessons of music or what-have-you.

Ian argues for the development of mental powers over and above the conception of what is involved in certain approaches to the curriculum, such as vocationalism, or indeed in the subject-based curriculum as supported by the philosophy of Hirst and Peters (1970) and their argument for seven basic 'Forms of Knowledge'. Bolton (1984) quotes Elliott (1975, p. 49) on the kind of mental powers in mind, which are 'the basic tools of most intellectual effort':

> Such powers are exercised, for example, in retention and anticipation; in synthesis and synopsis; in the reduction of whole to parts; in the discernment of relations and discovery of structures; in 'bracketing' properties and aspects; in discovering the objects of feelings and impressions; in guess-work; in pushing ideas to their limits; in shifts of perspective of many kinds; in weighing pros and cons and sensing the balance; and so on. It is about 'natural understanding', 'genuineness as a human being', the 'life of the mind'.

No doubt as Ian and his staff came to target the National Curriculum they would be under pressure, and 'a lot of other things were happening', but,

I think most of us are in teaching because we actually care about kids and the kind of people that they grow into, and that we need if, as a society, we're going to survive. Teachers may get bogged down in assessment, profiling, etc. etc., but finally they say 'My God! There's an individual underneath here and I'll give that some more time because that's crucial.'

Conclusion

Godspell was not only a critical event, but a multiple one. There were three phases. Each phase and especially the first two, showed the classic structure of conception, preparation and planning (during which several were sceptical and unwilling to make full investment of self); divergence (featuring the chaos of creative experimentation, containing both confusion and highly constructive innovation); convergence during which the best features were selected and matched together and refined as part of the whole; finally, there was the celebration, the public presentation, when it 'all came together', the mass of complicated activity becoming integrated in all its details and at each level.

The second phase, from December onwards, was a repeat of the first, but on a higher plane. They could not repeat phase 1 in exactly the same circumstances. How to pick up the traces again, therefore, was a serious problem. Two things were distinctive. First, the circumstances were different. The first phase was a 'school career', geared for presentation to pupils and parents at the school. Phase two was a 'national career' requiring fine-tuning for competition with the best student drama in the country. The process was the same, but the intensity was greater. To launch them on this second phase required the services of a 'critical other'. During the second phase they 'went up a level'. Not only did they reach new heights in their own performance, they encountered new learning experiences. The whole week they spent at Cambridge brought them in touch with what Kevin described as 'more subtle and particular analyses'. Also the Cambridge experience had aided their integration by the process of differentiation from other groups, who were not only in competition with them, but were also, apart from one, senior to them in age and experience. Again, therefore, they stood out, and their reception confirmed their distinctiveness. By the time they arrived at Derngate on their third career — a 'general public' one — they had become thoroughly professional. Sara was sure 'we could not have achieved it if we'd had just five nights of performance. We could never have reached the height of feeling that we did in just a week's production, because it's just this process of learning, a gradual mutual understanding and appreciation of the play'.

Those who took part in Godspell will always remember it. It will figure among the high peaks of their achievements. In giving people a sight of the ultimate, an indication of possibilities, some hitherto undreamt of, and new views of themselves, it established a platform for even greater endeavours.

Chapter 6

Conclusion: Outcomes and Prospects

In this final chapter I review the educational outcomes from critical events and how such events might feature in the National Curriculum.

Educational Gains

Student Gains

Students have received a considerable boost to their personal development from these events. This is especially marked in relation to, firstly, attitude to learning. Increased, or new-found confidence in oneself is frequently mentioned, as is motivation for learning. There is enhanced disposition and skill in listening to others, and being listened to. Secondly, there are several reports of self-discovery, a realization of abilities and interests, and a 'coming-out' of a new-found self which might coincide with a 'blending-in' to the culture of a group hitherto impenetrable. Such was the case with Sara in Chapter 5, Stephen in Chapter 2, Ellie in Chapter 3, Ben in Chapter 4. Emotional development was also prominent, especially in Chapter 5. Egan (1992) sees this as essential to 'imaginative learning'. Hard work is necessary, certainly, and it cannot always be pleasurable, but

> if we accept that imaginative engagement is a necessary condition of educationally valuable learning then we will want to find ways of ensuring a place for emotion, for engaging with students' hopes, fears and intentions, and for evaluating qualities of experience and richness of meaning. (Egan, 1992, p. 52)

Hope, fear, anger, ecstasy, love, happiness, joy, sadness, excitement, fervour, boredom, wonder, pride, surprise have all featured in these pages. The manifestations in these events have contributed to students' emotional development, but have also enhanced other forms of learning. The emotional engagement with Godspell, and how this contributed to personal and social development is perhaps the best example. As with Nias, Southworth and Campbell (1992, p. 74), 'teachers were overwhelmed by the realization that children were able to achieve standards of which they had never before thought them capable'. Interestingly, in the schools of their research, where the staffs were engaged in whole school curriculum development, there was not 'serialized, step-by-step planning and implementation' (ibid., p. 44). Particular developments were 'sometimes spontaneous, at others they seemed opportunistic, as heads or members of staff capitalized upon the curricula interest or classroom experiments of an individual' (ibid.). There has to be planning, and linear, gradually cumulative development. But much will be missed — including self-discovery — if these opportunities are lost. Everybody here was involved in hard work, but it featured a high degree of enthusiasm, excitement, and fun. These events stirred the adrenalin, sharpened senses to the peak of awareness, marshalled all one's energies and abilities, even summoned up new and unsuspected ones. They were cathartic, providing a spark which touched off individuals and groups alike, and which led to revelations about oneself and others.

Thirdly, there has been refinement of the 'art of learning'. Imagination and creativity has been stimulated, but within a disciplined framework. Students have learnt skills of communicating in a variety of media. They have learnt how to research, how to find things out, how to conceive, develop and express ideas. They have learnt the ability to self-evaluate, and to reflect critically on their own work and that of others. They have been challenged, stretched, fulfilled, in what for them has been 'real' learning, in a contrast to what Stephen in Chapter 2 called 'number-crunching'. So much learning is unreal in the sense that it is not about person development or pure education but about the peripheral, instrumentalist structure of it which so often works against the best intentions of teachers, as in learning about the structure of questions rather than their content (Mehan, 1986), of 'pleasing the teacher' strategies (Woods, 1990b), or classroom culture (Hammersley, 1977b), or learning material with the sole aim of passing a test, or in 'procedural display' (Bloome, 1987). A great deal also is compartmentalized, sectioned, disembodied, striated, unrelated to other forms of knowledge or areas of learning or aspects of life. In real learning, the artificial controls of traditional schooling are removed and students are liberated and empowered in the sense that they have acquired a considerable resource with which to face the world (Freire, 1970). Teachers cannot liberate pupils from society, but 'they can remove the artificial controls of traditional schooling . . . [and] make their classrooms communities of learning . . . [in which] pupils are free to invent ways of dealing with their functional needs . . .' (Goodman and Goodman, 1990, p. 238). Real learning has a measure of student ownership and control, is relevant to their needs and is pitched at a level where they will be stretched. It is notable that some of the contributors to Rushavenn considered it a celebration of childhood, while I saw Godspell as a celebration of youth. Real learning also is holistic. It is multidisciplinary; it combines cognitive, affective, aesthetic, physical and spiritual experience to general enhancement, and it regards the world as school. It is no accident that a great deal of the work done in these projects took place outside school and in or out of school hours; nor that so much of the outside world came into the schools to support and enrich the activity.

Learning about oneself was matched by learning about others. These include not only one's fellow-students, but teachers, other professionals, and members of the community. Barriers of sex, age, social class, status, role and structure were transcended to some degree. They learnt the nature and benefits of working cooperatively in a group, democratic procedures, decision-making. They realized they could both enhance the group, and be enhanced by it; that their own worth was valued, and that they could value the work of others — surprisingly so in some cases. There was respect and dignity for both self and others. D. Hargreaves (1982) and Pring (1987), among others, have argued for a rediscovery of 'community' within the school, cultivating a certain quality that resides in the common humanity of persons (Tawney, 1938). Pring (1987, p. 15) feels that there should also be a wider sense of community, 'a re-examination of values, a focus upon the personal, a concern for individual dignity, and a sense of solidarity which is shared with different constituencies in society'. These events show one particular form of expression of this idea.

Students have developed skills and acquired knowledge in relation to the event. Literacy and oracy have improved, designing and planning, camera work, drama skills, and so on. They have seen how a book is conceived, written, and published; how members of a village community spend their spare time and how those activities comprise a community; how plans and designs for a building are initiated, effected and processed, and so on. They have had their awareness raised in respect of pressing current issues, such as the environment, citizenship, the community, how to live together.

These events have provided aesthetic education in some measure. All of them have aspired to a truth that they have not previously known, one that has required considerable groundwork, trial and error, effort and ingenuity, frustration and triumph. They have all been concerned with the production of a work of art, unique and beautiful in its own right. They have helped make it, so it is theirs. Part of their selves is enshrined within it, and, in turn, their selves are enriched by it. There was, at times, a 'magic' or 'mystery' about it, something outside their normal experience. It seemed on some occasions an emotional experience, on others an aesthetic experience. In either case, it was difficult to describe and explain, but they did their best to convey the character and purport of the experience. Reflecting upon it, and talking about it, arguably increased the sense of ownership.

The character of the learning has thus been something special. It gains the highest rating in their educational careers from the students. Stephen still looks for his name in *Rushavenn Time* in the public library. Ian can look back on 'Godspell' and feel that he helped to please so many people. For Matthew, the experience was at least the equivalent of his considerable academic achievements. The Laxfield pupils still look back on their film as an educational high-point. In short, they achieved a standard of accomplishment which surpassed other learning experiences they had known. It stands as a benchmark for the future, reveals what is possible, and will perhaps inform and enthuse other endeavours in other fields.

The Gains of Others

Nias (1989a) has drawn attention to the importance of the 'self' in considering the teacher's role, and the Meadean concepts of the socially constructed 'me' and the autonomous, creative and more spontaneous 'I'. The creative 'I' is the source of initiative, novelty and change; the 'me' is the agent of self-regulation and social control. The 'self' consists of the interaction between the two, with the 'I' inciting, and the 'me' regulating (Woods, 1992). People may have multiple selves, perhaps a substantial self, which represents the 'real me', and 'situational selves' that are adapted to particular situations (Ball, 1972). The latter may be a way of coping with the world, and particularly institutional, depersonalized life.

Critical events have important consequences for the teacher's self. Firstly, they allow expression to the 'I'. At times, external regulation is predominant, and teachers have little opportunity for experiment. They may be discouraged from taking risks — an essential gambit in all creative endeavours. But the fact that these teachers are reflective practitioners ensures that their gambits will be closely monitored. Given opportunities to experiment they can achieve the heights that come from fruitful interaction between the 'I' and the 'Me', acting at their most refined and at full power and in perfect balance. This yields the most profound satisfaction, fulfilment, exhilaration even. It is the high point of teaching, the 'great moment of teachability' (see Chapter 1). Peter (Chapter 2), Melanie (Chapter 3), Sally (Chapter 5) all express this very well.

Secondly, critical events promote the unification of the self. Norquay (1990) argues that the self is not unified. At least there is no 'single narrative of a unified self, but rather several tellings with which we present and represent ourselves within different contexts and configurations of our locations in our gender, race and class' (p. 291). This may well be the case in general as people became subject to changing historical and social forces. But in critical events at least, the inner core that is the substantial self, comprising 'the most highly prized aspects of our self-concept and the attitudes and values which are salient to them' (Nias, 1989a, p. 21), achieves maximum expression. It is not on the defensive, hidden, and protected by layers of adaptation as often may be the case. It is given its head. The inner core becomes all-embracing. Situational selves are seen in perspective as the substantial self predominates and grows and develops as, perhaps, unsuspected potentials are realized. As Huberman (1992) reports with regard to one of his studies (Huberman and Miles, 1984), 'It was the experience of increasing skill in delivering and varying the programmes, along with the attendant headlines of actually obtaining results one had thought beyond one's reach, that produced ownership' (p. 10). It is, then, a moment of profound truth. In contrast to being deskilled and demoralized — a not uncommon experience among teachers — these teachers through these experiences are enskilled and remoralized.

There are several examples in the events described. For Sally (Chapter 5), the experience had 'changed her life'. She would not be the 'same person' again after it. Her expressions speak to the unificatory and uplifting aspects of the experience. It had made her 'happier' and 'more positive', given 'meaning to life', made 'everything worthwhile', given her 'confidence', 'hope,' and 'insight'; it had been 'the ultimate production' for her, the 'most satisfactory', and she had developed it 'as fully as possible within the job that we do'. For Peter (Chapter 2) also, it was an apogee, an experience that brought everything together. Everything prior to that had been leading up to it. As the project unfolded, things began to 'fall into place'; it provided 'the key to a whole range of earlier experiences'; showed how 'things could be changed and improved to the advantage of everyone'. In terms of self, his substantial self, which erstwhile had been marginal, became central, employing the vision gained from marginality to spectacular effect.

There were other products in terms of knowledge, skills and relationships that have been recorded in the text. Of these, perhaps relationships have been the most notable. At times, they have risen above the restrictions of role in the view of their students. In some instances they have become friends and colleagues. The perception of others, therefore, of the teacher's self has also been changed, to mutual benefit. They have become more human and 'person-like' in their eyes, fuelling the ability of the teacher to assist the student in the construction of learning. This relationship has also enabled the teacher to learn from the student, which would be difficult in a more instructional, hierarchical situation. Further teacher development ensued from the research on the events, which I discuss in the Appendix.

How Have They Learned?

Alexander (1992) has pointed out that the dominant ideology of primary education — that of child-centredness, deriving from Piaget and Plowden — is 'alive and well' in spite of the 1988 Education Reform Act. He argues that this ideology has been 'frequently constraining and oppressive while ostensibly libertarian', and for many 'has become a mere shell of slogans and procedures'. 'All the sacred cows and shibboleths — the resistance to subjects, integration, thematic work, topics, enquiry methods, group work and so on — must be subjected to clear-headed scrutiny' (p. 194). The research reported in this book illustrates how, in some instances, the ideology has not remained at the level of ideas and wishful thinking, but has been implemented in strikingly successful ways. In the general debate about teaching styles and classroom practice that is currently in train, these achievements should not be lost sight of.

Further, as is clear from these examples, the ideology in some instances has been modified along constructivist lines. Scaffolding has been strongly in evidence as a general strategy for aiding the student through the zone of proximal development (ZPD) (Vygotsky, 1956), that is the area of understanding between the point that the child can reach on his or her own and the point that can be reached with assistance from teacher and from peers. The extent of the ZPD can clearly be considerable. One passage may then inform other passages, as well as lending experience and confidence to learning generally.

Great attention has been paid to context. The importance of this for student learning as it applied to the classroom was well-expressed by Peter in Chapter 2, and clearly was of crucial significance for all the events. An interesting feature of all the events was the extent of out-of-school and extra-curricular time and space that was used. This aided the sense of holistic and real learning, and counteracted any bureaucratic tendencies of the institutional structure. The more general context of the school was also important. These events, in fact, were a product of their schools. It was difficult for some to see them occurring in any other type of school. Institutional values were empathetic, school organization facilitated, resources were made available, and heads and others lent support.

The context had to be chosen or designed to serve the principles of cooperation, collaboration and negotiation. Interestingly, shades of the competitive spirit hung on in all the events, but subsided as the benefits of cooperation took hold. Thus at Laxfield (Chapter 3) they 'wanted to win' but in the end 'it didn't matter'. At Winchester (Chapter 4), some initially 'wanted to be best' and saw it as a competition, but finally settled for working to do their best design and appreciating the best in others. As for *Rushavenn Time* (Chapter 2) and Godspell (Chapter 5), they both won prestigious competitions, but neither had set out with that aim in view, and indeed were only entered after excellence had been established.

The collaboration took a number of forms. Students had to work together in teams; then the teams had to relate together in the interests of a greater whole. They had to learn the benefits of democratic procedures, and how to use the mediation of the teacher to maximum effect. On the teacher's side, a special relationship was developed with students, characterized by mutual respect and warmth. Generally, the primary teacher's relationship with her students is the most valued component of her job (see, for example, Nias, 1989a). In these cases the relationship was even more special, and this feeling was clearly reciprocated by the students.

The projects benefited also by the quality of team-work developed by the central teacher as critical agent, and other teachers and professionals as critical others. Nias (1987) has described how a head and deputy head worked in close liaison almost as one in the running of a school. Here, also, we have critical agents and others acting together in interlocking roles, increasing the skills and knowledge level, sparking each other off in new directions in their own expertise, and constructing a highly productive compound role. This is well illustrated here by Theresa and Peter (Chapter 2), Sally, Lesley and Nick (Chapter 5), and the architects and teachers (Chapter 4). This team-work took place against a background of a 'culture of collaboration' within the school as a whole. Nias *et al.* (1992, p. 203) characterize this as showing a willingness to 'confront the existence of professional differences and to try to resolve them constructively'. They showed equal concern for the individual and for the group. Prominent features are openness, facilitating personal expression and security, since all are valued and have a sense of interdependence and mutual respect.

Content was another key factor. The book, film, design, play was relevant to students' concerns and needs. It was meaningful to them and they could personally identify with it. It was real, not mocked-up, second-hand, cold, substitute (Atkinson and Delamont, 1977). Above all, perhaps, it caught their imaginations. It elevated them above the conventional, offered them a new perspective, a new vision, helping them to become 'autonomous thinkers, able to see conventional ideas for what they are' (Egan, 1992, p. 47). The content, then, provided a splendid vehicle for the journey across the ZPD. It offered footholds, opportunities, challenges in a stimulating framework.

At the centre of operations, arranging the context, setting up the collaboration, selecting, mediating and perhaps modifying content, encouraging, inspiring and organizing, is the critical agent, committed, constructivist, child-oriented, and creative. The critical agent is a skilled observer of students, recognizing ZPDs as they occur naturally, knowing when and how to offer support in the role of mediator,

> supporting the learning transactions but neither causing them to happen
> in any direct sense nor controlling the learning. In this way the forces of
> invention and convention are unfettered, and the teacher supports the
> learner in achieving equilibrium. (Goodman and Goodman, 1990, p. 236)

These teachers have high levels of 'planning genius' (Chapter 3). Their readiness to tackle new initiative has them and others 'bubbling like a hot spring'

(Nias, 1989b). While it is true that teachers must have opportunities to teach (Woods, 1990a), they can, to some extent, given appropriate general conditions, create opportunities. All the critical agents here, for example, secured additional resource, recruited skilled and technical assistance, initiated enthusiasm, managed the tempo of the event, and above all, perhaps, created time. Much of the work in all instances took place outside official school time. There was no compulsion about this in the sense of making students work against their will — quite the reverse — it was the natural thing to do given the subject-matter of the projects and the enthusiasm of the participants. They even carried on the work in many cases in their own homes. Secondly, because such strong motivation was generated, the best possible use was made of time. High levels of awareness, full engagement of the senses, deep personal involvement, exercising of creative talents, ensured that more was crammed in to their time available, than might be the case in routine work. These were indeed 'golden moments'. Time was invented where previously it was not suspected that it existed. We are all constrained and our actions are structured in important ways by time in one form or another (Berger and Luckmann, 1967). Timetable norms are constructed in schools to mark out the allocation and sequencing of knowledge and skills-acquisition and the passage of the pupil career (Roth, 1963). But people can have different time perspectives (Horton, 1967), and they can experience different 'rhythms of work'. Blauner (1964) points to different ways in which a manual worker can associate with work — from being involved and engrossed in a situation where skills are fully employed, emotionally engaged with the immediate activity and problem-solving, and looking to the completion of the task; to, at the other extreme, in unskilled routine jobs, a repetitive-cycle work rhythm, where one is detached from the task, looks forward to the cessation of the activity rather than the completion of the task, and where 'the meaning of the job is largely found in instrumental future-time rewards' — in the case of pupils examination or test passes, job chances, or more prosaically, an easy time. This is similar to the distinction made by Hall (1984) between monochronic and polychronic conceptions of time. The former focuses on linear progression rather than doing several things at once, completing schedules rather than transactions, tasks and procedures rather than relationships, has little sensitivity to context, is typical of bureaucratic organizations and is common throughout the western world. It is associated with a technical-rational view of the world. Lyman and Scott (1970) make a similar distinction in their notion of humanistic-fatalistic 'time-tracks':

> By humanistic time tracks we refer to the complex subjective experience that activities are governed by personal decision, and are exhibited through self expression. By fatalistic time tracks we refer to the subjective experience that these activities are matters of obligation or compulsion, are outside the active domination of the social actor, and are vehicles of coercive or conformist rather than individual expression. (Lyman and Scott, 1970, pp. 191–2)

McLaren (1986) shows how the students of his research experienced the two kinds of time differently. In one, 'time became "death" — an enemy to avoid' (p. 198). This led students to 'waste time', and when one does that, 'one actually lays waste to time'. In the other, students 'owned' the time; time passed quickly, 'dissolving' into whatever activity the students were doing (ibid.). Lyman and Scott point out that these experiences are generated by social arrangements — the context. In setting these up, the critical agent makes one of her most crucial inputs. It influences the rhythm of work, the time-frame and the time-track on which participants engage.

Critical others also played a key role. An author, an expert in role-play, planners and architects, a drama expert were integrally involved. They lent an authenticity to the proceedings, raised the activity to a new level, injected novelty as well as expertise. On occasions, they played an important part in moving the process from one key stage to another (as in Chapter 5). They contributed to the sense of holism, bringing the outside, real world into the school, or rather, incorporating the school into the real world. They provided a new kind of role-model for students, extending their horizons, and making bridges between professional and person. Students learnt to appreciate these others as human beings, and were encouraged to exercise part of the professional's role.

With the extension of context, content, and personnel went an extension of method. The use of multi-methods has been evident in all the events. There was a basic fitness-for-purpose behind this, but it had a deeper significance. Firstly, it was a response to a belief that all children have ability, and that it is a teacher's responsibility to find it and help children use it. As was shown in Chapter 2, the use of a range of methods, perhaps through different media, achieved breakthroughs and enabled some children to 'come out'. Secondly, it enabled new heights of excellence to be reached, for example, in the second stage of Godspell (Chapter 5), where the introduction of new techniques refined the production and cemented the 'communitas'. Thirdly, the use of multi-methods acts as a kind of triangulation, enhancing the validity of one's work. This occurred in all the events, but the application in the Laxfield study (Chapter 3) is particularly interesting, for here the children were acting as researchers and employing the same kind of techniques as researchers in trying to find things out and in testing their validity.

Finally, while the emphasis so far has been on extension in various respects and the provision of opportunities, a feature of all the events has been the skilful way in which the burgeoning and highly creative activities that were engendered have been disciplined and structured. Careful and detailed planning in the first instance, based on previous work in the school, ensured that the creativity was directed towards relevant ends. The structure of the project ensured a productive tension between creativity and discipline. An optimum balance was achieved between the pleasure of inventing and the pain of application. The focus on the final product and its celebration ensured a most effective symbiosis.

Critical Events in the National Curriculum

The events described in this book took place before the National Curriculum, established by the Education Reform Act of 1988, began to take effect. Some consideration should be given, therefore, to the compatibility of critical events with the National Curriculum. Are they possible within its framework, desirable, essential even? The conditions pertaining to the critical events described in this book include legitimation within the curricular structure; critical agents, strongly committed to teaching, espousing constructivist learning theory and using democratic-participatory procedures; a measure of teacher and pupil ownership of knowledge and control of teaching and learning processes; and resources, including a supportive school ethos, and time to conceive, plan, prepare and carry out the event. The situation with regard to the National Curriculum is not clear-cut in any of these respects. There are grounds for both pessimism and optimism. There are both constraints and opportunities for critical events in the National Curriculum.

Constraints in the National Curriculum

The Education Reform Act of 1988, and related events have seemed to some to deal a blow to the kind of education depicted here, and to challenge the philosophy on which it is based (Dadds, 1992). The organization of a National Curriculum into subjects, the specification of attainment targets, the requirements of national assessment, all seemed to indicate separation rather than integration, delivery rather than initiative on the part of teachers. Instrumentalist and rationalist philosophies appear to have displaced the naturalism and experimentalism of Rousseau, Dewey and Plowden. Central has replaced local control. Teachers trained as generalists, many of them avowed integrationists, are having to teach a range of subjects, some of them, like technology, completely new, others, like science, in much greater concentration. Commentators like Brighouse (1990, p. 71) wonder if the National Curriculum will be 'so rigid in its framework that there is no room for the teacher to try interesting diversions and take the opportunity for exploration of unmapped territory'. Will it become 'the deadening grind of something we have to do?' (p. 72). Tann (1988, p. 16) notes that 'the more curriculum issues are decided "outside" the classroom . . . the more the opportunities may be diminished for a "topic work" way of teaching and learning'.

Certainly, for the moment at least, of the teachers featuring in this book, Melanie (Chapter 3) for one thought that things had changed:

> I don't think one feels as open and as ready to take the risks of that kind of long-term commitment, of spending a year on something which is essentially about community and media use . . . I don't feel I have the freedom of scope to do such a project. I haven't been able to get one off the ground. It's been very small, separate things that we've done.

Her headteacher felt there was 'so much ground to cover in the National Curriculum', that it would be a complicated job 'seeing what attainment targets you've covered' in a long-term project, and that the almost inexorable trend was towards 'compartmentalization in teaching in blocks', though they 'would resist that in primary schools, because we try to integrate things as much as we can'. His feelings are echoed by Winkley (1990, p. 113), who notes, 'content-driven curriculum is always in danger of reducing the quality of transactions between teacher and child by becoming a handing-out of packages'. They may allow no space for learners to develop activities, they may be badly integrated, not recognize that learners develop in different ways at different rates, and need to be motivated; and they may embroil teachers in administration and bureaucracy. A redefinition of the teacher's job is taking place. Their role has expanded to cover a number of other specified duties including administration, parents, in-service and curriculum development meetings, and for some, managerial duties. Headteachers are experiencing a new form of role conflict. Peter (Chapter 2), for example, has protested that; 'Nobody has worked out what the head's role should be. I'm under pressure to take more part in financial management on the one hand, and to remain heavily involved with classroom teaching and staff support on the other. If I concentrate on one, the other suffers, and I can't do both.' With five years to go before he chooses to retire, his aim is not to go on to more experiments in creative teaching, but to defend what he has achieved while overcoming all the problems brought to the school in the wake of the Reform Act, and to leave the school in good order for his successor.

Evidence from the PACE project (Primary Assessment, Curriculum and Experience) shows that children value activity, autonomy, stimulation, engaging with other children, things they can succeed at, and opportunities to be creative (Pollard, 1991a, p. 36). Pollard draws attention to the release of the imagination and the connection with previous experience which is implicit in many of the priorities given by the children' (ibid., see also Egan, 1990, 1992). But teachers, under pressure of required demands were moving away from work designed to stimulate children's interest in fantasy and imagination. A number felt their relationships with the children were also suffering, through lack of time and through stress on the teachers' part. They were sad to lose the spontaneity and flexibility of old, and the ability to respond to children's learning initiatives. Furthermore, the areas of the curriculum most associated with creative work — Arts education, and especially that to do with the creative arts: art, music, drama, dance — have been given a lower priority. Drama is seen as an offshoot of English, which might be viewed as diminishing its importance. Art, music and physical education (which is deemed to include 'dance') were the last subjects in the National Curriculum to be introduced into schools. They are not be tested, and the programmes of study and statements of attainment are non-statutory. Art and music can both be dropped at age 14. There is a fear, therefore, that these subjects may become marginalized. This is already happening in primary schools. Pollard (1991a), for example, found a shift among his teachers towards the prescribed core subjects (mathematics, English and science) and away from 'creative' areas. A number said they were doing less art and music; and that the type of activities had changed, for example, less creative writing in English, less 'art for art's sake'. As for secondary schools, Godspell was produced entirely outside classroom hours, but its success built on skills in interaction and self-expression learnt through classes in dance, drama and music, which now have to fight for time in the curriculum. This hardly meets Mary Warnock's (1977) point that art activities are crucial since they encourage finer and more thoughtful perception and deeper emotional experience, well illustrated in the projects here. On the other hand, the National Curriculum states that everyone must be offered some 'aesthetic experience' between the ages of 14 and 16. While this is somewhat vague, the drama, dance and music activities in Godspell would meet this requirement. Further, the Education Reform Act of 1988 stipulates that the curriculum should 'promote the spiritual, moral, cultural, mental and physical development of pupils at the school and of society'. The events depicted in this book show what a contribution they can make to these aims (see also Robinson, 1991). These stipulations, however, do have the flavour of generalized afterthoughts, less compelling than the more detailed prescriptions.

On the whole, this seems a less favourable set of conditions for the production of critical events than obtained formerly. The trend is towards standardization and against exceptionality. In their comparison of primary teaching in the French and English systems, Osborn and Broadfoot (1992) feel that while English teachers show a strong determination not to sacrifice the child-centred methods in which they believe, as the pressures grow it may be inevitable. The French experience suggests that there will be a shift of emphasis from process to product.

One of the pressures is on time. While critical agents are adept at constructing high-quality polychronic time, alternative monochronic demands may squeeze out their creativity in that respect. Thus, one of the conditions for creativity, as suggested earlier, is time for planning and reflection (Woods, 1990a), but teachers, following the Reform Act, have little of it free of the activity of teaching. HMI have noted that many schools have had time distribution difficulties among core (especially) and foundation subjects (DES, 1990), and severe lack of time for preparation (DES, 1989). Campbell and Neill (1990) showed that the teachers they studied in teaching key stage 1 (up to age 7) had on average only twenty-two minutes per week free of teaching in in-school time. Nine out of ten teachers were working beyond what they all considered a reasonable number of hours. On the distribution of time, large amounts were being spent on preparation and in-service training as compared to teaching. In the late 1960s/early 1970s, Hilsum and Cane (1971) showed teachers spending 58 per cent time on teaching, 42 per cent on non-teaching; for Campbell and Neill's teachers, it was 43.9 per cent and 56.1 per cent respectively. They felt that this considerable shift was likely to produce stress and disaffection, since work with children was the source of most intrinsic satisfaction.

In another study, Campbell *et al.* (1991) found infant teachers still enjoying their interaction with pupils, but they pointed to a number of sources of dissatisfaction, including:

> teachers saw their classrooms as less joyful places, with less attention to display, less time listening to children talk about their lives and preoccupations, on singing and painting, and following up children's spontaneous interests. This was because their work had become more cognitively pressurised, focusing on national curriculum targets. (Campbell *et al.*, 1991, p. 11)

Teachers were still as conscientious as ever, and supported the National Curriculum in principle but the tremendous drive we have seen in devising and running events has been eaten up by the demands of the National Curriculum requiring long hours at work. Campbell *et al.* (1991) call this 'the trap of conscientiousness' — devotion to the task that has become a fault, since 'it was damaging their personal lives, their health and, ironically, the quality of their pupils' learning and relationships with them'. (p. 22). There was less warmth in the personal relationship with children. This all aggravated the 'guilt' syndrome (A. Hargreaves and Tucker, 1991). One teacher explained that at the end of the day she was now thinking about what she had not done, whereas previously she used to feel, 'Great, we have done this.' (p. 36) Campbell *et al.*, felt there was an 'uneasy notion of accountability' promoting a paranoiac and fearful attitude that pervaded their teaching. A sense of low morale emerged from the sample. One thought it a 'soul-destroying, exhausting job at the moment'. Several had lowered their career aspirations. One specified the lack of consultation as the major blow — a clear perception of de-skilling. 'Most worrying of all,' in Campbell *et al*'s., (p. 67) view, was that 'these class teachers perceived that the vigour, enthusiasm and liveliness which they had previously brought to their work was being damaged.' These findings, generally, have been supported by other studies. Osborn and Pollard (1990), Broadfoot *et al.* (1991) and Pollard (1991a), for example, show that while many teachers welcome some of the ideas in the National Curriculum, they feel demoralized and frustrated over the lack of resources needed to implement change.

Morale is a key factor in the performance of any job, and is especially important when commitment and dedication is strong. Brian Simon (1990) in offering what he sees as essential conditions for effective learning puts teacher morale top of the list 'by a long way'. Fullan (1992) agrees, arguing that 'the main problem in teaching is not how to get rid of the deadwood, but rather how to motivate good teachers throughout their careers' (p. 121). A number of factors have contributed to teacher alienation. Disempowerment is one of them. Giving teachers back a voice in decision-making and control over their own teaching would go some way to restoring balance. The teachers featured in this book are all committed to educating the young to maximum effect. Success leads to gratification, which fuels inspiration for even higher achievement. Deprived of the opportunities for this, they will lose an important part of their 'selves'. Nias (1991) has shown how some teachers feel a sense of bereavement if they are not allowed to put their whole selves into their teaching, selves which have been constructed around child-centred philosophies and validated in their own experience. The changing nature of teaching as work could have profound consequences for critical events in education.

Opportunities in the National Curriculum

Paisey (1975) has drawn attention to optimistic and pessimistic assumptions about human nature. Hammersley (1977a) has shown how the traditional type of teaching approaches, which he terms 'discipline-based' and 'programmed', have pessimistic assumptions in this respect. Progressive types, among which would be included child-centredness, and constructivism are optimistic. They believe that human beings, in the right conditions, like and enjoy work, are self-regulating if committed, seek responsibility and are ambitious. They feel that the capacities for imagination, ingenuity and creativity are widely distributed, and that intellectual potentialities are only partially realized (Paisey, 1975, pp. 15–16). The promoters of critical events need to be optimistic, both in relation to particular happenings and with regard to the National Curriculum and its assessment working itself out at least partially in their favour.

As it is, there is much to offer them encouragement. Curiously enough, perhaps, after the previous section, the National Curriculum would appear to *require* exceptional events — and more of them. Consider, for example, the first three attainment targets for English, one of the three core subjects:

1 Speaking and listening: The development of pupils' understanding of the spoken word and the capacity to express themselves effectively in a variety

of speaking and listening activities, matching style and response to audience and purpose.

2   Reading: The development of the ability to read, understand and respond to all types of writing, as well as the development of information-retrieval strategies for the purposes of study.

3   Writing: A growing ability to construct and convey meaning in written language matching style to audience and purpose.

It is clear how all three targets were reached in our events in particularly effective ways, especially in the Rushavenn and Laxfield projects. At the time of writing, Wragg (1992) reports that while many teachers 'were nervous about a National Curriculum in English, they now feel it still allows for creative work' (p. 7).

In Technology, in Profile Component 1, Design and Technology, there are the following attainment targets:

1   Identifying needs and opportunities: Pupils should be able to identify and state clearly needs and opportunities for design and technological activities through investigation of the contexts of home, school, community, business and industry.

2   Generating a design: Pupils should be able to generate a design specification, explore ideas to produce a design proposal and develop it into a realistic, appropriate and achievable design.

The other two targets relate to 'planning and making' and 'evaluating'. The programme of study at Key Stage 2 (age 11) mentions 'organizing and developing practical activities and proposals', 'learning about the selection of materials and the ways in which they can be combined and safely used, while also developing some concept of aesthetic design', using 'drawings, models and graphics to explore and communicate ideas', 'understanding the needs and preferences of customers', and so on (see Sweetman, 1992). Chippindale seems ready-made for the promotion of these aims.

Drama is described as 'not simply a subject, but also a method . . . a learning tool. Furthermore, it is one of the key ways in which children can gain an understanding of themselves and of others' (NCC, 1990b). It contributes to 'the development of pupils' verbal communication skills'. It enables them to 'reconsider their feelings and attitudes' (ibid., p. D11), The guidance on 'media education' similarly recommends that 'children should produce media texts', among them 'video tapes'. The subject 'aims to develop systematically children's critical and creative powers through analysis and production of media artefacts'. Topics in this area can be used as a way of 'integrating work across the curriculum' (ibid., p. D16). Experiences like Godspell and Laxfield would appear to be serving these purposes, among others.

Further, this type of activity speaks strongly to the 'cross-curricular' elements of the National Curriculum. In particular, these events are promoting four of the six skills mentioned, namely those of communication, of studying, of problem-solving, and personal and social skills, all of which are 'transferable, chiefly independent of content and can be developed in different contexts across the whole curriculum' (NCC, 1990b). Of the five cross-curricular themes, the events depicted in this book are ministering to environmental education and education for citizenship, though whether all agree on what some of these things, such as 'citizenship', constitute, is another matter. They are also offering equal opportunities, one of the cross-curricular 'dimensions', in particular ways, overcoming to some degree, for example, differentiation by age and gender.

There are many other ways in meeting attainment targets and carrying out programmes of study that events like those discussed in this book offer to meet the requirements of the National Curriculum. Further, there are no prescriptions or proscriptions of teaching methods. Teachers are free to select those methods they judge best designed to accelerate progress toward the targets. However, teaching itself, as opposed to curriculum, is coming under scrutiny as it becomes increasingly recognized that 'it is pedagogy rather than content which constitutes the most basic reality of teaching' (Alexander, 1992, p. 169). and that radical change in one implies radical change in the other. A government commissioned report has sought to initiate discussion (Alexander, Rose and Woodhead, 1992). It is seen by some, mistakenly perhaps, as traditionalist in orientation. The key-note appears to be 'balance' — not dissimilar to an essential feature of the events described here. For example, it states:

> If it can be shown that the topic approach allows the pupil both to make acceptable progress within the different subjects of the National Curriculum and to explore the relationships between them, then the case for such an approach is strong on both pedagogic and logistical grounds.

It might be argued that the case is made by the events in this book. Webb (1990) also presents evidence for such a case. She points out that there are many common elements among the core subjects such as collaboration, the use of Information Technology (IT), and the development of information skills; and that schemes of work need to contain activities that integrate subjects to some extent (p. 98). She concludes that while the National Curriculum is providing a challenge, 'topic work now has the potential to be rigorous and systematic while maintaining the diversity, creativity and spontaneity that have made it popular with both pupils and teachers' (p. 123). Anning (1991) reports 'initial angry reaction' among infant teachers to the National Curriculum proposals, followed by 'knuckling down to making the best compromises they could' (p. 104). In the course of this, 'their protestations about a commitment to an integrated approach to curriculum planning forced many school staffs to become more rigorous in their long-term planning of themes and topics than they had ever been before' (ibid.). In this respect, the National Curriculum is cathartic, forcing teachers to re-examine their teaching, the principles on which it is based, its coherence and its effectiveness. If it reins in some of the undisciplined freedom that might be present in some schools, this might well be in the best interests of creativity, topics, themes, integrated learning, and critical events. Fowler (1990) also has illustrated how National Curriculum core elements can be integrated in a topic approach, though 'careful planning and recording of progress is vital, and the concept of a progressive subject approach must not be lost' (p. 75). HMI (1991), in their report of the first year of implementation of the Act, noted that 'the planning of topic work generally improved, and to be effective it required 'a firm commitment by staff to work as a team, sharing expertise and responsibility for decision-making' (p. 16). Certainly the Act appears to have brought teachers together in several ways. But what of collaboration among pupils? The competitive underpinning of the Act (Wragg, 1988) and the new scheme for assessment do not seem designed to promote such relationships. The current pressure is for more whole-class teaching (Alexander *et al.*, 1992). However, it is generally recognized that there is a basic organizational problem in primary schools with generalist class teachers required to deliver a subject-based curriculum, monitor and assess work in classes of thirty or more children. Galton and Williamson (1992, p. 193) conclude that 'the increase in collaborative group work, with its emphasis on inter-dependency between pupils offers a practical solution to some of these more pressing problems and a sound basis for today's children as they prepare to face adult life in the twenty-first century'.

In general, as things begin to settle down, some research and commentary suggest that the prospects for more changes for a different kind of approach do not seem so remote. Jones and Hayes (1991, p. 215) report hectic change in the schools of their research and crises of conscience for some headteachers, for example, remaining true to their own philosophies of education and 'convincing staff that the "new philosophy" (as perceived) is able to be accommodated, even welcomed'. Whether the Act will provide for success or despair remains to be seen, but 'the portents are promising' (p. 219). Moon (1990, p. 24) felt that within a year of the passing of the Act, there were signs that 'the crusading zeal of the polemicists was being eroded through the implementation process'. He detected in a number of documents a move away from the emphasis on subjects. A DES (1989) document talked of statements of attainment rather than subjects. It made it clear that *how* schools taught the stipulated programmes was for the schools to decide. The integrated day and modular approaches were not excepted. The original assessment proposals have been modified, and the subject working parties have produced balanced programmes on the whole.

The longitudinal study of primary teachers' adaptation to the National Curriculum by Wragg *et al.* (1989) and Bennett *et al.* (1992) shows progressive accommodation. Teachers see themselves as more competent now in science than in 1989, such that Bennett *et al.* (1992, p. 76) conclude, 'The net result is that primary science appears to have benefitted greatly from the introduction of the National Curriculum'. The same goes for IT, but teachers were experiencing less latitude in the humanities. Their perceived competence in English and mathematics also showed a decrease. Perhaps, the authors suggest, they were being more realistic. The study on the whole points to the inadequacy of INSET made available, yet there were signs that teachers were coming to terms with the National Curriculum.

Nias *et al.* (1989, p. 124) point out that 'primary schools are constantly changing, in unpredictable ways'. In the schools of their research, after some initial anxiety,

> aspects of the National Curriculum were actively used to foster policies and practices which already existed . . . As this happened, teachers and headteachers began to absorb the National Curriculum into their thinking and to serve their own purposes through it. In the process they collectively reasserted their own sense of control over and personal identification with the school curriculum . . . (Nias *et al.*, 1989, pp. 49–50)

Teachers used the new opportunities 'to increase their own learning and, through the acquisition of new knowledge and skills, to expand their own classroom potential' (ibid.). Whether this control is still being sustained as assessment pressures come to bear is another matter. For the moment, however, these teachers are continuing to feel that they 'own' the curriculum for which they are responsible. Nias *et al.*, give the examples of science, technology and mathematics in three of the schools where the staff have adapted what otherwise might have been seen as an external constraint to their own educational concerns.

Even more to the point, perhaps, is the extent to which children will feel that they own and control their own learning. The place of the constructivist learning theory underpinning the events depicted here is not clear in the National Curriculum. To Pollard (1991b), for example, it seems more behaviourist in orientation. The learning path is seen as external to the pupils along which they are to be channelled and directed, in what Hammersley (1977a, p. 38) has described as 'discipline-based' teaching. However, as Pollard (1991b, p. 41) says, 'It remains to be seen to what extent constructivist models of learning can be incorporated into the new structures so that children are given opportunities to control parts of their own curriculum. It is certain, though, that primary teachers will work very hard on this'. As Pollard (pp. 60–5) shows, certain constructivist activities in primary schools cover a range of National Curriculum topics and promote learning in 'real' and meaningful ways. In fact, Watts and Bentley (1991, p. 171) go so far as to claim that 'constructivism is to be found as the root rationale behind parts of the National Curriculum' — especially science. However 'assessment it would seem, is much more about conformity to orthodox ideas' (ibid., p. 179). They conclude that 'collaboration with teachers is needed, to take the work forward in revision of the National Curriculum itself (ibid., p. 180).

It is still, therefore, too early to say what the effect of recent changes on classroom teaching will be. There are some positive, some negative effects. There is divided opinion about whether teachers are being de-skilled or en-skilled. There is some of each in the fall-out. Most would agree, perhaps, that things are still in a state of flux. There is still room, perhaps, for educational argument. Simon (1990, p. 40) argues that we must 'grasp back from the politicians the central area of teaching and learning in our schools'. Another rallying call comes from Drummond (1991, p. 120) who urges teachers 'not to see our child-centred principles nibbled away at, corrupted, abandoned. This involves being clear about what it is we will stand for through thick and thin . . . It is only this clarity, this principled understanding, that will sustain us in the tug-or-war between the requirements of the 1988 Act and the need to conserve our child-centred heritage'. She points to learning as an emotional enterprise, and to curriculum being based on human relationships, not just cognitive development. 'Unless we are careful', Whitehead (1947, p. 196) wrote 'we shall organize genius right out of existence'. This book is offered as a contribution to an antidote to that tendency, testimony to the genius of teachers and pupils and how it can flourish under the right conditions.

Appendix

Researching Critical Events

One of the problems in researching these activities was in employing ethnographic methods, which I judged to be the most suitable in this kind of research, for matters that had happened in the past. The long-term engagement in the situation as things actually happen, which is one of the most prominent features of the approach, was not possible here. Another problem was in identifying and characterizing the criticality. I hoped to capture the emotional and aesthetic import of the experience and to represent it as felt by the participants. A third concern was how to maximize any benefits from the research for teacher, pupil and educational development. In this article, I explore some of the main approaches used in meeting these questions.

Historical Ethnography

It is difficult to study critical events as they are happening. This would be ideal, since not only would the process be observed at first hand, but comparative studies could be undertaken of events that worked to differing degrees of success. Invariably, however, the subject for study cannot be identified until it has occurred. As Kelchtermans (1991, p. 7) has observed, with regard to critical incidents, 'The "critical" character of an event is defined by the respondent . . . events can only become "critical incidents" afterwards, retrospectively'. Therefore it is not possible to make a general list of potential, critical incidents. Hence the need for historical ethnography. This is the exploration of events that have occurred in the past, using qualitative, naturalistic methods that aim to explore meanings and understandings and re-create cultures and contexts in the evocative manner typical of ethnography. The chief methods are extensive interviewing; use of documentary evidence, such as tapes, film, reports, children's work, all made at the time of the event; and visiting scenes. A measure of observation was involved, especially in witnessing several celebratory functions. By comparing a number of such events, it is possible to see what they have in common.

Among the advantages of historical ethnography is that the 'progressive focusing' (Hammersley and Atkinson, 1983) has already been done to some extent, and one can go ahead immediately to 'saturate' (Glaser and Strauss, 1967) knowledge of particular aspects of the event. The event is clearly demarcated, integrated and developed, and participants are able to reflect on the event in its entirety and in more general educational context. Because these are such notable events, there tends to be a great deal of evidence available. Lots of people know about them, and are eager to share their experiences. There were none of the traditional difficulties that occur when negotiating access (Burgess, 1991). Indeed I had a sense that my enquiry was seen as integral to the event. My activity seemed in some ways to be part of the celebration, but leading mainly to a new evaluation/recording phase.

Historical ethnography as an approach is not to be confused with what Rist (1980) has termed 'blitzkrieg ethnography', involving just two or three days of fieldwork, nor with those studies which isolate outcomes from processes or a small subdivision from a larger whole. Nor is it the 'condensed fieldwork' that Walker (1986) recommends, since the rationale for that was more or less immediate feedback to the teachers concerned in order to inform their teaching. While feedback was seen as important, it was never conceived of as anything close to 'immediate'. It lacks the classical ethnographic character of studying processes as they occur over a lengthy period, but other salient features are in place. What it loses in time, it makes up for, to some extent, in intensity. It retains the focus on natural settings with film, tape, witness and visit; and it employs multi-methods, and time, people and place sampling (Ball, 1990) to enrich the description and enhance the validity. There is the same employment of multi-methods in the attempt to build up the picture as it was experienced by participants. There is the same emphasis on trust and rapport, and while in traditional ethnography this takes time to develop, it was quickly established in these cases. The critical event embraced us all. Having been granted entrance, I was a member of the club, membership then being consolidated by the lengthy conversations that took place.

The initial burst of interviewing took place over two or three days. All were followed up in some form or other, both extending the range of interviews, and intensifying the discussion with the major participants. In the case of the headteacher involved in the event described in Chapter 2, the detailed discussions have led in the three years of our association to a full-scale life history. This further illustrates the earlier point about the importance of these events within these teachers' lives. In general, they drew on their biographies extensively to explain the meaning of the event to them (see also Goodson, 1991). Life history techniques were used here, building on previous work in Woods (1987, 1990a) and Sikes, Measor and Woods (1985). The schools, teachers and some of the pupils involved in the events in Chapters 3, 4 and 5 have all been re-visited, and their current opinions and perspectives on the event sought — another form of triangulation.

The interview, therefore, is seen as a process involving pre- and post-interview strategies and reflection, and several and varied interviews among a range of people connected with the event as they, together, progressively over time *construct* an account of the event. Between them they re-create and analyse the event in three respects bearing on (a) information-gathering, (b) evoking the past, conveying feelings associated with the event, and (c) testing out various explanations, which then become grounded in the data. A succession of interviews, talks or conversations (Woods, 1985) took place, therefore, generally until no new material or thoughts were being generated (Glaser and Strauss, 1967).

Collaboration

There has been considerable interest in collaborative research between teachers and researchers recently (Carr and Kemmis, 1986; Hustler *et al.*, 1986; Day, 1991; Louden, 1991; Biott and Nias, 1992). This research was in this broad tradition. Just as the teacher as critical agent coordinated the event, I coordinated the research. Like the events, it is a collective product. I have collected, selected and organized the material and written the accounts, but I have tried to remain faithful to teachers' perceptions. The events are not written-up as an outsider looking in, with the traditional analytical distance, but from the inside, combining my own 'researcher-mode' form of appraisal with the 'reflective practitioner' mode of the teachers. I have argued the strengths of this combination elsewhere (Woods and Pollard, 1988). The approach will not work with teachers who are more 'technical rationalist' (Schön, 1983) in orientation.

'Critical-agent' teachers were something more in this case than the 'traditional informant'. They were providing not only a vast range of information, but their own considered evaluation. They have a number of qualifications as evaluators. Firstly, they are highly credible people, concerned to get accounts right. They want proof for claims made, and are not content with first impressions. Secondly, they were centrally involved and possess detailed and wide knowledge of the event, more than anybody else, and certainly more than people from outside could have. As Egan (1992, pp. 149–50) has observed, in judging how successful we have been in engaging students' imaginations, extending the range of their emotional sensitivity and human understanding, 'the finest instrument we have for evaluating degrees of success in such a unit is the teachers' sensitive observation.' They have experienced it as participant observers, seeing, thinking, feeling, discussing at first hand. But they have not just been involved, for there are times when, thirdly, they have been detached, and reflected on the event at a distance as it were, in discussion with others, in writing reports, or in considering the implications for the improvement of their own teaching. As 'reflective practitioners' (Schön, 1983), they cast a critical eye over their work. If it is not being productive they want to know why. They are able to confront (Smyth, 1991) normal processes and ask 'why' questions as well as 'how' ones. They bring a certain rigour to their self-appraisal. Their claims have to be supported and put to the test, just like the researcher's. This leads to the fourth point, for they have already collected a considerable amount of evidence in the form of pupils' work; taped, photographed or filmed recordings of teaching episodes; letters, diaries, reviews and so forth; records of discussions with pupils and 'critical others'; and field notes that log the structure and processes of the event. This forms part of the corpus of evidence together with that collected independently by the researchers, and with the testimony and judgments of others. Fifthly, their evaluation can be compared to the evaluation of others, some of whom might have been involved in the project, some not — such as pupils, parents, members of the community, inspectors, education officers, other professionals with a particular interest, education correspondents, academics.

The collaboration, therefore, was not consensual in the sense that accounts from either side were accepted beyond question. When I began the study of each event, certain analytical frameworks were already in place. I provided a means of testing these, by comparing them with the views of others, and with an assessment of the evidence. I could bring in another comparative element from my work on the other, related events, and experience generally. My description and analysis was then tested against their, and others', understandings. I wrote a draft, and sent copies to critical agents and critical others for comment. Some factual inaccuracies were corrected and some missing information provided. In some cases, further interviews were held. In this manner the event was reconstructed between us.

Considerable attention has been paid in recent years to giving teachers 'voice' (Elbaz, 1991; Goodson, 1991). A Hargreaves (1991c) summing up this line of argument, states, 'Failure to understand the teacher's voice is failure to understand the teacher's teaching. For this reason, our priority should be not merely to listen to the teacher's voice, but also to sponsor it as priority . . .' (p. 11). To this might be added the need for that voice to be given the opportunity to speak of processes, of what actually happens, and not just characteristics of their teaching style, job satisfaction etc. In research terms, this means seeing teachers less as objects and subjects of research, and more as people who have something to say of worth in its own right. They are, in a sense, co-research workers, with equal rights, and subject to the same strictures, concerning, for example, the burden of proof, as researchers. This is empowering in at least two senses. First, they share in the construction of the account. Critical theorists have pointed to the power enjoyed by researchers and authors in setting agendas and writing the report (Smyth, 1991). Teachers are often seen as 'material to be used'. While independent research into their public practice is a legitimate pursuit, there are occasions when joint enquiry is indicated. These occasions will be more often rather than less if one's aims include educational improvement, since this has to be done through teachers. Secondly, in researching the event in collaboration with an external researcher they have deepened, integrated, and codified the account, and added to the legitimation of the practice. Schön (1984, p. 43) argues that, for professionals, 'a crucially important dimension [of their work] . . . tends to remain private and inaccessible to others'. Smyth (1991, p. 28) points out that 'because awareness of our own thinking usually grows out of the process of articulating it to others, as practitioners we often have little access to our own reflection-in-action'. In encouraging articulation and externalization, the research, one might claim, promoted identification and ownership of that particular kind of knowledge. It enabled them, also, in Clark's (1992, p. 93) terms to 'blow their own trumpet', not in a 'showing off' way, but in 'confronting and answering difficult questions like "What have I been doing lately that is worthwhile and interesting? What ideas and insights have I had that might be useful to others? How do I want to frame and remember the positive side of this year?"' It means 'making coherent and public the ways in which your professional development is developing'. The research, in other words, contributed to the criticality.

Connelly and Clandinin (1990), in their work on teacher narrative claim that, 'in our story telling, the stories of our participants merged with our own to create new stories, ones that we have labelled *collaborative stories*. The thing finally written on paper (is) . . . a mutually constructed story created out of the lives of both researcher and participant' (p. 12). Similarly, they both take part in the process — 'the narratives of participant and researcher become, in part, a shared narrative construction and reconstruction through the enquiry' (p. 205). To this collaboration in process and product might be added an initial affinity in values. In this respect I might be considered a late entrant to the group 'communitas' spoken of earlier. I sympathize with the education philosophy, teaching approach and style of management espoused by these teachers. No doubt this was a factor in the selection of events, and in the rapport that was established. There was a communality of aim, therefore, and of spirit. I was almost as excited by these events as they were. In a way they were critical events for me also, in the confirmatory sense. They were all providing evidence in their different ways of the efficacy of an approach with which I identified, but which had recently come under attack; and illustrates the possibilities that existed within the system if only certain conditions applied. I played a dual role, therefore, of involvement — trying to get as close to people's understandings and feelings about their experience as possible, by almost becoming one of them (a kind of historical participant observer!); and of detachment — in trying to gain a view of the whole, and introducing some forms of analysis.

Evaluation

Evaluation as well as research and teacher development was also a prominent aspect of the enquiry. I was concerned both to generate theory from the case studies, intrigued by the nature and functions of critical events; to aid teachers in their reflectivity; and to evaluate the events as educational activities. These modes of enquiry are often separated in the literature as discrete activities. I find it difficult to separate them. Understanding their nature enhances one's appreciation of the effects of critical events. Being concerned with a number of them permitted generalization, and the development of the concept beyond the particular instance of it. Particular cases can then be compared to the general model. Its properties provide a hypothetical framework for the analysis.

Yet though the events had common properties, they were also unique — a prominent feature of their criticality. There will be other critical events in their lives, but not quite like this one. It is necessary, therefore, to bring out its special quality, to try to capture its spirit. This, however, is not easy since it is to do with emotionally charged aesthetic appreciation which is not readily translated into words (D. Hargreaves, 1983). Yet the highly articulate teachers and pupils involved in these events did their best to capture, or re-capture the essential likeness.

It will be seen that this is an artistic pursuit. The enquiry had certain scientific properties in its concern for a range of sampling among the participants, the use of multi-methods, exhaustive interviewing, cross-checking of accounts, continuous comparative analysis at various levels, and theory-generation. These largely apply to the sociological product. As an educational activity, however, one has to focus on what Eisner (1985) calls the 'expressive objective'. This is

> an outcome of an activity planned by the teacher on the student which is designed not to lead the student to a particular goal or form of behaviour but, rather, to forms of thinking-feeling-acting that are his own making. The expressive curriculum activity is evocative rather than prescriptive, and is intended to yield outcomes which, although educationally valuable, are not prescribed or defined beforehand. The task of the teacher is to look back, as it were, to evaluate what happened to the student rather than to ask whether the student achieved '90 per cent

mastery of a set of items placed before him during a forty-minute period'. The expressive activity is one in which the creative personalistic use of skills gained in instructional activities can be employed, developed and refined. The expressive objective is the outcome of such activities. (Eisner, 1985, p. 77)

Eisner identifies a third kind of objective, one that lies between instrumental and expressive, and that provides a clearly specified brief, but leaves the range of possible solutions open. The teacher is encouraged to provide 'high degrees of structure in setting the problem' but leaves 'the avenues for potential solutions wide open' (p. 79). Evaluation here takes the form of an appraisal after the enquiry of 'the relative merit of solution to the objective formulated'.

Both these types involve artistic activity. Eisner believes that educational evaluators should not 'seek recipes to control and measure practice, but rather to enhance whatever artistry the teacher can achieve'. (p. 91) Diagnostic (not prescriptive) theory can help in the cultivation of what Eisner calls 'educational connoisseurship', basically 'the art of appreciation', and 'educational criticism' which is 'the art of disclosure'. The latter is no straightforward task, for it involves the expression of the ineffable. The task of the critic is 'to adumbrate, suggest, imply, connote, render . . . In this task, metaphor and analogy, suggestion and implication are major tools . . . The task of the critic is to help us to see' (pp. 92–1).

This research is within this mould. As a collaborative activity, the teacher — and pupils — were also involved in 'connoisseurship' and 'criticism'. The enquiry aimed to round up and draw out a range of views and materials on the event. It sought to aid teachers in their own reflection and criticism. It gave voice to pupils as well as to teachers. Who are better qualified to speak of their own learning? As Nias (1989a, p. 205) says, 'teachers rely in the last resort for recognition upon their pupils, for no one else knows, or can know, how effectively they have taught' (see also Guba and Lincoln, 1981; Riseborough, 1985; Sikes *et al.*, 1985). On the political front also there is a case to be made for collaboration with pupils. As Qvortrup (1990, p. 94) argues, 'If we seriously mean to improve life conditions for children we must, as a minimum precondition, establish reporting systems in which they are heard themselves as well as reported on by others'.

This is a very modest demand of, or on behalf of, a population group which at a societal level is mute, and is being kept mute by adults, the dominant group' (see also Rowland, 1987). Pupils are heard here, therefore, quite strongly. They even shared in the analysis presented in Chapters 1 and 4.

The research aimed to be a creative activity in itself. Firstly, in collating the responses an integrated whole was externalized. Secondly, in seeking to 'articulate the ineffable' and pursuing this as far as possible, meanings and understandings were enhanced. It was not a matter, simply, of collecting information and opinions. The participants were encouraged to plumb the depths of their subconsciousness and to experiment with words and phraseology to find the formula to embody and convey their experience and feelings. Here, one is trying to 'exploit the potential of language as an artistic medium, not merely as a descriptive one'. (p. 141) The 'evaluator' acts as sounding-board here, and in following the usual interviewing techniques as recommended for example, by Dean and Whyte (1969), and responding to the interviewee, prompting, summarizing, putting a point into other words, tries to help elucidate and sharpen the teacher's own mind. 'I never even thought of it like that' said Sally (Chapter 5), 'but that's probably exactly what happened'. In this way, the evaluator hopes to be able to give a 'vivid rendering of how that game is played' (Eisner, 1985, p. 131), and 'to capture the richness of the consequences of wide forms of knowing' (p. 132). The idea is to do this so that 'the reader will be able to empathetically participate in the events described' (p. 138), and to experience with those involved their feelings, understandings, hopes, fears, triumphs, failures. With this in view, a large part of the story is told by the people who made it. This keeps faith also with the collaborative principle, seeking to present the account in their terms, and to ensure that their 'voice is heard to speak throughout the construction of the story' (Day, 1991, p. 545).

Respondent Validation

Lincoln and Guba (1985) argue that the standard for qualitative research where the objective is to reconstruct events and the perspectives of those being studied is the demonstration that the findings and the researchers' interpretations are credible to those who were involved. I was interested to find out, therefore, from the participants whether I had represented their views correctly and whether I had 'recaptured' the event as they knew it. The task as I saw it was an artistic as well as scientific one. It had to be accurate, but it also involved putting material together in such a way as to construct an integrated and coherent whole, and to convey the feel and excitement participants associated with it (Van Maanen, 1988). Since 'feel' is not a matter of words, this presented some difficulty, both for participants and for me. It is easy both to understate and overstate the case. Again, they could judge how closely I had represented their experience. What were my participants' responses?

Theresa Whistler wrote (Chapter 2), 'It is a most interesting and living memento of what was such a happy and absorbing experience — it brings back the very feel of it . . . what strikes me most is the great interest of having so many articulate and extended quotes from the children's own reflections looking back. I am astonished at the vividness and fullness of their memories . . .' She thought the group 'became very attracted by the chance to take this long reflective look at what they already know their lives would not have again . . . the project helped them to know themselves'. Melanie (Chapter 3) 'found it most exhilarating to have our work compared to the model of critical events,' and hoped the book 'will have some influence in the current trend away from projects'. Whilst she had done some interesting work with her pupils since the research, 'the video project still rates as tops for creative excitement and relationships with the children'. She went on, 'I have enjoyed reading your very able analysis of our project. It is interesting to see how, what seemed to be my own ideas of how to go about things, tally with certain educational theorists.' She was 'delighted with the overall structure, and feel very rewarded by your interest, and supported by the links with educational theory'.

Debbie Kerr (Chapter 4) read the draft 'with great interest', and was 'very happy with what you have written from Western's point of view and feel it reflects accurately our experience of the venture.' Pam Turner 'really enjoyed' reading the draft. Phil Turner thought it 'an excellent draft and an enjoyable read, contributing a great deal to their understanding of our environmental education project.' He was particularly impressed with 'the comments of other contributors'.

I had an opportunity to discuss with Peter his reaction to Chapter 2 at greater length . . . He was 'impressed by the authenticity' of the account. He referred, firstly, to the factual evidence, and the way this was 'carefully recorded and re-assembled in the script'. He noted 'the many and sometimes lengthy consultations we had had, the drafting and re-drafting, the gradual accumulation of evidence, the memory search over a lengthy period'. At a second level, he thought that the text had 'as far it is humanly possible, recaptured the ethos of the event, and the feelings, the emotions, all of the exhilaration, excitement, wonder, occasional frustrations and set-backs and how they were overcome, the pushing into new frontiers, the way in which we felt so different in this situation compared to school, all part and parcel of discovering and rediscovering our essential selves . . .' He had gained some new insights, particularly from what the students had said. They had been 'extremely enlightening', and this would have been 'essential reading' had he been going on with the project. This endorses the point made earlier about the benefits of pupil evaluation. He summarized his view on the text:

> You can re-live it intermittently over time, but what you've required me to do is to sit down, and over a period of time recall as many aspects of our experiences as I possibly could. You've put all this together and re-created almost in total in fact what actually happened. It's as if I was in possession of the pieces of a jigsaw which a long time ago had been complete but over a period of time had got scattered. As I found them again I gave them to you, and you've re-created the picture I originally had.

Several points are being conveyed by these comments. First, the accounts contain a certain truth in the perspectives of the participants. Then, their understanding of the event is heightened, particularly by the input of others and by the analysis using educational theory. They are pleased that something special in their teaching, and an unrepeatable experience, has received attention and been recorded. And they have derived reassurance and a sense of reward from my interest. This last point might be considered by some a further aid to validity — if, in fact, the participants were left stronger and better equipped to do their job in the ways they thought best. Peter, for one, said he welcomed being involved in the research as 'it helped give him a sense of proportion and balance at a time of confusion and uncertainty in schools'.

As noted earlier, the articulation of 'tacit knowledge' (Polanyi, 1958) leads to more definite ownership. The knowledge has been given shape and substance. However confident in one's own intuition, one must be more open to criticism from others and to moments of self-doubt without the benefit of articulation. As a teacher told me in another study, 'Now the more we talk about it, the more the uncertain things become, you know, fixed . . . it is mine. The minute I put it into words, *my* words, I've got it'. (Woods, 1987, p. 125)

Others benefit also. As Tyler (in Hosford, 1984) notes, 'the professional practice of teaching, as well as that of law, medicine and theology, is largely a product of the experience of practitioners, particularly those who are more creative, inventive and observant than the average' (p. 9). It might be claimed that this applies to the participants in this research, and that their 'putting it into words' helps others both in providing examples of exceptional professional activity, and in aiding their own self-reflection and efforts to articulate key, but hitherto unexpressed, aspects of their practice. This might be an example of what Fullan (1992, p. 120) terms 'interactive professionalism', operating not in a face-to-face situation, but in a more general sense of a profession keeping itself informed and marking new developments for general advancement. It is one way in which teachers would be 'continuous learners in a community of interactive professionals' (ibid.).

Though teachers' testimony was very important, it was subject to the same kinds of tests of validity as my own report would be. Thus, I have not included everything that I was told, points, for example, that were relayed at second or third hand, or that seemed otherwise to require substantiation that was not forthcoming. I was able to press for clarification, for example, for documentation, and to challenge things that did not ring true. I had both an insider and outsider role, the one taking me close to their experiences, the other distancing me from them and putting claims to critical test. This, I would argue, counters any suggestions of romanticism that might be made about these accounts, a point often made about the kind of teacher thinking involved when it is not put into action. Definitions of 'romanticism' include 'an imaginative lie', 'talking extravagantly or with an infusion of fiction', 'extravagant, wild, fantastic'. These events are some of these certainly. They are fantastic, magical in the sense of amazing, as I have defined it, they do involve imagination, a great deal of it, and sentiment. They are extravagant in the sense that they go beyond normal bounds. But they are not lies, or fiction, or wild. They are carefully controlled, they deal in real education, and, for those involved, strike an uncommon truth (see also Goodman and Goodman, 1990). The onus is on the researcher and writer to represent this extravagance accurately, neither more nor less than that experienced.

There is a sense, too, in which these evaluations are offered to the teaching community as providing some benchmarks for their own experiences, and for which they will bring these experiences to bear in considering. The validation, in part, is done by them as they assess the credibility of these cases through their own experience, their personal, practical knowledge and their private theories, and put them into practice in their own teaching with renewed confidence and vigour. This view of validity places emphasis on 'the insider's perspective', and follows logically from the principles of collaboration on which the research was based (Lather, 1986; Erickson, 1986; Lincoln and Guba, 1985). In identifying such cases in their own work, they may find something of value here in aiding their own reflectivity, and possibly bring something further to bear on the phenomenon. If it brings a measure of reassurance at a time of depression and sustains hope for an educational approach seen by many as currently under siege, then the book will have achieved its aim.

References

ALEXANDER, R.J. (1984) *Primary Teaching*, London, Holt, Rinehart and Winston.

ALEXANDER, R.J. (1992) *Policy and Practice in Primary Education*, London, Routledge.

ALEXANDER, R.J., ROSE, J. and WOODHEAD, C. (1992) *Curriculum Organisation and Classroom Practice in Primary Schools: a discussion paper*, London, Department of Education and Science, HMSO.

ANNING, A. (1991) *The First Years at School*, Milton Keynes, Open University Press.

AOKI, T.T. (1983) 'Experiencing ethnicity as a Japanese Canadian teacher: reflections on a personal curriculum', *Curriculum Inquiry*, **13**, 3, pp. 321–35.

APPLE, M.W. (1986) *Teachers and Texts: a political economy of class and gender relations in education*, New York, Routledge and Kegan Paul.

ARMSTRONG, M. (1980) *Closely Observed Children*, London, Writers and Readers.

ARMSTRONG, M. (1981) 'The case of Louise and the painting of landscape', in NIXON, J. (Ed) *A Teacher's Guide to Action Research*, London, Grant McIntyre.

ARMSTRONG, M. (1990) 'Does the national curriculum rest on a mistake?', in EVERTON, T., MAYNE, P. and WHITE, S. (Eds) *Effective Learning: into a new ERA*, London, Jessica Kingsley Publishers.

ATKINSON, P.A. (1975) 'In cold blood: bedside teaching in a radical school', in CHANAN, G. and DELAMONT, S. (Eds) *Frontiers of Classroom Research*, Slough, National Foundation for Educational Research.

ATKINSON, P. and DELAMONT, S. (1977) 'Mock-ups and Cock-ups: The Stage Management of Guided Discovery Instruction', in WOODS, P. and HAMMERSLEY, M. (Eds) School Experience, London, Croom Helm.

AVANN, P. (1982) 'Information skills teaching in primary schools: progress report on a Coventry survey', *Education Libraries Bulletin*, **25**, pp. 15–23.

BALL, D. (1972) 'Self and identity in the context of deviance: the case of criminal abortion', in SCOTT, R.A. and DOUGLAS, J.D. (Eds) *Theoretical Perspectives on Deviance*, New York, Basic Books.

BALL, S.J. (1980) 'Initial encounters in the classroom and the process of establishment', in WOODS, P. (Ed) *Pupil Strategies*, London, Croom Helm.

BALL, S.J. (1990) 'Self-doubt and soft data: social and technical trajectories in ethnographic fieldwork', *International Journal of Qualitative studies in Education*, **3**, 2, pp. 157–72.

BARRAULT, J.L. (1972) 'Best and worst of professions', in HODGSON, J. (1972) *The Uses of Drama*, London, Eyre Methuen.

BECKER, H. (1966) Introduction to Shaw, C.R. *The Jack-Roller*, Chicago, University of Chicago Press.

BENNETT, S.N., WRAGG, E.C., CARRÉ, C.G. and CARTER, D.S.G. (1992) 'A longitudinal study of primary teachers' perceived competence in, and concerns about, National Curriculum implementation', *Research Papers in Education*, **7**, 1, pp. 53–78.

BERGER, P.L. (1971) *A Rumour of Angels*, Harmondsworth, Penguin Books.

BERGER, P.L. and KELLNER, H. (1964) 'Marriage and the Construction of Reality', *Diogenes*, **46** (i), pp. 1–23.

BERGER, P. and LUCKMANN, T. (1967) *The Social Construction of Reality: a treatise in the sociology of knowledge*, Harmondsworth, Penguin.

BEST, D. (1991) 'Creativity: education in the spirit of enquiry', *British Journal of Educational Studies*, **34**, 3, pp. 260–78.

BIOTT, C. and NIAS, J. (Eds) (1992) *Working and Learning Together for Change*, Milton Keynes, Open University Press.

BLACKIE, P. (1980) 'Not Quite Proper', in REEDY, S. and WOODHEAD, M. (Eds) *Family, Work and Education*, London, Hodder and Stoughton.

BLAUNER, R. (1964) *Alienation and Freedom*, Chicago, University of Chicago Press.

BLOOME, D. (1987) 'Reading as a social process in a middle school classroom', in BLOOME, D. (Ed) *Literacy and Schooling*, Norwood, Ablex.

BOLTON, G. (1984) *Drama as Education*, London, Longman.

BONNETT, M. (1991) 'Developing children's thinking . . . and the National Curriculum', *Cambridge Journal of Education*, **21**, 3, pp. 277–92.

BRICE-HEATH, S. (1982) 'Questioning at home and at school: a comparative study', in SPINDLER, G. (Ed) *Doing the Ethnography of Schooling: Education Anthropology in Action*, New York, Holt, Rinehart and Winston.

BRIGHOUSE, T. (1990) 'What does it mean to the youngster?', in BRIGHOUSE, T. and MOON, R. (Eds) *Managing the National Curriculum: some critical perspectives*, London, Longman.

BROADFOOT, P., ABBOTT, D., CROLL, P., OSBORN, M., POLLARD, A. and TOWLER, L. (1991) 'Implementing National Assessment: issues for primary teachers', *Cambridge Journal of Education*, **21**, 2, pp. 153–68.

BRUNER, J.S. (1983) *Child's Talk*, London, Oxford University Press.

BRUNER, J.S. (1986) *Actual Minds, Possible Worlds*, Harvard, Harvard University Press.

BRUNER, J.S. and Haste, H. (1987) *Making Sense*, London, Methuen.

BURGESS, R.G. (1991) 'Sponsors, gatekeepers, members, and friends: access in educational settings', in SHAFFIR, W.B. and STEBBINGS, R.A. (Eds) *Experiencing Fieldwork*, London, Sage.

CAMPBELL, R.J., EVANS, L., ST. J. NEILL, S.R. and PACKWOOD, A. (1991) *Workloads, Achievements and Stress: two follow-up studies of teacher time in Key Stage 1*, Policy Analysis Unit, Department of Education, University of Warwick.

CAMPBELL, R.J. and ST. J. NEILL, S.R. (1990) *Thirteen Hundred and Thirty Days*, Final report of a pilot study of teacher time in Key Stage 1, commissioned by the Assistant Masters and Mistresses Association.

CARR, W. and KEMMIS, S. (1986) *Becoming Critical*, Lewes, Falmer Press.

CARR, W. (1989) *Quality in Teaching: arguments for a reflective profession*, London, Falmer Press.

CARRINGTON, B. and SHORT, G. (1989) *'Race' and the Primary School*, Slough, NFER-Nelson.

CLARK, C.M. (1990) 'What you can learn from applesauce: a case of qualitative inquiry in use', in EISNER, E. and PESHKIN, A. (Eds) *Qualitative Inquiry in Education*, New York, Teachers College Press.

CLARK, C.M. (1992) 'Teachers as designers in self-directed professional development', in HARGREAVES, A. and FULLAN, M.G. (Eds) *Understanding Teacher Development*, London, Cassell.

CLARK, D. (1987) 'The concept of community education', in ALLEN, S., BASTIANI, J., MARTIN, I. and RICHARDS, K. (Eds), *Community Education: an agenda for reform*, Milton Keynes, Open University Press.

COLLINGWOOD, R.G. (1966) 'Expressing one's emotions', in EISNER, E.W. and ECKER, D.W. (Eds) *Readings in Art Education*, Lexington, MA., Xerox College Publishing.

CONNELL, R.W. (1985) *Teachers' Work*, London, Allen and Unwin.

CONNELLY, F.M. and CLANDININ, D.J. (1985) 'Personal practical knowledge and the modes of knowing: relevance for teaching and learning', in EISNER, E. (Ed) *Learning and Teaching and Ways of Knowing*, NSSE Yearbook, Chicago, University of Chicago Press.

CONNELLY, F.M. and CLANDININ, D.J. (1990) 'Stories of experience and narrative enquiry', *Educational Researcher*, **19**, 5, pp. 2–14.

DADDS, M. (1992) 'Monty Python and the three wise men', *Cambridge Journal of Education*, **22**, 2, pp. 129–41.

DAY, C. (1991) 'Roles and relationships in qualitative research on teachers' thinking: a reconsideration', *Teaching and Teacher Education*, **7**, 5/6, pp. 537–47.

DEAN, J.P. and WHYTE, W.F. (1969) 'How do you know if the informant is telling the truth?', in McCALL, G.J. and SIMMONS, J. (Eds) *Issues in Participant Observation*, Reading, MA., Adison-Wesley.

DEPARTMENT OF EDUCATION AND SCIENCE (1989) *Standards in Education 1987–88*, London, HMSO.

DEPARTMENT OF EDUCATION AND SCIENCE (1989, 1990) Series of HMI reports entitled: *The Implementation of the National Curriculum in Primary Schools*, London, HMSO.

DESFORGES, C. (1990) 'Understanding learning for teaching', *Westminster Studies in Education*, pp. 17–29.

DEWEY, J. (1934) *Art as Experience*, New York, Minton Balch and Co.

DONALDSON, M. (1978) *Children's Minds*, London, Fontana.

DRUMMOND, M.J. (1991) 'The child and the primary curriculum — from policy to practice', *The Curriculum Journal*, **2**, 2, pp. 115–24.

EDWARDS, D. and MERCER, N. (1987) *Common Knowledge: the development of understanding in the classroom*, London, Methuen.

EGAN, K. (1990) *Romantic Understanding: the development of rationality and imagination, ages 8–15*, London, Routledge.

EGAN, K. (1992) *Imagination in Teaching and Learning: ages 8–15*, London, Routledge.

EISNER, E.W. (1979) *The Educational Imagination*, London, Collier MacMillan.

EISNER, E.W. (1985) *The Art of Educational Evaluation: A Personal View*, Lewes, Falmer Press.

ELBAZ, F. (1991) 'Research on teachers' knowledge: the evolution of a discourse', *Journal of Curriculum Studies*, **23**, 1, pp. 1–19.

ENVIRONMENTAL BOARD (1979) *Environmental Education in Urban Areas*, London, HMSO.

ERICKSON, F. (1986) 'Qualitative methods of research on teaching', in WITTOCK, M. (Ed) *Handbook of Research on Teaching*, New York, MacMillan.

FOWLER, W.S. (1990) *Implementing the National Curriculum: the policy and practice of the 1988 Education Reform Act*, London, Kogan Page.

FREIRE, P. (1970) *Pegagogy of the Oppressed*, New York, Seabury.

FRY, D. (1985) *Children Talk About Books: seeing themselves as readers*, Milton Keynes, Open University Press.

FULLAN, M. (1982) *The Meaning of Educational Change*, Columbia, New York, Teachers' College Press.

FULLAN, M.G. (1992) *Successful School Improvement*, Milton Keynes, Open University Press.

FULLAN, M. and HARGREAVES, A. (1992) *What's Worth Fighting For in Your School?*, Milton Keynes, Open University Press.

GALTON, M. (1989) *Teaching in the Primary School*, London, David Fulton Publishers.

GALTON, M. and WILLIAMSON, J. (1992) *Group Work in the Primary Classroom*, London, Routledge.

GAMMAGE, P. (1990) 'Primary Education: where are we now?', in PROCTOR, N. (Ed) *The Aims of Primary Education and the National Curriculum*, London, Falmer Press.

GEERTZ, C. (1973) *The Interpretation of Cultures: Selected Essays by Clifford Geertz*, New York, Basic Books.

GERSHMAN, K. (1988) 'Surviving through time: a life history of a high-school drama production', *International Journal of Qualitative Studies in Education*, 1, 3, pp. 239–62.

GLASER, B.G. and STRAUSS, A.L. (1967) *The Discovery of Grounded Theory*, London, Weidenfeld and Nicolson.

GLASER, B.G. and STRAUSS, A.L. (1971) *Status Passage*, Chicago, Aldine.

GOODMAN, Y.M. and GOODMAN, K.S. (1990) 'Vygotsky in a whole-language perspective', in MOLL, L.C. (Ed) *Vygotsky and Education: instructional implications and applications of sociohistorical psychology*, Cambridge, Cambridge University Press.

GOODSON, I.F. (1991) 'Sponsoring the teacher's voice: teachers' lives and teacher development', *Cambridge Journal of Education*, 21, 1, pp. 35–45.

GRUGEON, E. and WOODS, P. (1990) *Educating All: multicultural perspectives in the primary school*, London, Routledge.

GUBA, E.G. and LINCOLN, Y.S. (1981) *Effective Evaluation*, San Francisco, Jossey-Bass.

HALL, E.T. (1984) *The Dance of Life*, New York, Anchor Press/Doubleday.

HAMMERSLEY, M. (1977a) 'Teacher Perspectives', Units 9–10 of Course E202, *Schooling and Society*, Open University Press, Milton Keynes.

HAMMERSLEY, M. (1977b) 'School learning: the cultural resources required by pupils to answer a teacher's question', in WOODS, P. and HAMMERSLEY, M. (Eds) *School Experience*, London, Croom Helm.

HAMMERSLEY, M. and ATKINSON, P. (1983) *Ethnography: Principles in Practice*, London, Tavistock.

HARDING, D.W. (1977) 'Psychological processes in the reading of fiction', in MEEK, M. *et al.* (Ed) *The Cool Web*, London, Bodley Head.

HARDY, G. (1977) 'Narrative as a primary act of mind', in MEEK, M. (Ed) *The Cool Web*, London, Bodley Head.

HARGREAVES, A. (1978) 'Towards a Theory of Classroom Strategies', in BARTON, L. and MEIGHAN, R. (Eds) *Sociological Interpretations of Schooling and Classrooms*, Driffield, Nafferton Books.

HARGREAVES, A. (1986) *Two Cultures of Schooling: The Case of Middle Schools*, Lewes, Falmer Press.

HARGREAVES, A. (1988) 'Teaching Quality: a sociological analysis', *Journal of Curriculum Studies*, **20**, 3, pp. 211–31.

HARGREAVES, A., BAGLIN, E., HENDERSON, P., LEESON, P. and TOSSELL, T. (1988) *Personel and Social Education: choices and challenges*, London, Blackwell.

HARGREAVES, A. (1990) 'Teachers' work and the politics of time and space', *International Journal of Qualitative Studies in Education*, **3**, 4, pp. 303–20.

HARGREAVES, A. (1991a) 'Teacher preparation time and the intensification thesis', Conference of the American Educational Research Association, Chicago, Illinois, (3–7 April).

HARGREAVES, A. (1991b) 'Curriculum reform and the teacher', *The Curriculum Journal*, **2**, 3, pp. 249–58.

HARGREAVES, A. (1991c) 'Restructuring restructuring: postmodernity and the prospects for educational change', Unpublished paper, Ontario Institute for Studies in Education.

HARGREAVES, A. and TUCKER, E. (1991) 'Teaching and guilt: exploring the feelings of teaching', *Teaching and Teacher Education*, **7**, 5/6, pp. 491–505.

HARGREAVES, D.H. (1982) *The Challenge for the Comprehensive School*, London, Routledge and Kegan Paul.

HARGREAVES, D.H. (1983) 'The teaching of art and the art of teaching: towards an alternative view of aesthetic learning', in HAMMERSLEY, M. and HARGREAVES, A. (Eds) *Curriculum Practice: Some Sociological Case Studies*, Lewes, Falmer Press.

HARGREAVES, D.H. (1991) 'Coherence and manageability: reflections on the National Curriculum and cross-curricular provision', *The Curriculum Journal*, **2**, 1, pp. 33–41.

HARTLEY, D. (1985) *Understanding the Primary School: a sociological analysis*, London, Croom Helm.

HAYHOE, M. and PARKER, S. (1984) *Working With Fiction*, London, Arnold.

HEATHCOTE, D. (1970) 'How does drama serve thinking, talking and writing?', *Elementary English*, **47**, December, pp. 1077–81.

HEATHCOTE, D. (1972) 'Drama as challenge', in HODGSON, J. (Ed) *The Uses of Drama*, London, Eyre Methuen.

HER MAJESTY'S INSPECTORATE (HMI) (1991) *Education Observed: the implementation of the curricular requirements of ERA*, London, HMSO.

HILSUM, S. and CANE, B.S. (1971) *The Teacher's Day*, NFER, Windsor.

HIRST, P.H. and PETERS, R.S. (1970) *The Logic of Education*, London, Routledge and Kegan Paul.

HODGSON, J. (1972) 'Drama as a social and educational force', in HODGSON, J. (Ed) *The Uses of Drama*, London, Eyre Methuen.

HOLT, J. (1964) *How Children Fail*, Harmondsworth, Penguin.

HORTON, J. (1967) 'Time and cool people', *Transaction*, 6th April.

HOSFORD, P. (1984) *Using What We Know About Teaching*, Alexandria, VA., Association for Supervision and Curriculum Development.

HOYLE, E. (1980) 'Professionalization and deprofessionalization in education', in HOYLE, E. and MEGARRY, J. (Eds) *World Yearbook of Education 1980: professional development of teachers*, London, Kogan Page, pp. 42–54.

HUBERMAN, M. (1992) 'Critical introduction' to FULLAN, M. (Ed) *Successful School Improvement*, Milton Keynes, Open University Press.

HUBERMAN, M. and MILES, M. (1984) *Innovation Up Close*, New York, Plenum.

HUSTLER, D., CASSIDY, A. and CUFF, E.C. (Eds) (1986) *Action Research in Classrooms and Schools*, London, Allen and Unwin.

JACKSON, P.W. (1977) 'The way teachers think', in GLIDEWELL, J.C. (Ed) *The Social Context of Learning and Development*, New York, Gardner Press.

JONES, G. and HAYES, D. (1991) 'Primary headteachers and ERA two years on: the pace of change and its impact upon schools', *School Organization*, **11**, 2, pp. 211–22.

KELCHTERMANS, G. (1991) 'Teachers and their career story: a professional development', Paper presented at the *Fifth Conference of the International Study Association on Teacher Thinking*, Guildford (UK), 23–27 September.

KING, R.A. (1978) *All Things Bright and Beautiful*, Chichester, Wiley.

KING, R.A. (1989) *The Best of Primary Education: A Sociological Study of Junior Middle Schools*, Lewes, Falmer Press.

LACEY, C. (1977) *The Socialization of Teachers*, London, Methuen.

LARSON, S.M. (1980) 'Proletarianisation and educated labour', *Theory and Society*, **9**, 1, pp. 131–75.

LATHER, P. (1986) 'Research as praxis', *Harvard Educational Review*, **56**, 3, 257–77.

LAWSON, B. (1990) *How Designers Think: the design process demystified* (2nd edition), London, Butterworth Architecture.

LEE, J. (1915) *Play in Education*, London, MacMillan.

LEE, V. and LEE, J. (1987) 'Stories children tell', in POLLARD, A. (Ed) *Children and Their Primary Schools*, Lewes Falmer Press.

LINCOLN, Y.S and GUBA, E.G. (1985) *Naturalistic Inquiry*, New York, Sage.

LITTLE, J. (1990) 'Teachers as colleagues', in RICHARDSON-KOEHLER, V. (Ed) *Education Handbook*, New York, Longman.

LORTIE, D.C. (1975) *Schoolteacher*, Chicago, University of Chicago Press.

LOUDEN, W. (1991) *Understanding Teaching: continuity and change in teachers' knowledge*, London, Cassell.

LYMAN, S.M. and SCOTT, M.B. (1970) *A Sociology of the Absurd*, Appleton-Century-Crafts, New York.

McLAREN, P. (1986) *Schooling as a Ritual Performance*, London, Routledge and Kegan Paul.

MAROWITZ, C. (1978) *The Act of Being*, New York, Secker and Warburg.

MARTIN, I. (1987) 'Community education: towards a theoretical analysis', in ALLEN, G., BASTIANI, J., MARTIN, I. and RICHARDS, K. (Eds) *Community Education: an agenda for educational reform*, Milton Keynes, Open University Press.

MASLOW, A. (1973) *Further Reaches of Human Nature*, Harmondsworth, Penguin.

MEAD, G.H. (1934) *Mind, Self and Society*, Chicago, University of Chicago Press.

MEASOR, L. (1985) 'Critical incidents in the classroom: identities, choices and careers', in BALL, S.J. and GOODSON, I.F. (Eds) *Teachers;' Lives and Careers*, Lewes, Falmer Press.

MEASOR, L. and WOODS, P. (1984) *Changing Schools: pupil perspectives on transfer to a comprehensive*, Milton Keynes, Open University Press.

MEHAN, H. (1986) 'What time is it Denise? Asking known information questions in classroom discourse', in HAMMERSLEY, M. (Ed) *Case Studies in Classroom Research*, Milton Keynes, Open University Press.

MEIGHAN, R. (1991) *Unfashionably UnFascist? A selection of quotations on education*, Nottingham, Educational Heretics Press.

MOON, R. (1990) 'The National Curriculum: origins and context', in BRIGHOUSE, T. and MOON, R. (Eds) *Managing the National Curriculum*, London, Longman.

MORENO, J.L. (1964) *Psychodrama*, New York, Beacon House.

MORENO, J.L. (1972) 'Drama as therapy', in HODGSON, J. (Ed) *The Uses of Drama*, London, Eyre Methuen.

MUSGROVE, F. (1976) 'Marginality, education and the reconstruction of reality', *Journal of Curriculum Studies*, **8**, 2, pp. 101–9.

MUSGROVE, F. (1977) *Margins of the Mind*, London, Methuen.

NATIONAL CURRICULUM COUNCIL (1989) *A Framework for the Primary Curriculum*, York, National Curriculum Council.

NATIONAL CURRICULUM COUNCIL (1990a) *Curriculum Guidance 3*, York, National Curriculum Council.

NATIONAL CURRICULUM COUNCIL (1990b) *English Non-Statutory Guidance*, York, National Curriculum Council.

NIAS, J. (1987) 'One finger, one thumb: a case study of the deputy head's part in the leadership of a nursery/infant school', in SOUTHWORTH, G. (Ed) *Readings in Primary School Management*, Lewes, Falmer Press.

NIAS, J. (1988) 'Informal education in action: teachers' accounts', in BLYTH, W.A.L. (Ed) *Informal Primary Education Today*, Lewes, Falmer Press.

NIAS, J. (1989a) *Primary Teachers Talking: a study of teaching as work*, London, Routledge.

NIAS, J. (1989b) 'On the move: a case study of Upper Norton C of E Primary School, a school in transition, 1988–9', Cambridge Institute of Education mimeo.

NIAS, J. (1991) 'Changing times, changing identities: grieving for a lost self', in BURGESS, R. (Ed) *Educational Research and Evaluation*, London, Falmer Press!

NIAS, J., SOUTHWORTH, G. and CAMPBELL, P. (1992) *Whole School Curriculum Development in the Primary School*, London, Falmer Press.

NIAS, J., SOUTHWORTH, G. and YEOMANS, R. (1989) *Staff Relationships in the Primary School: a study of organizational cultures*, London, Cassell.

NISBET, R. (1962) 'Sociology as an art form', *Pacific Sociological Review*, Autumn.

NORQUAY, N. (1990) 'Life history research: memory, schooling and social difference', *Cambridge Journal of Education*, **20**, 30, pp. 291–300.

O'HAGAN, B. (1987) 'Community education in Britain: some myths and their consequences', in ALLEN, G., BASTIANI, J., MARTIN, I. and RICHARDS, K. (Eds) *Community Education: an agenda for educational reform*, Milton Keynes, Open University Press.

OSBORN, M. and BROADFOOT, P. (1992) 'A lesson in progress? Primary classrooms observed in England and France', *Oxford Review of Education*, **18**, 1, pp. 3–16.

OSBORN, M. and POLLARD, A. (1990) 'Anxiety and paradox: teachers' initial responses to change under the National Curriculum PACE', *Working Paper No. 4*, Bristol, Bristol Polytechnic.

PAISEY, H.A.G. (1975) *The Behavioural Strategy of Teachers*, Slough, NFER.

PERINBANAYAGAM, R. (1975) 'The significance of others in the thought of Alfred Schultz, G.H. Mead and C.H. Cooley', *The Sociological Quarterly*, **16**, pp. 500–21, Autumn.

PHILLIPS, E.M. (1980) 'Cognitive development and design education', *Design Education Research Note 4*, Milton Keynes, Open University.

PHILLIPS, E.M. (1982) 'Design education and the development of affect', *Design Education Research Note 10*, Milton Keynes, Open University.

PLOWDEN REPORT (1967) *Children and their Primary Schools*, Report of the Central Advisory Council for Education in England, London, HMSO.

POLANYI, M. (1958) *Personal Knowledge*, London, Routledge and Kegan Paul.

POLLARD, A. (1982) 'A model of coping strategies', *British Journal of Sociology of Education*, **3**, 1, pp. 19–37.

POLLARD, A. (1985) *The Social World of the Primary School*, London, Holt, Rinehart and Winston.

POLLARD, A. (Ed) (1987) *Children and Their Primary Schools*, Lewes, Falmer Press.

POLLARD, A. (1988) 'Reflective Teaching — The Sociological Contribution', in WOODS, P. and POLLARD, A. (Eds) *Sociology and Teaching*, London, Croom Helm.

POLLARD, A. (1990a) 'The aims of primary school teachers', in PROCTOR, N. (Ed) *The Aims of Primary Education and the National Curriculum*, London, Falmer Press.

POLLARD, A. (1990b) 'Towards a sociology of learning in primary schools', *British Journal of Sociology of Education*, **11**, 3, pp. 241–56.

POLLARD, A. (1991a) 'The child's place in a conflict of interests', *ASPE Conference Papers*.

POLLARD, A. (1991b) *Learning in Primary Schools*, London, Cassell.

PRAWAT, W.S. (1992) 'Teachers' beliefs about teaching and learning: a constructivist perspective', *American Journal of Education*, **100**, 13, pp. 354–95.

PRING, R. (1985) 'Personal development' in LANG, P. and MARLAND, M. (Eds) *New Directions in Pastoral Care*, Oxford, Blackwell.

PRING, R. (1987) 'Implications of the changing values and ethical standards of society', in THACKER, J., PRING, R. and EVANS, D. (Eds) *Personal, Social and Moral Education in a Changing World*, Windsor, NFER-Nelson.

PROTHEROUGH, R. (1983) *Developing Responses to Fiction*, Milton Keynes, Open University Press.

QVORTRUP, J. (1990) 'A voice for children in statistical and social accounting: a plea for children's right to be heard', in JAMES, A. and PROUT, A. (Eds) *Constructing and Reconstructing Childhood*, London, Falmer Press.

READ, H. (1966) 'The aesthetic method of education', in EISNER, E.W. and ECKER, D.W. (Eds) *Readings in Art Education*, Lexington, Mass., Xerox College Publishing.

REIMER, E. (1971) *School is dead: an essay on alternatives in education*, Harmondsworth, Penguin.

RISEBOROUGH, G.F. (1985) 'Pupils, teachers' careers and schooling: an empirical study', in BALL, S.J. and GOODSON, I.F. (Eds) *Teachers' Lives and Careers*, Lewes, Falmer Press.

RIST, R.C. (1980) 'Blitzkreig ethnography: on the transformation of a method into a movement', *Educational Researcher*, **9**, 2, pp. 8–10.

ROBINSON, K. (1991) 'Stop the art breaker', *Times Educational Supplement*, 29 November, p. 16.

ROSS, M. (1978) *The Creative Arts*, London, Heinemann.

ROSS, M. (Ed) (1982) *The Development of Aesthetic Experience*, Oxford, Pergamon.

ROTH, J. (1963) *Timetables*, New York, Bobbs-Merrill.

ROWLAND, S. (1984) *The Enquiring School*, Lewes, Falmer Press.

ROWLAND, S. (1987) 'Child in control: towards an interpretive model of teaching and learning', in POLLARD, S. (Ed) *Children and Their Primary Schools*, Lewes, Falmer Press.

RUDDUCK, J. (1985) 'The improvement of the art of teaching through research', *Cambridge Journal of Education*, **15**, 3, pp. 123–7.

RUSSELL, B. (1950) *Unpopular Essays*, London, Allen and Unwin.

SCHAEFER, R. (1967) *The School as a Centre of Inquiry*, London, Harper and Row.

SCHILLER, C. (1979) *Christian Schiller: in his own words*, London, Black.

SCHÖN, D.A. (1983) *The Reflective Practitioner: how professionals think in action*, London, Temple Smith.

Schön, D. (1984) 'Leadership as reflection-in-action', in SERGIOVANNI, T. and CORBALLY, J. (Eds) *Leadership and Organizational Culture: new perspectives on administrative theory and practice*, Urbane, Ill., University of Illinois Press.

SCHÖN, D. (1987) *Educating the Reflective Practitioner*, New York, Jossey-Bass.

SCHUTZ, A. (1964) 'The stranger: an essay in social psychology', in BRODERSEN, A. (Ed) *Collected Papers, II*, The Hague, Martinus Nijhoff, pp. 91–105.

SCHWAB, J.J. (1969) 'The practical: a language for curriculum', *School Review*, **78**, pp. 1–24.

SCHOOLS COUNCIL (1974) *Children's Growth through Creative Experience: art and craft education 8–13*, Van Nostrand Reinhold.

SHIPMAN, M.D. (1975) *The Sociology of the School*, 2nd edition, London, Longman.

SHORT, G. and CARRINGTON, B. (1987) 'Towards an anti-racist initiative in the all-white primary school: a case study', in POLLARD, A. (Ed) *Children and Their Primary Schools*, Lewes, Falmer Press.

SIKES, P., MEASOR, L. and WOODS, P. (1985) *Teacher Careers: crisis and continuities*, Lewes, Falmer Press.

SIMON, B. (1990) 'How to achieve effective learning in spite of the Education Reform Act', in EVERTON, T., MAYNE, P. and WHITE, S. (Eds) *Effective Learning: into a new Era*, London, Jessica Kingsley Publishers.

SLADE, P. (1968) *Experience of Spontaneity*, London, Longman.

SMYTH, J. (1991) *Teachers as Collaborative Learners*, Milton Keynes, Open University Press.

SPARKES, A.C. (1988) 'Strands of commitment within the process of teacher initiated innovation', *Educational Review*, **40**, 3, pp. 301–17.

STANISLAVSKI, C. (1972) 'Emotional involvement in acting', in HODGSON, J. (Ed) *The Uses of Drama*, London, Eyre Methuen.

STENHOUSE, L. (1975) *An Introduction to Curriculum Research and Development*, London, Heinemann.

STEWART, J. (1986) *The Making of the Primary School*, Milton Keynes, Open University Press.

STONE, G.P. (1962) 'Appearance and the self' in ROSE, A.M. (Ed) *Human Behaviour and Social Processes*, London, Routledge and Kegan Paul.

STRAUSS, A.L. (1959) *Mirrors and Masks: the search for identity*, Free Press, Glencoe.

STRAUSS, A. and CORBIN, J. (1990) *Basics of Qualitative Research: grounded theory procedures and techniques*, Newbury Park, Sage.

SWEETMAN, J. (1992) *Curriculum Confidential Two: the complete guide to the National Curriculum*, Newton Regis, Bracken Press.

TANN, C.S. (1988) 'The practice of topic work', in TANN, C.S. (Ed) *Developing Topic Work in the Primary School*, Lewes, Falmer Press.

TAWNEY, R.H. (1938) *Equality*, London, Allen and Unwin.

TICKLE, L. (1983) 'One spell of ten minutes or five spells of two . . .? Teacher-pupil encounters in art and design education', in HAMMERSLEY, M. and HARGREAVES, A. (Eds) *Curriculum Practice*, Lewes, Falmer Press.

TURNER, G. (1983) *The Social World of the Comprehensive School*, London, Croom Helm.

TURNER, V.W. (1974) *The Ritual Process*, Harmondsworth, Penguin Books.

TURNER, V.W. (1979) *Process, Performance and Pilgrimage*, New Delhi, Concept.

VAN MAANEN, J. (1988) *Tales of the Field*, Chicago, University of Chicago Press.

VYGOTSKY, L.S. (1956) *Izbrannie Psibhologicheskie Issledovania (Selected Psychological Research)*, Moscow, Izdateel'stro Akademii Pedagogicheskikh Nak.

VYGOTSKY, L.S. (1962) *Thought and Language*, Cambridge, MA, MIT Press.

VYGOTSKY, L.S. (1978) *Mind in Society: the development of higher psychological processes*, London, Harvard University Press.

WALKER, R. (1976) 'Innovation, the School and the Teacher (1)', Unit 27 of Course E203, *Curriculum Design and Development*, Milton Keynes, Open University Press.

WALKER, R. (1986) 'The conduct of educational case studies: ethics, theory and procedures', in HAMMERSLEY, M. (Ed) *Controversies in Classroom Research*, Milton Keynes, Open University Press.

WALLER, W.W. (1934) 'Insight and scientific method', *American Journal of Sociology*, **40**, 3, pp. 285–97.

WARNOCK, M. (1977) *Schools of Thought*, London, Faber.

WATTS, M. and BENTLEY, D. (1991) 'Construction in the curriculum. Can we close the gap between the strong theoretical version and the weak version of theory in practice?', *The Curriculum Journal*, **2**, 2, pp. 171–82.

WAY, B. (1967) *Development through Drama*, London, Longman.

WEBB, R. (1990) 'Information gathering in topic work: the pupil experience; in WEBB, R. (Ed) *Practitioner Research in the Primary School*, London, Falmer Press.

WHITEHEAD, A.N. (1947) *Essays in Science in Philosophy*, New York, Philosophical Library.

WINKLEY, D. (1990) 'A view from a primary school', in BRIGHOUSE, T. and MOON, R. (Eds) *Managing the National Curriculum: some critical perspectives*, London, Longman.

WOLFF, J. (1981) *The Social Production of Art*, London, Macmillan.

WOOD, D. (1986) 'Aspects of teaching and learning', in RICHARDS, M. and LIGHT, P. (Eds) *Children of Social Worlds*, Cambridge, Polity Press.

WOOD, D. (1988) *How Children Think and Learn*, Oxford, Basil Blackwell.

WOOD, D., BRUNER, J.S. and ROSS, G. (1976) 'The role of tutoring in problem solving', *Journal of Child Psychology and Child Psychiatry*, **17**, pp. 89–100.

WOODS, P. (1979) *The Divided School*, London, Routledge and Kegan Paul.

WOODS, P. (1985) 'Conversations with teachers: aspects of life history method', *British Educational Research Journal*, **11**, 1, pp. 13–26.

WOODS, P. (1987) 'Life-histories and teacher knowledge', in SMYTH, J. (Ed) *Educating Teachers—Changing the Nature of Professional Knowledge*, Lewes, Falmer Press.

WOODS, P. (1990a) *Teacher Skills and Strategies*, London, Falmer Press.

WOODS, P. (1990b) *The Happiest Days? How pupils cope with school*, London, Falmer Press.

WOODS, P. (1992) 'Symbolic interactionism: theory and method', in LECOMPTE, M.D. and GOETZ, J.P. (Eds) *The Handbook of Qualitative Research in Education*, New York, Academic Press.

WOODS, P. and POLLARD, A. (Eds) (1988) *Sociology and Teaching*, London, Croom Helm.

WRAGG, E.C. (1988) *Education in the Market Place*, London, NUT.

WRAGG, E.C. (1992) 'Accent on a common language', *National Curriculum: Observer Schools Report*, London, Observer, 6 September, p. 7.

WRAGG, E.C., BENNETT, S.N. and CARRÉ, C.G. (1989) 'Primary teachers and the National Curriculum', *Research Papers in Education*, **4**, 3, pp. 17–45.

WRIGHT, D. (1971) *The Psychology of Moral Behaviour*, Harmondsworth, Penguin.

YEOMANS, R. (1987) 'Making the large group feel small: primary teachers' classroom skills—a speculation', *Cambridge Journal of Education*, **17**, 3, pp. 161–6.

Name Index

Alexander, R.J. viii, 2, 3, 5, 7, 10, 37, 145, 154
Alexander, R.J., Rose, J. and Woodhead, C. 3, 10, 154, 155
Anning, A. 7, 154
Aoki, T.T. 26
Apple, M.W. 3
Armstrong, M. 4
Atkinson, P.A. 92
Atkinson, P.A. and Delamont, S. 146
Avann, P. 2

Ball, D. 70, 144
Ball, S.J. 2, 158
Barrault, J.L. 113, 123
Becker, H. 1
Bennett, S.N., Wragg, E.C., Carré, C.G. and Carter, D.S.G. 155
Berger, P.L. 26
Berger, P.L. and Kellner, H. 3
Berger, P.L. and Luckman, T. 147
Best, D. 4
Biott, C. and Nias, J. 6, 159
Blackie, P. 32, 121
Blauner, R. 147
Bloome, D. 142
Bolton, G. 116, 117, 118, 139
Bonnett, M. 5, 6
Brice-Heath, S. 28
Brighouse, T. 149
Broadfoot, P., Abbott, D., Croll, P., Osborne, M., Pollard, A. and Towler, L. 152
Bruner, J.S. 5, 7
Bruner, J.S. and Haste, H. 5
Burgess, R.G. 158

Campbell, R.J., Evans, L., St. J. Neill, S.R. and Packwood, A. 151
Campbell, R.J. and St. J. Neill, S.R. 151, 152
Carr, W. 2
Carr, W. and Kemmis, S. 159
Carrington, B. and Short, G. 12
Chippindale, F. 72, 92
Clark, C.M. 160
Clark, D. 52
Collingwood, R.G. 116
Connell, R.W. 2
Connelly, F.M. and Clandinin, D.J. 3, 160

Dadds, M. 149
Day, C. 159
Dean, J.P. and Whyte, W.F. 162
Department of Education and Science 2, 151, 155
Desforges, C. 10
Dewey, J. 5, 80, 149
Donaldson, M. 5, 11
Drummond, M.J. 156

Edwards, D. and Mercer, N. 5
Egan, K. 141, 146, 150, 159
Eisner, E.W. 2, 11, 13, 161, 162, 163
Elbaz, F. 160
Environmental Board 101
Erickson, F. 165

Fowler, W.S. 154
Freeman, C. 44, 58
Freire, P. 142
Fry, D. 116
Fullan, M. 6, 12, 152, 165
Fullan, M. and Hargreaves, A. 6

Galton, M. 4
Galton, M. and Williamson, J. 7, 155
Gammage, P. 2
Geertz, C. 111
Gershman, K. 9
Gibson, R. 15, 35
Glaser, B.G. and Strauss, A.L. 1, 112, 158
Goodman, Y.M. and Goodman, K.S. 142, 146, 165
Goodson, I.F. 158, 160
Grugeon, E. and Woods, P. 12, 135
Guba, E.G. and Lincoln, Y.S. 162

Hall, E.T. 147
Hammersley, M. 142, 152, 156
Hammersley, M. and Atkinson, P. 157
Harding, D.W. 116
Hardy, G. 116
Hargreaves, A. 3, 8, 10, 13, 56, 160
Hargreaves, A. and Tucker, E. 151
Hargreaves, A., Baglin, E., Henderson, P., Leeson, P. and Tossell, T. 117
Hargreaves, D.H. 4, 5, 69, 70, 117, 143, 161
Hartley, D. 6, 8
Hayhoe, M. and Parker, S. 116
Heathcote, D. 32, 116, 119, 124
Her Majesty's Inspectorate 154
Hewison, R. 104
Hilsum, S. and Cane, B.S. 151
Hirst, P.H. and Peters, R.S. 139
Hodgson, J. 115, 123
Holt, J. 10, 70
Horton, J. 147
Hosford, P. 164
Hoyle, E. 11
Huberman, M. 144
Huberman, M. and Miles, M. 144
Hustler, D. Cassidy, A. and Cuff, E.C. 159

Jackson, P.W. 11
Jones, G. and Hayes, D. 155

Kelchtermans, G. 157
King, R.A. 8, 10, 37

Lacey, C. 3
Larson, S.M. 3
Lather, P. 165
Lawson, B. 79
Lee, J. 118

Lee, V. and Lee, J. 69
Lincoln, Y.S. and Guba, E.G. 163, 165
Little, J. 6
Lortie, D.C. 56
Louden, W. 159
Lyman, S.M. and Scott, M.B. 147

McLaren, P. 2, 7, 147
Marowitz, C. 116
Martin, I. 57, 69
Maslow, A. 2
Mead, G.H. 2, 106
Measor, L. 1
Measor, L. and Woods, P. 18
Mehan, H. 142
Meighan, R. 10
Moon, R. 155
Moreno, J.L. 32, 106, 107, 123
Musgrove, F. 7, 26, 117

National Curriculum Council 70, 153
Neelands, J. 14, 31
Nias, J. 2, 4, 6, 7, 11, 56, 70, 143, 144, 146, 147, 152, 162
Nias, J., Southworth, G. and Campbell, P. 2, 6, 141, 146
Nias, J., Southworth, G. and Yeomans, R. 6, 11, 155, 156
Nisbet, R. 6
Norquay, N. 144

O'Hagan, B. 69
Osborn, M. and Broadfoot, P. 151
Osborn, M. and Pollard, A. 152

Paisey, H.A.G. 152
Perinbanayagam, R. 12
Piaget, J. 68, 145
Phillips, E.M. 79, 111
Plowden Report 4, 145, 149
Polanyi, M. 164
Pollard, A. 3, 5, 7, 8, 10, 13, 150, 152, 156, 157
Prawat, R.S. 9
Pring, R. 2, 69, 143
Protherough, R. 133

Qvortrup, J. 162

Read, H. 90
Reimer, E. 11
Renton, A. 104
Riseborough, G.F. 162

Rist, R.C. 158
Robinson, K. 150
Ross, M. 111, 124
Roth, J. 147
Rousseau, J.J. 149
Rowland, S. 4, 162
Rudduck, J. 11
Ruskin, J. 90
Russell, B. 6

Schaefer, R. 2
Schiller, C. 111
Schön, D.A. 2, 11, 12, 83, 159, 160
Schools Council 89
Schutz, A. viii
Schwab, J.J. 11
Shipman, M.D. 117
Short, G. and Carrington, B. 69
Sikes, P., Measor, L. and Woods, P. 1,
    2, 158, 162
Simon, B. 152, 156
Slade, P. 107
Smyth, J. 159, 160
Sparkes, A.C. 1
Stanislavski, C. 115, 116, 123
Stenhouse, L. 11
Stewart, J. 2
Stone, G.P. 114
Strauss, A.L. 1
Strauss, A.L. and Corbin, J. 1
Sweetman, J. 153

Tann, C.S. 2, 149
Tawney, R.H. 143
Tickle, L. 103
Turner, G. 28
Turner, V.W. 7, 26, 117

Van Maanen, J. 163
Vygotsky, L.S. 5, 145

Walford, G. 105
Walker, R. 1, 158
Waller, W.W. 6
Warnock, M. 150
Watts, M. and Bentley, D. 156
Way, B. 117
Webb, R. 154
Whitehead, A.N. 9, 156
Winkley, D. 149
Wolff, J. 89
Wood, D. 5, 11
Wood, D., Bruner, J.S. and Ross, G. 5
Woods, P. viii, 2, 3, 12, 13, 92, 138,
    142, 143, 147, 151, 158, 164
Woods, P. and Pollard, A.159
Wragg, E.C. 153, 155
Wragg, E.C., Bennett, S.N. and Carré,
    C.G. 155
Wright, D. 47

Yeomans, R. 117

Subject Index

ability 16, 18, 62, 74–6, 103, 137
age 7, 18, 44, 69, 142, 154
artist 17, 21, 24, 41
artistry 44–5, 52, 80, 124, 161–3 *see also* teaching as an art and teacher as artist

bureaucracy 28, 145, 149–50

celebration 8, 45, 69, 138, 142
childhood 14, 22–5, 36–7
collaboration 65, 146, 155, 159–61, 165
collaborative cultures 6–7, 146, 156
commitment 5, 11, 45, 105, 136, 149, 152, 154
communication 5, 50, 78–9, 85, 153, *see also* skills
communitas 6–8, 18, 43, 101, 117–24, 134–5, 148, 160–1
competition 12, 55, 122, 140, 145, 155
confidence 4, 16–7, 18, 29, 52–3, 56, 60, 68, 73–6, 110–1, 122, 141, 144–5, 165
content 37–8, 43, 128–33, 146
context 12, 21, 27–9, 64–6, 68, 90, 102, 145
connoisseurship 162
cooperation 12, 47, 68, 76–7, 91–2, 102, 120–2, 132, 142, 145
creativity viii, 23, 28, 41, 80, 88–91, 106–10, 121, 133–5, 137, 142, 148, 151–2, 154
critical
  agents 11–2, 25, 35–7, 43, 66–7, 95–8, 135–7, 146–7, 159–60
  incidents 1–2, 157
  others 12, 67–8, 98–9, 137–8, 146, 148, 159–60

democratic participation 12, 33, 60, 62–4, 133–5, 142, 149
designing 73–6, 79–81, 88–91
development
  emotional 111–6, 141
  personal 2, 15–8, 52–5, 105–16, 141, 153
  social 18–20, 76–7, 117–24, 152–5
  teacher 2, 25–7, 55–7, 83–5, 126–8
drawing out 38–42

education
  aesthetic 41, 142–3, 150, 157, 161
  for citizenship 143, 154
  community 44–71, 72, 143
  environmental 72–103, 154
  media 44–71, 153
  reform act 145, 149–50
  religious 47
elitism 103, 139
empowerment 10, 121, 142, 152, 160
environment, 28, 72–103, 143
ethnography vii, 1, 157–65
evaluation 161–3

fieldwork 158
freedom 8–9, 30–1, 61, 89–90, 97, 117, 142

gender 7, 18–19, 44, 69, 114, 142, 144, 154

Holism 2, 5, 12, 43, 55, 92, 142, 145, 148

identity 2, 3, 12, 27, 114, 116, 128
imagination 16, 23, 44, 73–4, 101, 117, 141–2, 146, 150, 152, 159, 165

inspiration 11, 44, 56, 60, 75, 91, 108, 130, 135, 142
integration
  of community 57–60, 69
  of curriculum 149, 153–5
  of self 70, 144
intensification viii, 3
interviews 47–9, 158–9

knowledge
  personal practical, 3, 12, 165
  of self 14–8
  tacit 164

language 21–2, 41, 78–9, 92, 94, 162
learning
  art of 20–5, 52, 142
  constructivist theory of 4–6, 43, 60–4, 68, 148, 156
  piaget theory of 68
  real 4–6, 10–11, 23, 43, 72–103, 115, 142, 145, 156, 165
  rhythm of 9
legitimation 10, 148
life histories 158

marginality 26, 144, 150
mediary 49–52
motiration 5, 9, 55, 73–6, 97, 135, 147
multi-methods, 29–32, 148, 158

National Curriculum ix, 3, 10, 43, 84, 139, 141, 148–56
negotiation 4–5, 81–8, 96–7, 102, 145

orchestration 91

PACE project 150
participant observation 54, 159
place 15, 100
planning 12, 61, 79–81, 87, 142
progressive focusing 157–8

relationships 2, 3, 37, 51, 70, 91–2, 117–25, 128, 137, 144–6, 150, 155–6
religion 104, 122, 128–9
research
  collaborative viii, 159–61
  qualitative vii, 9, 157–65
resources 11, 64–8, 89, 95–101, 128–140
respondent validation 163–5
ring game 118

rites of passage 9
Role 115
  conflict 150
  models 12
  play 27, 29, 31–2
  see also teacher role
romanticism 23, 69, 112, 165

scaffolding 5, 43, 68–9, 134, 145
school
  ethos 11, 28, 35, 64, 99, 138–40, 149
  primary passim
  secondary vii, 17–18, 104–40
self 2, 4, 26, 109, 143–4, 152
  control 113
  discovery of 105–6, 127, 141
  substantial 70, 144
skills
  camera 50–1
  communication 45, 47–9, 153
  designing 79–81
  interviewing 47–8
  personal and social *see* development
  researching 47–9
  writing 21–5, 30, 43
social class 7, 142, 144
space 9, 81, 88, 145
sponsorship 100, 119
spontaneity 106–9, 133, 142, 150
status passage 112
stimulation 10, 30, 39–40, 150
structure 8–10, 31, 43, 61, 88–91, 102, 113, 116, 148
  social 7
subjects
  art 6, 17, 82, 150
  creative arts 13, 104–6, 138–40, 150
  dance 13, 150
  drama 13, 29, 104–40, 150, 153
  english 21, 24, 34, 55, 150, 152–3, 155
  mathematics 6, 55, 150, 155–6
  music 13, 24, 129–30, 150
  physical education 54
  science 6, 150, 155–6
  social and environmental studies 30
  technology 6, 73, 83, 153, 155–6

teacher
  action 3
  alienation 152
  artists 2, 11
  as person 32, 121, 145
  as reflective practitioner 11, 83, 102, 144, 159

career 25, 152
creativity viii, 1–2, 7, 55, 57
deskilling viii, 3, 144, 152, 156
guilt 151
morale viii, 68, 151–2
role viii, 32, 60, 87, 102, 127–8, 137, 146, 149–52
self 145, 152
socialization 1
strategies 3, 87–9, 142
stress 151
voice 160, 162–3
teaching
  as an art 6, 20, 44, 86, 89
  child centred vii, 5, 10, 12, 22, 27, 60, 145, 151, 156
  constructivist vii, 60–4, 68, 97, 133–5, 145

group 7
  opportunities 12–3, 138, 147, 152–6
  person centred 12, 135
  progressive vii, 4, 10, 152
  team 7, 36, 154
  technical-rationalist 12, 159
  traditional vii, 71, 152, 154
  whole-class 155
time 10, 15, 44, 102, 145, 147–9, 151
topics 2–3, 10, 145, 149, 153–4, 156
transition (primary-secondary) 18
triangulation 148, 158

vocationalism 139

zone of proximal development 145–6